OUT THERE

ESSAYS ON THE LOWER BIG BEND

Creative Texts Publishers products are available at special discounts for bulk purchase for sale promotions, premiums, fund-raising, and educational needs. For details, write Creative Texts Publishers, PO Box 50, Barto, PA 19504, or visit www.creativetexts.com

OUT THERE: ESSAYS ON THE LOWER BIG BEND
By Ben H. English
Published by Creative Texts Publishers
PO Box 50
Barto, PA 19504
www.creativetexts.com
Copyright 2020 by Ben H. English
Cover design copyright 2020 Creative Texts Publishers, LLC
Photographs Copyright 2020 Ben H. English
All rights reserved

The opinions expressed in our published works are those of the author(s) and do not reflect the opinions of the Publisher or its Editors.

ISBN: 978-1-64738-026-7

OUT THERE
ESSAYS ON THE LOWER BIG BEND

By

Ben H. English

CREATIVE TEXTS PUBLISHERS, LLC
Barto, Pennsylvania

TABLE OF CONTENTS

Dedicated to those who came before, and to those who still follow in their footsteps...

The 'Backwards BHE' logo stands for 'Ben H. English,' and represents a ranch brand that I designed for myself while attending fourth grade in Terlingua school. Unfortunately, the ranch never happened.

But the richly talented as well as hard-working staff at Creative Texts took note of my childhood dream, and conceived the stylized version contained in these pages. When someone asks why I selected this particular publishing house to sign with? Well, this is one of the reasons.

The logo is used to highlight the quotes at the beginning of each essay, some of which have been with me for about as long as that ranch brand idea. Each adds a special flavor to the article and I hope that you, the reader, benefits from them and how they tie into the individual story.

And to Creative Texts Publishers… Thanks Guys!

Ben H. English
Alpine, Texas

FOREWORD

There are those, including me, who would say that Ben English has been "out there" for most of his life. I would imagine those people would include many of his Marine Corps mentors, his teachers and professors, his supervisors and co-workers at the Texas DPS, and even his long-suffering wife, Cathy. But here's the thing: ask any of those people who they'd like to have "covering their six" in a fracas of any sort, and chances are Ben's name jumps to the top of the list.

So why is that? How can someone so "out there" be so highly esteemed in a pinch? I think I can sum it up for you. Ben is out there in relation to the times we live in, but he isn't really a man of these times. He's a man from an older time living in these times. Can he function here? Sure. Admirably, but his heart, soul, and morality are 19th century Texas, pure and simple.

I've had the privilege of knowing and working with Ben for several years now, and he's asked me to read each of his works before they were published. Sometimes I liked everything about them, and sometimes I didn't. When I didn't, we talked about it, and I always told Ben the same thing about his writing and life in this tumultuous century: people crave authenticity, and Ben has it.

When a good friend of mine visited from Boston one time, I took him to dinner at the Starlight Theater in Terlingua on a Saturday night. There was a great black blues band from Austin playing, and the place was jumping. The food was good, the people friendly, and the atmosphere raucous and fun. At one point my friend yelled to me, "Man, if we could franchise this place on the East Coast, we could retire rich!" I have great respect for that friend, but his comment saddened me. Franchises are copies. The Starlight is unique.

So is Ben, and so is his writing. He has a following precisely because he's authentic. His family goes back to Spanish rule in Texas. They were lawmen and ranchers and cowboys and merchants, but they earned their way honestly. They were what people once thought of when they thought of Texans. These days one has to come to West Texas to find such critters, and even then, they're rare. All the Indians run hotels these days, and most of the outlaws hold public office.

When Ben's grandfather ran the Trading Post in Lajitas, he gave Ben a jenny mule and sent him off to prowl the Big Bend. Ben speaks with reverence about his grandfather, so much so that it reminds me of a story I read recently about the beautiful five-year-old daughter of a wealthy Texas oilman. She was the apple of his eye, and he was her idol. One day a well-intentioned lady friend

i

of the family asked the young girl if she didn't think it was time for her to start attending Sunday School. The young lady replied without hesitation, "No, ma'am. I want to go to Hell with my Daddy!"

That's Texas. That's loyalty. That's Ben English. When you read these accounts, they're not coming from some Chairborne Ranger in NYC who has fast WiFi and three computers and monitors to research details on, they're coming from a guy who saddled up and walked the ground like the old scout sniper he is. If he talks about terrain, he walked that terrain. He knows whereof he speaks. He knows firearms. He knows history. He knows Spanish and English. He knows outlaws and bandidos, horses and mules, Dodge Chargers and Corvettes, corridas and ballads, Louis L'Amour and Mark Twain.

If he's a success, it's because he decided a long time ago to be one. It's because he gets up at 0600 every morning and gets after it until the Sabbath gives him rest. He and his wife are understated but overly successful. They raised two fine sons who were Eagle Scouts, class valedictorians and graduates of the US Naval Academy. That's the English tradition.

So enjoy this book as I did, knowing that it's the real deal. Ben English is his own franchise, and every book he publishes is a new addition to his franchise. I'm currently reading the pre-publication copy of his second novel, and I can say with some certainty that Ben's franchise is about to take off. I'm not sure if he has another natural history book like Out There in him, but I predict that his novels will someday rank right up there with Louis L'Amour, Elmer Kelton, and Zane Grey.

Get it while you can, folks. Our local boy has taken wing.

Mike Boren
Executive Director
Big Bend Natural History Association

PROLOGUE

In the past twenty years or so, it seems the world has finally discovered the enduring magic and magnificence of the Big Bend country in Texas. As with anything else akin to progress, such changes in the binding seam for the spirit of a land leads to unintended consequences.

For each gain there is an accompanying loss and often enough the scales become unbalanced if no one speaks for the past, and those who came before. Though I am now only reaching my sixtieth year, my family first came to the Big Bend some one hundred and forty years ago. Presently, six generations of my clan have called these mountains and desert home.

More so, they had an active and abiding curiosity as well as respect for this land, and the people who came prior. An old adage in our family is if you want to know where you are going, you must first know where you are coming from.

As the decades passed by and those family members have passed on, by necessity I became a repository for those memories and stories. Only recently have I began writing about them, along with so many others who can no longer speak for themselves. This has been a labor of love on my part, paired with the feeling of a deep responsibility in doing so.

It is my sincerest wish that you, the reader, take these stories and the associated lessons learned to heart. You collectively represent the future of the Big Bend, a future that if shaped properly must contain the fading images of the past.

May God be with you in such a vital endeavor, and guide you and those like you in the decisions you make. This country has always had a penchant for the forming of its people. Yet it is the people, in turn, who give it the defining aroma for its singular flavor.

Ben H. English
Alpine, Texas

CHAPTER ONE

BURRO MESA AREA

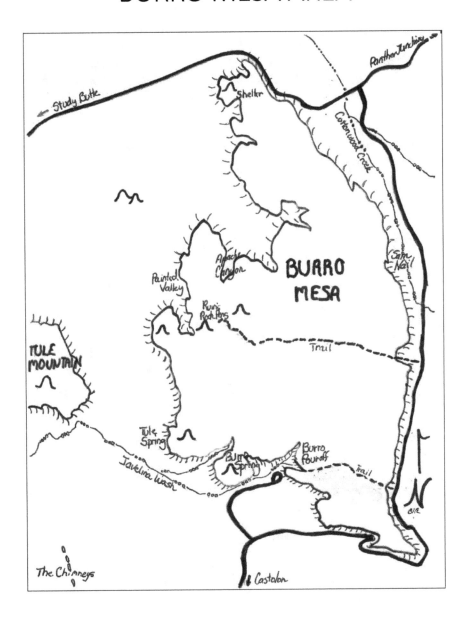

If truth be known, it was Bob Sholly who first really focused me on Burro Mesa. He and his brother Dan, along with their old schoolmate Bill Dodson, were with me not too long before Bob passed. Among these three men were decades of knowledge from a time before my own, so I was doing my best to keep quiet and listen to what they had to say.

We were driving up from Castolon and Bob began quizzing me on what I knew about the mesa. Soon enough he began pointing out approaches, water sources, points of interest and places I needed to see. It was like drinking from a fire hose turned full on and I made mental notes as best I could.

About a month later, I was saddling up near where Bob first began explaining the many intricacies of this craggy uplift. With his shared experiences and knowledge in my head, on that day I made my first trip across the mesa. It would not be my last.

And every time I go, I think of Bob Sholly.

Vaya con Dios, my friend.

"I am prepared to go anywhere, so long as it is forward."

--David Livingston

Burro Mesa sits west of the Chisos Mountains; a large chunk of soil and rock measured in several miles by several miles, and about as craggy and rugged as one can find anyplace.

It serves as a humbling reminder when some well-intentioned people exclaim that I must know all there is to know about the lower Big Bend; for in truth I will never possess a complete knowledge of even this one solitary feature, sitting amid so many other wondrous creations by God's Own Hand.

I suppose that is why I come here at every given opportunity. You could say that Burro Mesa is a thin slice of the pie that makes up the total grandeur of this country, and contains a little bit of just about everything to be found across this extraordinary land.

There are ruins, corrals, seeps, holes, springs, tinajas, cliffs, pour-offs, water tanks, dirt dikes, pictographs, metate holes, near gone fence lines, vanishing trails, roughhewn arroyos and rocks and boulders of every size, shape and description. All intertwined into a maze of different eras and times that form a mosaic of both natural as well as human history for this area.

The sights and experiences to be had in this one place alone could fill the pages of a volume narrating a well-lived life, with plenty left over when that life was done. Though not an easy piece of landscape to approach from most directions, I can think of at least a dozen different ways to get on top and each one is a different journey through its immediate surroundings, wondrous in its own way as to what can be seen and felt where spirit and soul abides.

With that comes other challenges. The weather itself can be as extreme as the rest of this environment; I've been on and around Burro Mesa when it was way over a hundred degrees, and six quarts of water and two of Gatorade were barely enough to get me from sunup to just past sundown.

Other times a northerner would come blowing dust so hard that it would sting your face, near freeze your fingers and make you wish for some of that 106 degrees from a few months before. But hot or cold, wet or dry, the wind blowing up a gale or as still and listless as inside of a dead man's tomb, it was always a glorious day to be there.

This photo was taken not long after the sun arose on a crystal-clear January morning, one of those times when all of those extremes measured themselves out against each other, and for a while managed to compromise themselves into a near perfect day.

I was enroute to the high point for the pass that sits between the mesa and Tule Mountain, looping my way along in a lazy to and fro pattern that would bring me to both Tule Spring as well as Burro Spring. Along the way would be dozens of views that you just wouldn't expect to see, other than realizing that is the one constant refrain out here.

And once again, I would offer up heartfelt thanks to a Benevolent God for the blessing of being here.

4

> *"Inspiration comes in flashes, to clothe circumstances; it is not stored in a barrel, like salt herrings, to be doled out."*
> *--Patrick White*

I do not know how Apache Canyon first got its name; there is ample archaeological evidence showing that Burro Mesa and its surrounding environs were inhabited by Indians long before the Apache ever came to this part of Texas.

In fact, the better-known tribes and clans of Apache, Kiowa and Comanche were all late comers to the lower Big Bend, compared to those who first came on the scene. More so, the three named were only here for a little while; the Apache the longest of the three but still only for about two centuries. Artifacts found in this area dictate that man has been present for some 12,000 years, possibly more.

But I can tell you that Apache Canyon is one of the most unusual, colorful and show stopping sights to be found in this national park, bar none. To be truthful, that statement could expand to the entire Trans Pecos region and beyond. I have been here from the top side, walked both of the rims and have come up through the mouth of the chasm from below.

By any approach the view is simply spectacular in a constantly surprising, even sometimes puzzling manner. There is so much that should not be there; let alone displayed in such a bizarre, jumbled up way. Rhyme nor reason seems to have had little sway in what resulted.

The rocks in this canyon are of all shapes, sizes and compositions. This is one of the reasons why ancient man came to this locale, every kind and style of rock he might need for his primitive implements can be found here or nearby. In my prowling about I have found more than one spot where such implements were made with plenty of tell-tale evidence left scattered about. Even with dutiful efforts, a full search and documentation of these locations would take years, maybe even decades.

5

Yet for modern man it is the sheer variety of colors themselves that are the most striking; I can only describe it as some sort of earth-bound rocky rainbow painted upon the craggy, broken bottoms and heights. Framed by the occasional green of desert plant life and crowned by a brilliantly blue sky, it all makes for a kaleidoscope of natural rugged beauty tucked away in a quiet little corner where few would ever think to look.

This photograph, so painstakingly taken at just the right angle, still only gives the palest facsimile of what the eye, and the spirit, can discern here.

"Its soul, its climate, its equality, liberty, laws, people, and manners. My God! How little do my countrymen know what precious blessings they are in possession of, and which no other people on earth enjoy!"
--Thomas Jefferson

The lower Big Bend area of Texas is rife with surprises, both big and small. That most are hidden in some way is the very nature of this land, like any living creature she conceals her greatest treasures with the greatest zealotry. One can take a certain creek, or nearly vanished trail or wagon track, numerous times but then wander a certain number of feet to either side and a different world opens to you.

Such was the case with this photo, taken during the latter part of one of my prowls between Burro Mesa and Tule Mountain. I had started near the pour off and worked my way through Burro Spring and across to Tule Spring, both being well worth the effort in their own right. The day was crisp and traces of green were sprouting along the lower elevations, and the springs were flowing with more water than the uninitiated would think possible.

After circling through the ruins at Tule Spring and walking along the old earthen dam, I pointed my nose along a nigh forgotten trail that once ran northwest to the high side of Tule Mountain, where another such dam and sources of water are situated. My plan was to move into the very head of Javelina Wash as part of some 'boots on the ground' research concerning my third novel.

About a quarter mile up from Tule Spring, I noticed an unusual splash of white along the northern side of a low, dark volcanic hill that sits just northeast of Javelina Wash. Sufficiently intrigued, I glassed the area with my Leupolds and made a mental note to swing further west on the way back to investigate.

I could discern craggy, chocolate colored boulders and what appeared to be low ground at the base of that hill, and just the general feeling that I needed to go and see.

After nooning at a half way point in the pass between Tule Mountain and Burro Mesa, I reversed direction and drifted down a northern branch for Javelina Wash. The day had turned glorious with a crystal-clear sky above a rainbow of colored rock and ground, mixed among the earth shades splashed about for good measure. Most folks don't know it, but there are parts of the Big Bend that will give the so-called 'Painted Desert' a run for its money any day of the week. This area is one of them.

Near where the low hill abruptly ended in white, I crossed the dry creek bed and walked into an almost surreal atmosphere. Large boulders of that dark volcanic tone were perched in every position imaginable, many sitting upon unlikely foundations of small spires formed from the whitish soil. It was almost like you had strolled into nature's own trophy room.

The area was only a couple of acres or so in size at best, but oh what a sight to behold while being hidden in plain view.

And then I passed on through, heading upon another course through that same zealous desert.

I would like to think that I will go there again someday, but there is still so much that I know I'll never see in this country.

And I was burning daylight.

"The idea that men are created free and equal is both true and misleading: men are created different; they lose their social freedom and their individual autonomy in seeking to become like one another."
--David Riesman

Close to the west rim for Burro Mesa and near due south of Apache Canyon, sit some crumbling ruins that were once a set of rock pens and matching line camp. The structure for the pens themselves is still mostly solid and with a little work could be serviceable again. In contrast, the long-abandoned dwelling has mostly collapsed within itself, with only the north wall still standing.

My guess is that both are close to a hundred years old, and maybe more. No one I know of is really sure of who built it or exactly when. This country started out as part of the G4 outfit in the late 1880s, and passed through different hands until Homer Wilson and Sam Nail gained divided ownership of this uplift.

Mr. Wilson was an intelligent, enterprising man bent on improving what he had, and the remains of his ideas put into action still remain up here. There are several water tanks scattered around the top of the mesa, as his plan involved having water available for his livestock spaced no more than a mile apart.

These remaining tanks are of varying style and construction, and made of dirt, rock, concrete or metal. The formally trained and educated engineer even developed a patented booster pump for bringing the water atop the mesa from sources below.

I nooned at these ruins one day, with an oven-like sun beating down hard upon everything exposed to it. There was no shade available at that time of the hour and with the thermometer on my old Suunto hovering around 106 degrees, I silently commended the constitution of the men who once lived here. It was now only early May; the real heat of summer was still weeks away.

From sunup to past sundown I covered somewhere around seventeen to eighteen miles on foot, looping around and crisscrossing the mesa while consuming the two gallons of water in my backpack during the process. It is a lonesome, wistful place with no sign of any living soul to be found. Only the crumbling ruins, the dry tanks, and this desolate, scorched land that refuses to be tamed.

Along with the windblown memories of those men who didn't know what the word 'quit' meant.

"...And, while with silent,
lifting mind I've trod
The high untrespassed sanctity of space,
Put out my hand,
and touched the face of God."
--John Gillespie Magee, Jr.

Those words always meant something special to me, I first remember reading them when I was about eleven years old in Robert L. Scott's classic war story entitled *God Was My Co-Pilot.* The poem in its entirety was likely the first I ever memorized.

Though Scott had included the verses in his book, the poet was a young man by the name of John Gillespie Magee, Jr. Of an American father and British mother and born in China, Magee was one of those precious few who lived a full life many times over during a scant few years on this earth.

Having learned early on there were no good wars but sometimes necessary ones, he volunteered for the Royal Air Force as a fighter pilot. In December of 1941, John Magee was killed while flying his Spitfire. He was all of nineteen years old.

Now here I was nearly eighty years later, walking in a desert that was probably as foreign to him as the cliffs of Dover and castles of Kent would be to me. But each in their own way have their own unique grandeur, the kind that makes one feel there is no other place on earth for him than where he is now.

For me it had been another day of prowling where hardly anyone else goes, for that is where the desert guards many of its greatest treasures. I had already found pictographs, Indian camps, springs, seeps, rock pens, ruins, rotting fence lines and pieces of ancient trails worn a good foot into the surrounding ground.

In short, it had been another good trip where even a bad one beats being most anyplace else.

The day had been cloudy and cool, and I had not seen the sun dance in full array since having risen that morning. But just as it descended lowest upon the Sierra Ponce, that golden orb peeped under the cloud banks and lit up the southwestern part of Burro Mesa.

With the Chisos beyond serving as background, together they made for a display of natural beauty that sticks in one's memory forever more. Kind of like the final lines to Magee's poem *High Flight,* it only takes once for the moment to become a part of you in a very permanent way.

And though I was not soaring above those lofty clouds of white at the controls of a Spitfire Mark 5b, I knew at that moment what it meant to put out one's hand and touch the face of God.

It was the perfect last photo for a perfect sort of a day.

Rest in peace, John Magee.

"The world is your school."
--Martin H. Fischer

One of the shorter hikes I recommend for others is a mouthful referred to as the Upper Burro Mesa Pour Off Trail. Though most would be best served by taking this path when the weather is mild, it is a fairly easy walk utilizing the bottom of a gravelly creek bed for some four miles round trip.

For those who are familiar with the paved spur that leads to the lower elevations of the pour offs, you are basically approaching this same area from the eastern side and above. This makes for a completely new understanding of the size and complexities of the watersheds that feed these arroyos, as well as an entry point into the more inaccessible upper sections along the mesa's south side.

Not many people go here, at least as in my case for using the trail as a launch site to explore those aforementioned upper sections. Please note that I use the term 'pour off' in the plural, as there are actually two major ones in the immediate area. One is fed by the watershed for Javelina Wash, which actually starts on the southwestern slopes of the Chisos Mountains.

The other course slices into the very heart of the mesa itself, extending north to where Apache Canyon Trail wanders by headed west. You can reach this remote area from the Apache Canyon route, or by angling off the Pour Off Trail and cutting across country in a northwesterly direction. Be forewarned, though: desert experience and knowing how to read a topographical map are essentials. This is rough country, and it does not suffer lightly mistakes or miscalculations while being challenged.

The basic thing to remember when navigating the south side of the mesa is that all of the runs snaking in from the north, as well as the east, connect together just below the double pour offs. This is where Javelina Wash expands dramatically in size and charges off to the west, and to the southern foot of Tule Mountain. Over the eons, those momentous forces that shaped this wash are the very same that have also so magically sculpted its surrounding environs.

A flash flood on the move can be a fearsome thing, and can generate a massive, sometimes supremely vicious power that few can fully appreciate unless you have witnessed it with your own eyes. The scene is thrilling, perhaps even a bit frightening for some and rightfully so. Mother Nature can have a mean disposition, especially when riding hell bent for leather upon massive storm clouds when they vent their pent-up fury upon this land.

"He looks out upon humanity, and sees that in one aspect the world is full of births, and in another full of deaths. Coffins and cradles seem the main furniture, and he hears the tramp, tramp, tramp of the generations passing over a soil honeycombed with tombs."
--Alexander Maclaren

But such a fury also shapes for sights to behold, whether while trailing along through these arroyos or walking the rock-strewn ridges above. There is so much to see and the pour offs themselves are only miniscule portions of the total sum. One can easily spend a week prowling around this part of the mesa and not find everything worth a visit. And perhaps, some contemplation.

I suppose that Burro Mesa has such a continuing pull on me as you never quite know what to expect when you round the next corner. The photograph illustrates this perfectly; those eons of sculpting by sun, water, wind and simple decay made for a show-stopping rock window frame highlighting a perfectly blue desert sky.

You can look at this one, single creation of nature from a dozen different angles, and not get the same perspective twice.

But you won't, because you know inside yourself there is so much more to experience and so little time to see it all.

So, you continue along your way.

It was one of those spots that somehow called to the spirit, where we sometimes discern far more about a situation or circumstance than our five physical senses can convey to us. I had been on the scout along the northwestern side of Burro Mesa, looking for the remains of an old trail and a spring while researching a future historical novel.

They both were noted on an Army tactical map from 85 years or so before, as well as other equally antiquated sources. I missed the entrance on the first try, having to double back over a range of craggy knolls to the exact location. It had been there plain as day before me, but my attention had been distracted by a far more dramatic, impressive crevice that turned out to be nothing but a dry run. Funny how that works in life, both with places and with people.

Soon enough I had found where the spring was, but it had apparently gone dry decades ago. The rotting husks of vegetation littered the ground where now only mesquite and greasewood grew, nothing saps water in this country like mesquite or salt cedar.

I ambled my way northward as rain clouds closed in behind me, bringing precious moisture to the desert in yet another way. Attracted to a massive boulder on the slope of a ridge, one could see a large overhang on the leeward side, affording shelter and perhaps a secret or two. Curiosity aroused but mindfully cautious, I half circled around to see better.

Under the overhang was a beaten area where man and animal had taken refuge from the elements for as long as both had been in the lower Big Bend. Rusted tin cans, a beaten down area to crouch or to lie down, big cat prints, a piece of vertebrae from some small prey, the blackened rock from campfires past and a crude reflector told a thousand different tales without uttering a single word.

Dropping my pack, I sat down nearby and just looked it over, drinking from a canteen and eating lunch from the victuals I brought with me. Once satisfied I checked the maps again, scanned the high ground with my binoculars to plot my future course, and shouldered my gear for the journey.

Then one more man followed in the ancient steps of so many others.

"There is not one blade of grass, there is no color in this world that is not intended to make us rejoice."
--John Calvin

On the western side of Burro Mesa, in the wide, low lying pass that sits between its vertical walls and the reaches of Tule Mountain; is a spot like few others in the Big Bend or most anyplace else. The photograph does it no justice whatsoever.

I call it 'Painted Valley,' though it never really had a name that I know of. But if you ever stood on this high ground after the spring rains come and before it gets too hot to burn off the wild flowers and accompanying greenery, and the evening sun gives the landscape that special golden glow, you'd know right away why that name stuck in my mind.

Painted Valley is a deceiving sort of place, other than prowling off into its boundaries you would never know it was there. No road passes within sight, not now or a hundred years before. Whatever trails once present are now slowly dissolving away from time and general lack of use. The few game paths are usually hard to find and when you do, they often wander off some direction other than where you want to go.

This area is also surprisingly rough when compared to an aerial photo or even a quad map. What goes on between those elevation lines can be downright depressing when you see the same obstacles from ground level.

I had first come here researching an idea for a novel, involving a fast-moving Mexican cavalry detail arrowing across this land. It turned out to be an involved process with a couple of false starts. Yet be that as it may, it is also part of the innate charm: the seclusive, the desolate, the hard to find as well as to traverse.

And then there is the eroded landscape itself, almost as if you stepped through some unseen portal into another dimension. Fantastic shapes and contrasting, almost unnatural colors clash and reform into making you half believe that you have not only strayed off into a different part of the Big Bend, but maybe also on to a different planet. Perhaps Mars with occasional wildflowers and breathable air, you might say.

But once you climb out of the small basin or drift down into the Alamo Creek area below, you gradually get your earthly bearings repositioned where they belong. It takes a bit longer to stop, scratch your head and look back to where you came from and wonder, "Now what was that all about?"

Then it'll only take a little longer to make up your mind to go back someday, and spend a little more time and effort to fully scout out the colorful depression, rather than just passing through.

Everyone with a sense of adventure should spend at least a couple of hours walking into a different world and taking in the sights.

Especially when you are otherwise strictly earth-borne like most of the rest of humanity.

"This is the narrow estate of man, his breath, his earth, and his thoughts; and this is his threefold climax therein, —his breath goeth forth, to his earth he returns, and his thoughts perish. Is this a being to be relied upon? Vanity of vanities, all is vanity. To trust it would be a still greater vanity."
--Charles Spurgeon

They call it Tule Spring, though it sits closer to the southwestern reaches of Burro Mesa than Tule Mountain itself. Furthermore, there appears to be more than one spring and last time I ventured to this spot all of them were flowing. Each comes out of ground pockmarked by small copses of stunted mesquite, drifting down and joining together at a fairly large pond formed by an old earthen dike. There used to be fairly large cottonwoods present, but not anymore.

From this angle you are looking past one of the long-abandoned dwellings on site and beyond the left corner of the ruin, the reflection of the pond partially disguised by cane. To the right are the southern foothills of Tule Mountain while the Rattlesnake range peeks over those foothills. Behind the Rattlesnakes, Anguila Mesa sits still higher.

On the horizon are the mountains of Mexico. Like my father so often said; "All the big mountains are across the river." He, like so many of my ancestors, would have known. Mexico had a powerful pull on them, even from the era of the Texas Republic.

Several fought, worked and ranched down there, and some are buried in that ground. To this day, I cannot look at any peak or mountain south of the *rio* without his words echoing through my mind. He's been gone for some time now but I still miss his presence and his knowledge, as well as his love for this land.

This day I was pressing on beyond, while spending a bit of my time first prowling through what remains here. Ultimately, I would push to the top of the pass between Tule Mountain and Burro Mesa, and the very northernmost traces for the watershed of Javelina Wash.

From there you can see the world stretch out to the Christmas Mountains and as far as Hen Egg and *El Solitario*, and many points in between. It was January and the day would turn warm after a crisp, clear morning; the kind of day where it seems that you can see forever. And more so, that you just might even live forever.

Along the way I made note of how there seemed to be more water here than previously. Only time and the dry seasons will tell, but I am finding that many of the long dormant springs and seeps noted a century and more ago are now flowing again. I hope so for there is royalty in this desert and water was crowned king eons ago. It is easy to understand why the remnants of so many Indian camps are found around Burro Mesa, if they had access to water in the quantities that once reigned here.

That evening, as the sun hung low and cast the stark shadows so often the signature of this country, my mind turned to those who came before. Those in their primitive camps, those who once lived in the rock dwellings at Tule Spring, and those of my own blood with such a deep, abiding sentiment for the Big Bend. Time has swallowed each in turn; devouring near whole their breath, their bodies, their earth and their thoughts of a lifetime.

And in that recollection, I realized what briefest of moments each our lives consist of. It makes one feel sort of small and insignificant, and humbled to be alive and be here, even for a moment.

"Vanity of vanities, all is vanity," the man said. The greatest vanity of all is found in our own perceived self-importance.

24

*"The most dangerous of our calculations
are those we call illusions."*
--Georges Bernamos

It was a Saturday some time ago spent atop Burro Mesa, prowling about the northern reaches of this impressive uplift and taking in the sights. It was very hot, very dry, and over fifteen miles of mostly hard going. From dawn until dark I consumed the water I brought with me, the only moisture present during the entire trip. The tank at the old rock pens near Apache Canyon was beyond depleted, showing no sign of any rain for a long time.

Along the way of my wanderings I made note of how the lifeless patches of wild grass were as parched as that earthen tank, so much that the shriveled strands crackled under one's foot. In the sandy creek beds, each step brought little puffs of dust and soon enough my boots and lower trousers were covered with the fine, powdery residue. It was as if this country had not felt the caress of a single rain drop in a millennium.

The bleak condition of the land added to the sense of isolation, and the nearby presence of an even more inhospitable lower desert below. It put me in mind of being up here about ten years ago, when this country was enjoying abnormally large amounts of rainfall and groups of wild flowers dotted lush, green foliage in every direction. That memory stayed with me throughout the day, like when you were a teenager and had that first dance with the girl you had a crush on.

When I got back to Alpine that night, I dug through my photographs of that prior journey and gazed upon the desert in all her watered glory. Taken over on the southern part of the mesa, it was just as verdant and colorful as I remembered.

But the truth of the matter is this was an unusual event, which like that first dance does not happen very often. Most human beings, especially those new to this challenging environment, have very short memories to draw from.

Many of them come to the lower Big Bend during times of a great deal of rain, and only later ruefully learn how rare that 'first dance' can be.

They'll call it a drought and begin to wonder what will happen to their water supplies, and complain about the extreme heat, the dust, the mummifying wind and that blistering sun that never seems to give a moment's respite. They'll swear at and curse this country and everything that comes along with it, and often enough follow through on their vow to pack up and never return.

But that is the normal state of affairs here and why they call it a desert. All else is little more than a temporary illusion in the midst of a harsh, existential reality.

And as far as that swearing, cursing, and vows made against this far reaching land? The ranting, the hurled insults and the threats of removing yourself from its presence?

You waste your breath in perfect futility as the desert could not care less.

"Hide yourselves in holes of the earth, grots in the ground, clefts of the rocks, where you may best secure yourselves from the pursuing enemy.

--John Trapp

On the northwestern edge of Burro Mesa runs a canyon, a place that I am drawn to like a flitting moth to a bouldered flame. Though I have approached it over the years from three different directions, it often appears as a hundred different parts and scenes of something that makes up more than the whole. You look, you puzzle, you scratch your head and then shake it or grin, depending upon your mood.

The crevice is called Apache Canyon, a name that likely goes back to the earliest pioneers in regard to the Mescalero Apache who once held sway over the Chisos Mountains. When these newcomers arrived there were innumerous remnants of Indian camps, pictographs, metates and other tell-tale signs scattered throughout, though many wouldn't know the Mescalero from the Jumano or Chisos tribes. Thus the sheer abundance of these sites, along with such a name already being well known, led to the crevice being christened 'Apache Canyon.'

No matter what route one chooses, getting there is part of the adventure. Burro Mesa is a rough and tumble piece of real estate that goes on for miles. Once at the chasm itself, it can be nigh impossible to get to the bottom or just as difficult to climb out on top. Some spots consist of volcanic rock while others opposite or adjoining contain varieties of chert, which makes for excellent material in crafting primitive weapons and points. With shelter, water and defensible positions being provided by the rugged escarpment, it was natural for prehistoric people to come here and make a life.

Then there are the colors! Red, yellow, orange, purple, near black and back to earth tones such as grays and tans and browns. There is even solid white; a small rise of quartz-like material sitting atop and out of sight, unless you climb out or walk in from a different direction. All in turn set off by assorted shades of green from the vegetation and crowned by a magnificent blue sky above. It is an ever-revolving kaleidoscope with the sun's rays catching this terrain in different ways and angles, or when the inquisitive visitor takes a few steps to either side and looks again.

And if you listen closely as the breeze wafts up the chasm, bringing a sought for coolness in the midst of a summer afternoon, you sometimes think you hear something else. Something there but not really, something that calls to sense and memory like the name of someone you knew long ago, but can't quite remember now.

Like an invisible spider web that traces so lightly across your face, yet you cannot see it.

Or was it only the breeze, still wafting in near silence through the rocks and foliage?

Quién sabes?

"And they covet fields, and take them by violence; and houses, and take them away: so they oppress a man and his house, even a man and his heritage."

-Micah 2:2

Along the westerly side of Burro Mesa runs the remains of an antiquated fence line; it starts at the tip of what I call 'Arrowhead Point' and runs far away into the lower badlands beyond the northern reaches of the mesa itself.

This fence is a fading tribute of the first pioneer ranching families here, long before there was a park. It serves no real purpose anymore other than a slowly dissolving reminder of what once was, and of the unending tenacity it took to begin to tame a land. It is a rotting, rusting, fallen-down relic of a time and place now long gone.

Here, between a solitary low hill and the tip itself you can see where a wire gap once stood between two anchor posts. No one ever comes here anymore, though it used to be how one accessed Apache Canyon and the adjoining areas of this part of Burro Mesa.

Yet this gap, anchor posts tottering and weather-beaten beyond belief, remains wired shut with the fence line practically gone on either side. It is as if someone was making a final, defiant statement from eighty or so years ago in trying to keep the encroaching world out.

You see, when the ranchers were given their walking papers during the creation of the park it was not that sentimental, kumbaya moment sort of process the National Park Service continues to portray it as.

Pioneer families who had given their all for decades and were just beginning to see those efforts finally come to fruition were in no uncertain terms forced out, sometimes by threats and intimidation. They were 'compensated,' if you can manage to stretch the word that far, by the federal government at a set sum per acre mostly dependent on the elevation of the land.

The improvements made to that land may or may not have raised the sum, but if so, the amount was again dictated by some faraway bureaucrat who likely never laid eyes on your never-ending efforts. You challenged those estimations at your own peril.

And anyone who has ever attempted to stand against any level of government for any reason knows what a fearsome, all-powerful opponent it can be.

To this day there are descendants of these families, both Anglo and Hispanic, who refuse to have anything to do with any park activities concerning the Big Bend. Those scars run deep, and they run through the hearts and spirits of a proud, independent breed of people.

And no, this is not a total and complete damnation of the Federal Government and the National Park Service.

And yes, in a very real way I feel blessed and privileged to enjoy the final results, and to acknowledge that without the NPS this land would now look like Lajitas or Terlingua Ranch.

But I hope that anyone who drives into Big Bend National Park will take a moment to consider what was lost in bringing this veritable treasure beyond any monetary amount to them.

And for as long as they are here, to try to remember and give homage to those who came before.

You are standing in the midst of other people's dreams, folks.

Do not ever forget that.

CHAPTER TWO

FRESNO CANYON AREA

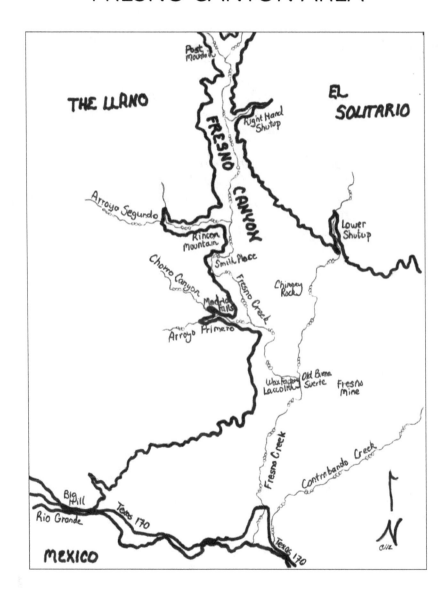

There are three major veins in the lower Big Bend that feed into the main artery known as the Rio Grande. These three creeks are where reliable water can be found in the driest of seasons, and then can carry a mind-boggling amount of flash flood runoff when those dry spells are broken in spectacular fashion.

They are known as the Fresno, the Terlingua and the Tornillo. I know each fairly well and have many good memories contained in them. All are essential to life in this desert region, and all have their own particular environment, history and lore. In a large part, they make for what is the lower Big Bend itself.

But of the three, my favorite has always been the Fresno. Running between what some call The Llano escarpment to the west, and El Solitario to the east, Fresno Canyon and its main tributaries cover some twenty miles in length from the head all the way down to the river, as well as being several miles wide in many spots.

Within those boundaries are multiple sources of large amounts of water; good water with copses of trees, shade and plenty of awe-inspiring scenery to feast one's eyes and spirit upon. Of all my childhood remembrances, most of my favorite lie here.

Mere words alone can never describe what that canyon means to me.

"Our cup is small, and we blame the fountain."
--Charles Spurgeon

So many people think the desert, any desert, has no water. The truth is there are usually places to find it nearby no matter where you may be, but water is still the rarest resource and the land knows how to hide those treasures well. If you do not have knowledge or a 'feel' for where it may be, you might as well be wandering around on the moon.

When you come upon Chorro Canyon anywhere more than a mile upstream from Madrid Falls, there is really not much of a canyon at all. At first it is more of a draw than anything else, with a fairly wide bed consisting mostly of rock, sand and gravel.

The surrounding terrain makes for easy enough approaches. You get to the wash from just about any heading, including by simply following along the creek bed from the Dos Hermanos campsite. Nothing but high desert in three directions, making for a leisurely sort of stroll that is quite deceiving as to what lies ahead. In fact, the terrain is unruffled enough to have a fairly good jeep trail going through the wash at about that same one-mile mark.

But downstream from there things start to change rapidly. The wide bed narrows, forming rocky walls that close in and constrict your movements amid sheets of stone and fields of irregularly shaped boulders. Taking advantage of this sudden bottling effect is an old stone dam now mostly filled in, an enduring monument to long dead men who struggled to utilize the nature of this country.

This section of the arroyo continues on for some distance as the walls become both higher and steeper, and the floor itself unsettled enough to consciously watch your step and plan your way forward accordingly. You also start seeing the signs of seeps and small tinajas that often contain moisture enough to keep man or beast going.

Where this rough run actually becomes something akin to a canyon starts at a twenty foot drop off into a fairly large waterhole. Reaching skyward is a solitary young cottonwood of some size, sitting serenely alongside the hole. Last time I was there a rope still hung from a branch on the tree, left by some filming crew who was shooting a 'reality' show about surviving in the Big Bend. They had also left some trash scattered about with only a cursory, half-hearted attempt to conceal it.

Moving past the tell-tale reminder of the damage that often accompanies the fool, you find assorted pools of water with tiny flowing rills leading from one to another. More seepage comes from the surrounding walls of rock themselves, feeding those ponds and adding to the strength of the rills as they move along.

This day was overcast and still, and while working your way down to the falls you think upon the analogy of a beautiful woman being wooed by a suitor. She ignores his desires at first but due to his continuing persistence decides to show him more and more of her heart, and the precious things contained within.

Then you come upon what is in the photo, only a couple of hundred yards from Madrid Falls itself. You pause slightly in awe at the sight, soaking your senses in the visage of what constitutes as a natural allure in most any man's estimation. The proverbial beautiful woman has not only showed you her heart, but her very soul.

And in this one little spot hidden away in a dry, desolate desert, you realize again why you believe there is a God in Heaven above.

39

"And how are things in old Magee Canyon,
How are the mountains I knew?
I've dreamed so long of old Magee
Canyon,
Gonna saddle my pony and ride it
through..."

--Dave Stamey,
'Old Magee Canyon'

In a bend of Fresno Canyon situated along the old Military Road, near the foot of Rincon Mountain, is a place where many of my best memories as a young boy reside. At that time, it was my favorite place to be and going was almost like a mini vacation, or as close as one could get while still being part of a ranching family in the lower Big Bend.

It has had several names over the past hundred years or so, but the one it is best known by is the Smith Place. Once one of the prettiest and most cared for homes in this region; time, circumstance and flash floods have presently reduced it to a mere decaying corpse of itself.

Ah, but the memories. That black and white photograph above was taken at the Smith around 1963 when I was five years old. Pictured are my Grandfather Ben and my Tia Maggie, who had just graduated high school in Alpine. It was a summer morning and the campfire had already served up an early breakfast, along with at least one pot of strong, black coffee in which the grounds were settled by a tin cup of spring water.

In the background sits the Smith headquarters. Nearly sixty years ago, the home and its surrounding environs still possessed some fading vestiges of its former splendor. The attention to detail and method of construction, the intricate tile work along the bottom of the walls, the large cottonwood trees that provided cooling shade, and the spring-fed creek made for a beckoning desert oasis even decades since it had been abandoned.

But like anything else built by man and then left to the harsh elements of the lower Big Bend, it now slowly devolves into the form from whence it came. Around 1976 an immense flood roared down this canyon, washing out the highway bridge for the River Road some eight miles below the Smith. That same surging wall of water did a great deal of damage here also, as the only weakness the place ever had was that it was built too close to the creek bed.

But the ruins still remain, as do the memories. More so, our family memories are still being made at this same spot. In the color photo below taken a few years back stands my older son Benjamin Levi. He was home on leave while in training as a Marine aviator, this was his first trip to the Smith after hearing all those stories.

Note the smile on his face and where he happened to be positioned, only mere feet from where his great-grandfather stood a half century before. Someday, somewhere off in the future, I know that his children will stand there, too.

As for me, when I go down for the final count it is my wish to have half of my ashes placed in Terlingua Creek and the other half overlooking the Smith. Maybe some of those same children will be grown by then, and can be the ones to put me there.

And I'll finally be back for good.

"It is always a comfort when you can see the footprints of another man in the mire and the slough, for if that man passed through unharmed, so may you, for his God shall also be your Helper."
–Charles Spurgeon

You are atop the very tip of the southern uplift for Chorro Canyon, about a quarter mile east of Madrid Falls. These falls, which are usually not much more than a seep, are supposedly the second highest in the State of Texas. Chorro Canyon has been one of the most reliable sources for plentiful amounts of water in this country for as long as anyone can remember.

Below and out of sight due to an intervening ridge at mid-frame is the old Madrid Place, a nineteenth century ranch headquarters that lent its name to the nearby falls. When viewed on traditional 1:24,000 USGS topographical maps, this immediate area is divided into quarters that come together at the top of that same intervening ridge.

That means the uninitiated sojourner needs to carry four different maps to keep his bearings and plot a successful course through these parts. It makes for a headscratcher at times, and a lot of rocks on the ground to keep your maps from blowing away while you orient yourself. Nothing is ever really easy in the lower Big Bend.

But oh, the views and sensations to be experienced while passing through. Center frame you can see Chorro Canyon and Arroyo Primero coming together, along with a wagon track that ran the shoulder of Chorro Canyon from the ranch headquarters, and into a dead end near the base of the falls.

The bottoms for the two crevices join together not a hundred yards from the Madid ruins. Together, they sway back and forth in a slow West Texas waltz while wandering their way to the still larger Fresno. You can follow their slow dance by the green dots of cottonwood trees, a sure sign of water in the Chihuahuan Desert.

On the horizon at a good thirty-five buzzard miles away are the Chisos Mountains, with both Casa Grande and Emory Peak plainly visible. Still further beyond center right and nigh a hundred miles away, you can make out the lofty far blue ridges of the Sierra del Carmen.

Below them on our side of the river is the unique shape and colored shades of Cerro Castellan, guarding the northern approach into the long defunct farming community of Castolon. Immediately to the right and closer in is the distinctive triangular form of Sierra Aguja, often called Needle Peak. It, in turn, is partially masked by the beginnings of the jumbled-up jigsaw puzzle that makes up the northeastern part of Mesa de Anguila.

That's a lot of rough country, the kind that makes one feel sort of small and insignificant when compared to the far grander scheme of things around you.

I think we all can use a little dose of that feeling every now and then, you tend to both give and receive more in life that way.

44

"Manifold and marvelous, O Lord, are thy works, whether of nature or of grace; surely, in wisdom and loving-kindness hast thou made them all; the earth, in every sense, is full of thy riches!"
--Thomas Hartwell Horne

It was a very early spring and we were scouting out Arroyo Segundo, a large canyon that acts as a feeder into the even larger Fresno Canyon. The arroyo enters the Fresno north of the Smith Place, and just north of Rincon Mountain.

In the photograph you are standing on the north side of Arroyo Segundo looking down into a drop off made of craggy, twisted, multi-colored walls of eroding rock. They serve as a handy hiding place for a series of water seeps and tinajas.

This spot was recently named 'Mexicano Falls' by Texas Parks and Wildlife, I am unaware of any other name save for 'the pour off in Arroyo Segundo.' This shot emphasizes the sheer roughness of this country, and how fervidly it guards whatever sources of water there might be available.

Inside the lip of the drop off are the tinajas, the last one being near inaccessible from any direction. Seeps from a nearby spring keep these tinajas replenished and they beckon in beguiling fashion. But just below is a plunge of at least fifty feet straight down, adding sauce for the goose if you desire to work your way into that last one. Imagine Wiley E. Coyote plummeting off one of those cartoon mesas should you make a wrong step, or shift your weight at just the wrong moment.

Approaching from the west, you have to climb out of the canyon as there is no real way to work yourself down the drop off unless you have plenty of rope. I know, because we tried that day from several different angles. To gauge the scale of this, keep in mind that some of those cottonwood trees in the frame stand more than twenty feet high, and that larger waterhole is about twelve feet wide. Past this point and on to the Fresno is a comparatively easy stroll in the sun, but you must get into the canyon floor first.

Once below you enter into a new world in some ways. The Fresno runs the length of the west side of *El Solitario* and is fed by numerous runs coming off the immense laccolith. Opposite is the Llano escarpment and canyons the size of Arroyo Segundo. With the rest of the watershed beyond and the creek itself snaking to and fro, it makes for plenty of territory to prowl and many sights to see.

As a child my family leased much of the lower area along Fresno Canyon, as it was far easier for us to reach it from Lajitas than to work those sections from off the escarpment.

Looking at this photograph, I think you can understand why.

> *"For man, as for flower and beast and bird, the supreme triumph is to be the most vividly, most perfectly, alive."*
> *--D. H. Lawrence*

You are looking easterly down the canyon from above Mexicano Falls, with Rincon Mountain to the direct front. As far back as I can recall, and as far back as my research has taken me, this chasm was always known as Arroyo Segundo. However, TPWD has recently started referring to this chasm as 'Arroyo Mexicano.'

But beyond some controversy as to what exactly to call what, the fact remains this particular state park is one of the biggest, most dramatically striking and seldom visited state parks found in the United States. The acreage alone would make up about half the state of Rhode Island, and the sheer ruggedness of the terrain makes it stand alone in our current state park system. We, the citizens of the great state of Texas, are blessed to have it.

On a more individual level I am doubly blessed, for some of this country constituted a personal playground for me during much of the time I was growing up. I have many fond, lingering memories of this land that few others can fully appreciate, or even really understand.

Contrary to my beginning quote, there are no flowers in this photograph. It was still too early in the year for the most part, as well as the traditional spring rains lacking in their presence. But in the midst of this roughhewn, isolated, chunk of the Chihuahuan Desert, I do know what the poet meant about that supreme emotion of being so vividly alive.

In the pell-mell, rush here and there rat race of what we call modern life are many people who possess other, less harmonious, emotions to deal with. These are best described as an enduring sadness, a lack of fulfillment or of belonging to something worthwhile.

48

So many know not where they go or who they are because they remember not where they came from, or who they were. It is as if they are a storm-racked ship at sea, sails torn and tattered with compass spinning madly about and no one at the helm.

I believe this driving feeling of despair is part of our human condition, and on occasion all of us must sup from that table of bitterness and bile. We seek, yet we know not what we seek for. We know that something is amiss within us but have no idea of where to find it, or even where to begin to look.

But for what it is worth to the listless and lost, these are places where I have found my bearings many times before. It comes as no surprise that ancient prophets of both the Old and New Testaments had their life-altering epiphanies and visions while alone in the desert.

A solitary place where they found replenishment for their spirit and meaning in the world around them, as well as the world to come.

For me it is here, in spots like this of the lower Big Bend.

> *"We learn something every day, and lots of times it's that what we learned the day before was wrong."*
>
> **--Bill Vaughan**

You are standing on the southern end of the escarpment that overlooks Chorro Canyon, and that is Madrid Falls directly to your front. Behind you the Chorro meets up with Arroyo Primero, near the old adobe ruins of the Madrid Ranch headquarters. On the earliest topographical maps for this area it is referred to as the 'Madril', another one of those spelling quirks by some cartographer that is so common in the historical records for the lower Big Bend.

Madrid Falls is supposedly the second highest waterfall in the state of Texas, and you can't see all of it due to the angle of this particular photograph. But you can see enough to realize that it is fairly high, and about as lush and green a spot as can be found in this part of the Chihuahuan Desert.

Much of the surface water present is actually above the falls, where a couple of good springs provide ample amounts even in the driest of conditions. Most of the time, except when following a good rain, the drop off itself is almost dry. Water trickles down the face of the rocks to the bottom and then seeps underground again. From there on, occasional pools can be found under copses of cottonwoods all the way to the Fresno.

When it does rain in this country, these canyons can carry raging torrents of water that have shaped the cliffs, crevices and folds of the Fresno for eons. They must make for a spectacular sight coming off the falls, but unfortunately one that I have never been blessed to see. Perhaps one day I shall.

Shortly after my grandfather passed in early 1977, some reporter for *Texas Monthly* wrote a long, somewhat sensationalist article about the lower Big Bend. The reporter referred to Madrid Falls as having been lost for decades but recently 'rediscovered' by a survey team. He went on to rhapsodize about it being the closest thing to Eden in West Texas, among some other rather tall talk about other area locales.

Even while still under the shadow of our patriarchal loss, my family managed the humor to find this article amusing. Years ago we worked cattle up and down through this land, and nooned more than once at the abandoned Madrid Ranch headquarters. It was my grandfather who first showed me these falls.

But beyond my personal childhood recollections, Madrid Falls was still part of the living memories of hundreds of other people at that time. These people included other members of our clan as well as friends, acquaintances and families who lived in the general area. Many have passed on since then, but like my grandfather shared their knowledge and memories with whomever might have an interest.

I guess you could sum this irony up best when my Dad joked: "Lost? Hell, I didn't even know they had turned up missing. Maybe somebody didn't ground hitch 'em right and they wandered off for a while."

And somewhere in the Great Beyond, my grandfather likely spit a stream of Beechnut tobacco and just shook his head.

"Enlightened people seldom or never possess a sense of responsibility."
--George Orwell

Most might think this photo was taken somewhere along Limpia Canyon in the Fort Davis Mountains but in actuality it is Arroyo Segundo, above what is now called Mexicano Falls. This area is replete with stunning vistas and strange, almost surreal sights; those that make one's mind work beyond its usual sphere and refill the spirit in ways never fully explained by mere words.

Many of these places have traditional names that stretch back over a century and more. Yet for some unknown reason beyond my own sense of propriety, certain bureaucrats for Texas Parks and Wildlife took it upon themselves to rename a portion of the landmarks found in this area.

This renaming has occurred throughout the park and often been conducted with little to no rhyme or reason. In the process, these efforts run contrary to USGS topographical maps as well as generations of local knowledge.

They also manage to sow confusion among newcomers who are relying upon those maps to guide by. Arroyo Segundo becomes Arroyo Mexicano, Post Mountain becomes La Posta, Burnt Camp becomes Papalote Ramon, and the list goes on.

What is being lost in this errant reshuffling? Well, as an example Burnt Camp has quite a bit of history to it, even literary history as the setting for a Louis L'Amour short story. Yet they changed the name of the camp while still calling the trail that leads through it Burnt Camp Trail.

Then they wonder why *turistas* get lost down here.

Go figure.

Not long before he passed, I was visiting with Lonn Taylor, a historian of some regional as well as national repute. He was asking me questions about Fresno Canyon. While doing so he mentioned being hired by Texas Parks and Wildlife to detail the historical significance for these landmarks, as well as their names.

Evidently Lonn put considerable time and effort into that research, turning in some hundred and fifty pages worth of findings. According to him, his report hit the circular file in almost record time.

I asked why TPWD would do such a thing and Lonn laughed in his characteristically hearty chuckle, followed up with that knowing smile of his.

"Money and politics," he replied. The report ran contrary to the personal agendas possessed by certain powers that be.

But putting aside what occasionally happens to our collective history, in size, singularity and remoteness the Big Bend Ranch State Park is surely a crown jewel in the Texas park system. It does not matter where you have been before in this region, you have not really experienced the lower Big Bend unless you have spent some time here. Throughout my life I have traveled this area on foot, on horseback, by mule and by vehicle. Much like the lower Big Bend itself, I still have not seen anything close to it all.

One other point that needs to be made and I would be terribly remiss by not doing so: There are really fine, knowledgeable people working for TPWD and this land is truly their passion. They are the ones who actually live on site and work in these environs, sometimes for decades.

They are not the anointed, 'enlightened' type who sit behind an oversized desk in some congested city, justifying their positions by rebalancing the scales between political contributions, returned favors, and related general skullduggery.

I tip my hat in sincere appreciation to the former. What I think of the latter is best left unsaid.

*"Out where the handclasp's a little stronger,
Out where the smile dwells a little longer,
That's where the West begins."*
--Arthur Chapman

This particular quote and photograph was first emailed to my Tia Maggie, who had sent me a treasure trove of family photos from a lower Big Bend now mostly dead and gone.

Among them were those of a hunting trip via horseback and mule along the west side of Fresno Canyon. Many years later, I took nearly the same shot from the same angle along that same trail leading down to the Smith Place. This trail has been in use since the late nineteenth century, and is now part of the state park backcountry network. It is one of the few spots where you can get off the escarpment and into the canyon fairly easily.

After I moved to Alpine, Tia Maggie began conversing back and forth with me in emails and Facebook. Some of you reading these lines might remember a few of those posts, as Tia had a mind like a bear trap on a hair trigger. A very quick wit, too, and she could recall dates and places and events as if they had only occurred yesterday.

By that period in her life, Tia was suffering from health problems and couldn't get around much anymore. Walking was becoming difficult for her and she could only see at distance with the aid of a rifle scope, and that was for putting venison on the table.

Tia Maggie always appreciated my photos and essays. By her own admission, they would take her back vicariously to what she always considered 'home.' Often enough she would respond with a thought or a story of people and times long passed.

Two of those stories involve this particular spot and the nearby surroundings. I will try to relate them as best possible, while attempting to retain the spirit in which she told them. The first she called 'Granny and the Mountain Lion.'

"One time your Papa and Granny, as well as your Dad and I along with a few hands were working cattle up by the Smith Place. Granny was riding her mule on the side of the escarpment, pushing some half-wild cows sheltering below the rim back into the canyon.

All of the sudden the horses started squalling and pitching, and no one was quite sure what was going on other than they needed to hang on. Cattle were bellering and scattering in every which direction. The hands down in the bottom were trying to hold them as best they could, amid their own personal little rodeos.

Meanwhile, Granny eased off the high side of the canyon to help and after about two hours' worth of resettling the situation, we finally figured out what happened. In her pushing those cattle down into the Fresno, she had also pushed an irate mountain lion into our midst.

There was nothing to laugh about when that cat bolted into the middle of us but after we thought about it a bit, we had to climb down and sit on the ground to have a good laugh.

I am still not sure who was the scaredest, us or that cat."...

The second one she called 'Baby Brother Ab.'

"Your great uncle Ab had wanted to be a cowboy so much that he quit high school, and your Papa was never real pleased about that. He and your Granny had helped raise his baby brother, and I suppose Papa wanted more for him.

Anyway, Papa told Uncle Ab to come on out to the Big Bend. That if he could cowboy there without breaking his fool neck, he could cowboy anyplace. First real workday after Ab arrived was in the Fresno above the Smith Place, and Papa had picked out Ab's mount.

That horse was like molasses in January. From the get-go Ab did little more than just stumble through that ol' canyon. Meanwhile, your Papa was all over Ab like a bulldog on a postman, riding him hard about keeping up and making himself useful. Uncle Ab got plumb flustered and that made the situation even worse, because that was when Papa really started needling him.

This went on all day long until they made camp that evening at the Smith. That was when Ab began examining his horse more closely and then angrily exclaimed, 'Ben, this horse is blind!'

Ab tried to light into Papa, but your grandfather was literally rolling beside the campfire from laughing so hard. He had pulled a good one on his baby brother, and was teaching him a life's lesson about wanting to be a cowboy.

Needless to say, Ab was real good about checking his horses from that day forward."...

Tia Maggie later admitted she shed tears while relating those stories, tears from wonderful memories of that country and the loved ones she shared it with. She also said that my essays and photos took her back to many of the happiest days of her life.

Now, I sit with this photo before me and the words I have just written about a few of those shining times. Tears are forming in my own eyes, the same as in hers for they are the kind brought on by joy, gratitude and love.

This one's for you, Tia.

Muchisimas gracias para todo.

"We have seen rugged strength devoid of beauty, we have also seen elegance without strength; the union of the two is greatly to be admired."
--Charles Spurgeon

You are standing in Chorro Canyon, some ways down from Madrid Falls. This line of sight takes you easterly toward the Fresno and beyond there, *El Solitario*. Many folks have called this spot 'Madrid Canyon' over the decades due to the waterfall. It was also part of the Madrid Ranch, one of the earliest ranches around and dating back to the late nineteenth century.

The adobe headquarters sits upstream in the canyon, about a quarter mile above where this photo was taken. As a child I used to hear some unusual stories about the place but not anything that I could ever independently confirm. Behind the ruins sits a good-sized cave, another site carrying a bit of vague mystery and lore from a long time ago.

To make it even more confusing to the newcomer, the remnants of the Madrid place actually sit just inside Arroyo Primero, which joins Chorro Canyon at that point. On most any topographical map, the stretch in the photo is labeled officially as Arroyo Primero. So this one crevice is known by at least three names that I am aware of, and each has a certain amount of veracity that comes with the naming.

As I have written before, the ebb and flow of humanity through this country over the past 150 years has led to many an enduring puzzlement. Furthermore, so many come to the lower Big Bend and think they have discovered some sort of new land, never giving any thought to those who came before.

This 'tradition,' if you will, carries on into the present. Even now someone, somewhere, has already either renamed a landmark or is thinking about doing so. Human nature, I suppose.

In the end, it is far better to know the lay of the land than what someone might be calling it at that particular moment. Proof positive to this are the copious amounts of good water shown in this photograph, as well as the shade provided by those cottonwoods. No one would likely know this rock-walled oasis even exists, other than having been there before.

Keep in mind this was taken during the height of a dry spell that many people mistakenly called a 'drought.' The enduring presence of such well-watered spots, amid an otherwise harsh, arid environment, are likely the main reasons the Madrid family settled here.

Trees and water are the true silver and gold of the lower Big Bend, everything else is just gravy.

"There is always one moment in childhood when the door opens and lets the future in."
--Graham Greene

Not too long ago I spent some time prowling beyond the northern edge of Contrabando Mountain. This general area, framed by Lajitas, Fresno Canyon and the southwestern reaches of *El Solitario*, holds many a good memory for me. I grew up here, my very foundations in becoming a man are rooted in what you see in this photograph.

Looking west across the rugged land from Whitroy Mine, past the heights of the Wax Factory Laccolith, and on to the western escarpment above Fresno Canyon, I stood on land where prior generations of my family had stood before.

If memory serves me, back then the Whitroy was known as the White and was not much more than an old rock house situated near some prospective diggings. My grandfather, along with my dad and other men such as Ray Atkinson, Cliff Wilson, Tull Newton, Chon and Ramon Armendariz and others used the house as a base camp.

Sometimes that was for working cattle and sometimes on hunting trips, depending on what the circumstances or mood of the moment. Not too far away, just over the fence line on the east side, my Tia Maggie and Uncle Tommy acted as caretakers for the Fresno Mine, along with the Lone Star and others in the immediate area.

Tia washed their clothes in a warm spring hidden in a rocky arroyo somewhere to the north. I think those two covered every square inch of the surrounding country on foot, as that was what they did for entertainment.

I hear many folks refer to Fresno Mine as 'Buena Suerte' these days and that is factual in part. But when we were here, that name was reserved for the original site at the foot of Wax Factory Laccolith inside Fresno Canyon. Though the town as well as the name were moved to Fresno Mine in the early

1940s, those who had been around for a while persisted in remembering the locales as they were. It was a habit I picked up from them.

More particularly, it was a habit learned from my grandfather and there was reason for that. If there was anyone who served as my role model and who I tried to emulate in every way possible, it was him. As a boy it was my estimation they did not come any tougher or more capable, or more respected because of such manly qualities.

Decades later after I became better acquainted with his surviving peers, I found my estimation confirmed in their words and recollections. That discovery has been a very precious thing for me, as he passed before we could relate to each other as men. Someday I shall see him again, we have a lot to talk about.

But for now I stood where he once did and about as old as he was when passing on to the other side. While thinking of him and the many other poignant memories of growing up here, it occurred to me just how blessed I had been throughout my life in so many different ways.

And how so many of those immeasurably precious blessings started here; in this rough, desolate, timeworn land known as the lower Big Bend.

It makes a man, whether young or old, want to fall to his knees.

Just to give thanks.

61

THOSE TO RIDE THE RIVER WITH:

*"Now from a distance I look back on
what the Corps taught me:
To think like men of action,
And to act like men of thought!
To live life with intensity,
And a passion for excellence!"*
--John Mattis

More often than not these days, when I go into the back country my journey is a solitary one. Both of my sons are grown now, and often times far away in the service of our nation.

They and a few friends make up my list of trusted companions, as I would rather go it alone than with someone I cannot count upon for physical strength, unflappable courage, good sense and an abiding respect for God's Great Handiwork. The few comprising that list mostly are men, real men, and they'll do to ride any river or cross any desert with.

Now and then we still get together and head 'out yonder,' wherever that particular yonder might be at the time. When this photo was taken, the 'yonder' was up, down and through parts of the western forks of Fresno Canyon.

As one can discern easily from my prior essays this is rough country, sometimes very rough and nigh impassable in numerous spots. That is when those qualities of good sense and abiding respect step to the forefront. This land does not suffer fools gladly, and when a fool makes a mistake out here it often proves costly to all involved.

This group photo was taken while trailing up Arroyo Segundo, making our way toward Ojo Mexicano. From left to right is my older son, Captain

Benjamin Levi English, USMC (Annapolis Class of 2011), myself, Michael Valaik, former Captain, USMC (Annapolis Class of 1988), Nathaniel 'Nate' Valaik, Lieutenant, USMC (Annapolis Class of 2013) and my younger son, Ethan L'Amour English, Lieutenant, USN (Annapolis, Class of 2013).

The Valaiks are family friends of ours, an exemplary breed of Americans who have served our nation ably through the generations. They are the kind of men I have in mind when I speak of those trusted companions, and they as well as the others on that short list have proven that trust time and again.

This essay is dedicated to the men in this photograph, and to those special ones I have journeyed down life's path with. Of all the blessings the All Mighty has seen fit to bestow upon me, they and their kind surely constitute a part of the greatest. To all who have shared that path with me at one time or the other: many, many heartfelt thanks.

You know who you are...

> **'Over the Mountains**
> **Of the Moon,**
> **Down the Valley of the Shadow,**
> **Ride, boldly ride,'**
> **The shade replied,—**
> **'If you seek for Eldorado...'**
> **--Edgar Allan Poe**

You are standing near what the state park now refers to as Chorro Vista Trailhead, looking east across Fresno Canyon into the western reaches of *El Solitario* Rim. From here you can see the flat irons of the Solitario; the craggy, corkscrewing canyon walls of the Lower Shutup and the small, almost invisible spire that makes up Chimney Rock. Above and to the far right on the horizon are the Chisos Mountains, all blue and with no visible terrain features, telling you just how far away they really are.

Today we were headed down into the Fresno itself, to visit a collection of treasured childhood memories most folks call the Smith Place. It had been a long time since I was there, but now the park was finally open and I could visit my recollections of long ago on this majestic spring day.

I spent many an hour there lazing under the shade of cottonwoods on a hot summer afternoon, and sneaking in some wading in the water holes nearby. Ate a lot of noon meals by its walls while working cattle with my grandfather, even camped out there once or twice.

From the Smith Place all the way down to Fresno Farm at the mouth of the canyon, over to Lajitas and back around the east side of Contrabando Mountain had been my own personal playground as a child. Even at five years old on the back of an old jenny named Becky, I felt like a knight in training who could roam his fiefdom at will.

And roam I did, filled with the imagination that only a child can possess and yearning to go and see what lay over the next hill or around the next bend. My grandparents seemed to understand that yearning as they were much the same in thought and character, though theirs was more seasoned by the crow lines in their faces as well as the graying of their hair.

In many ways I suppose that seasoning taught me much in becoming an adult, while they in turn were remembering what it was like to be a child. There are many things in this world that strive to alienate the generations but in this case, and in this dry, desolate, isolated land, there was something supremely precious that bound the generations together.

So many wondrous sights, adventures and challenges worthy for the training of that young knight-to-be abounded all about. Few children ever had a grander playground or a better proving trail by what you see in this photograph.

Then I grew up and the world beckoned from afar, and I rode off to answer the call.

CHAPTER THREE

GLENN SPRING AREA

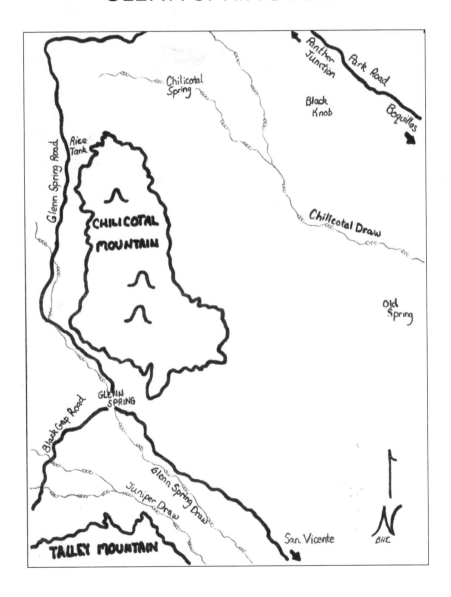

There are places in the lower Big Bend where the voices of those from time immemorial speak out to the sojourner wandering into their environs. Shaman Cave comes to mind, along with Persimmon Gap, Comanche Crossing, Payne's Waterhole, Manos Arriba and Apache Canyon.

Glenn Spring surely belongs to that list, though like the others the name has been changed repeatedly even from languages that no longer exist. Human activity in these spots go far into the past beyond the era of the Comanche, Kiowa and Apache, who were in truth very much latecomers to this desert.

The site was known as Jordan Spring before a surveyor was killed on the east side of the Chisos, done in by the last remnants of Apaches who once called those mountains home. His last name was Glenn and the spring was renamed in his memory.

But no matter the name, this site has figured large into the tapestry of mankind since he first came to this region. According to those who know far more than I, that is estimated to be more than 12,000 years ago.

Those are the voices in now unknown tongues you occasionally think you hear as you explore the immediate area of Glenn Spring.

Tread lightly and leave nothing in your passing, my friend. For the ghosts of countless others are watching you.

"Tomb, thou shalt not hold Him longer;
Death is strong, but Life is stronger;
Stronger than the Dark, the Light;
Stronger than the Wrong, the Right;
Faith and Hope triumphant say
Christ will rise on Easter Day!"
--Phillips Brooks

Almost invariably the most popular spot for the casual sightseer in most any abandoned community is the graveyard. Arguably the Glenn Spring area has more than one. The site shown in this photo is by far the most popular as it is the largest and easiest to find.

The terrain features and landmarks seen here are somewhat emblematic of the importance of Glenn Spring through the centuries. Most all of the crosses pictured mark the resting spot for Mexican workers and family members who came looking for a better life.

Directly behind you can see the clefts for Glenn Spring Draw. This eroded arroyo, which gathers its power from Juniper Canyon and Hayes Ridge along the eastern side of the Chisos, stops only long enough to give shelter to the spring before making for the Rio Grande about eight miles away. From these gravesites you can see the greenery marking where the river lazes to and fro, working its way to Boquillas Canyon and the Sierra del Carmen.

The high mountains pictured are on the Coahuilan side of that brown water boundary line, angled to form a natural funnel to San Vicente Crossing. That was the original fording for the eastern main branch of the Comanche War Trail, and was also used by other tribes long before any Comanche ever saw a horse.

After Irish expatriate and Spanish Army officer Hugo Oconór strategically placed a presidio overlooking the crossing, the Comanches shifted mainly to

Paso del Chisos to continue their depredations and buccaneer-like line of commerce. That location is out of the frame in this shot, sitting below the southernmost reaches of the Chisos called Punta de la Sierra.

As the land was settled and civilization embedded a far larger footprint, unimproved roads were run throughout the lower Big Bend connecting one area-wide point of importance to another. Glenn Spring acted as a hub for such activities, with several vehicular tracks and branches of tracks leading to and through.

A candelilla wax factory came into being here in 1914 and a community sprang up around it, calling itself 'Glenn Springs' in the plural. Most of the population was Mexican and as I mentioned before, so are the graves. They came here not only for the economic opportunities and betterment in life, but also because their homeland was in the midst of a fevered violence of near-genocidal proportions.

Those sweeping waves of incessant brutalities sometimes spilled over the northern banks of the river, and so it did in Glenn Springs on Cinco de Mayo, 1916. A large raiding force swept in with a vengeance, leaving four dead, multiple injured, a store looted and several buildings burned to the ground. The dead included a four-year-old boy.

The community tried to rebuild and for a few years was partially successful, but after the end of World War One and a crash in wax prices most everyone moved on to other places and had other lives.

Now all that is left of Glenn Springs are the ruins and the graves, waiting in mute patience for the resurrection to come and serving as a reminder of the dying that has already occurred.

"No less dear than a brother, the brother-in-arms who share my innermost thoughts."
--Homer's Odyssey

A few years back I was interviewed by film director Andrew Shapter concerning a planned PBS documentary on the Porvernir Massacre. Unfortunately, that documentary was never completed as envisioned, as Mr. Shapter died from cancer not too long after our meeting. He was a talented man, and with the ability to look at history with no particular personal axe to grind while telling its story. I admired him for that.

During the filming we also talked about the Brite Ranch Raid, which was a prime instigator for what later happened in Porvernir. But when I began speaking of the other attacks conducted against American citizens prior to what happened at the Brite, such as the Santa Ysabel Massacre and the Glenn Spring Raid, Shapter said he had never heard of those before.

He was not alone, most people haven't.

But on the weekend of Cinco de Mayo of 1916, a best-estimated force of between 150 to 200 Mexican raiders swept across the Rio Grande and into the lower Big Bend, striking against what was then Boquillas, Texas (now Rio Grande Village campgrounds), the ore tramway terminal near Ernst Basin, and Glenn Springs. These invaders have been variously described as Villistas, Carranzistas, or garden variety bandits. However, they were commanded by a Lt. Col. Natividad Alvarez under General Francisco 'Pancho' Villa, which seems to clearly identify the main culprit.

Alvarez's main force struck Glenn Springs around 11:00 PM that night. The ensuing battle lasted for hours as nine soldiers of the Fourteenth Cavalry, stationed as a token force due to the persistent border troubles, engaged the raiders. The cavalrymen, awakened by shots being fired into their tents, grabbed their weapons and made for an adobe building to make their stand.

Outnumbered, outgunned, but not about to be outfought, the men of the Fourteenth Cavalry resisted with whatever they had. As the sounds of confusion and exchanged gunfire echoed off Chilicotal Mountain, the fighting went on at a steady rate as both sides sought to secure their respective positions.

After a few hours of near stalemate, the raiders managed to set fire to the thatched roof of the adobe structure, forcing the cavalrymen into the open. Three were killed in the ensuing fusillade, while the surviving six were mostly wounded and or burned before they could reach cover.

This attack, among others, set into motion a large military effort led by General John J. 'Blackjack' Pershing to secure the border. Many of the young officers under his command would ultimately lead our nation to victory on the global battlefields of World War II.

This photo is of the general area where the adobe building once stood and those soldiers died. No memorial stone marks their service, no flag flies at perpetual half-mast, no specific Memorial Day remembrances are given in note of their sacrifice.

Just dead cottonwoods, low heaps of rocks or busted brick, some rusty barbed wire, eroding firing pits and an occasional shell casing from a Springfield .30-06.

The scene has always saddened me.

"Even a lonely lodging in the desert was preferable to the soul anguish he experienced in the midst of his people."
--Charles L. Feinberg on the prophet Jeremiah

Glenn Spring is one of those places I have passed through somewhat frequently when wandering through this country, and on occasion this site has been my main destination. I enjoy prowling the surrounding hills and arroyos, there is so much more present than what first meets the eye.

One of those oddities sits to the southeast of what most folks consider as Glenn Springs proper, beyond where the candelilla wax factory once stood and situated close to the edge of a low rise. It is the burial spot for James T. Lewis, a young man who died at the way too early age of thirty in February of 1917.

The grave marker stands alone, by itself and apart from anything else that presently bears the mark of man. I have tried to find out more about Mr. Lewis, who he was and how it came to be that he was buried here in this manner. So far, I have come up with next to nothing. Perhaps someone reading this can shed some light of knowledge on this.

But the strangest thing is the marker itself, a rather large and impressive one put up by the Woodmen of the World. Many years ago while in the Marine Corps I was a member of this organization, and helped with youth programs they sponsored. They were best described as a fraternal insurance company, and were quite popular a century ago in many parts of our nation.

An interesting tidbit to their story is having started the first television station in the state of Nebraska, appropriately christened WOW-TV. One of their first daily program hosts was a young local man and former amateur boxer by the name of Johnny Carson.

I have seen many of their memorial markers, which usually appear as a stump or a tree-shaped headstone with an inscription upon it.

But nothing quite like this, so perfectly preserved after more than a century and in such a quiet, isolated place.

"The desert does not mean the absence of men; it means the presence of God."
--Carlo Carreto

I had gotten a later start than hoped for and the blistering sun of mid-day was pulling sweat from every pore. Standing in the saddle of a low ridge, my eyes surveyed the dry, broken land spread before me.

Fishing out the compass from my war belt, I rechecked my azimuths to Ernst Canyon, Talley Mountain and the top of Chilicotal, figuring the magnetic declination for each in my head. I was still too far north by a good half mile and adjusted the straps of my pack to begin anew.

My goal was a pinprick on a map that was a hundred and sixteen years old, set on a 1:125,000 scale leaving plenty of room for error. The dot was labeled 'spring' and no other record of it could be found over the past nearly ninety years. That was a long time in a desert where springs go dry and never come back, leaving little more than the melancholy sense of a natural open grave.

As I drew closer to yet another piece of high ground, my attention went to the remains of a small trail, now almost gone. Its ghost wandered up the side of the next uplift and toward where the spring was supposed to be.

Two more gulleys and some intervening mesitas went by. The terrain changed from sand and dirt to rocky folds stacked upon each other, running to and fro like the solidified waves of an unsettled sea. That trail had faded off into nothingness and I found myself moving forward on the desert bred instincts that have served me so well.

I checked the azimuth again to the summit of Chilicotal Mountain, it was lined up just as it should be. If that spring was still here and that map was correct, I had to be close. Real close.

Then I spied another trail, this one working up a bare slope to where it slipped over the rise. Thing was the path took the slope at an angle leaving one to wonder whether it was going to water or away.

Deciding to play it safe, I circled to where the ridges were higher and could see more of what was around me. When I looked over my right shoulder, I observed what I had come for about a hundred yards away. That trail had led right to it.

This was one of the many photographs taken during the next half hour or so. In it you can see the remains of one of two dead shade trees, the other laying to the left beyond frame. Further still was a small, scraggly cave of eroded dirt that appeared ready to collapse.

Beyond camera lens to the right, the lip of the bowl ascended into a rock shelf that provided shelters for man and animal alike. No telling how long they had done so, or when man first discovered such an unlikely place exactly where it was not supposed to be.

The bowl itself was made up of surrounding small ridges, emptying out on this end. Water oozed from several seeps under large rocks and small boulders that ran across the lip, pooling in large spreads of lush, green grass. Easing beyond the edge of verdancy, the tongues of moisture sunk into parched, never satiated sand.

Later I would make a wide loop, swinging a good mile and a half further toward Glenn Spring. The maze extended in every direction, as if the desert itself was providing protection to its greatest treasure of all. Other trails, now mostly unused, drifted in from three directions.

I approached the spring again from the opposite side as day shifted into early evening, wanting to make certain the location was etched in my memory. That pinprick on a map was just as elusive in reality as it was on paper.

And then I wondered how many other men had done the very same for a thousand years and more.

"History is the witness that testifies to the passing of time: it illumines reality, vitalizes memory, provides guidance in daily life, and brings us tidings of antiquity."

--Cicero

When most people see Glenn Spring these days (or 'Glenn Springs', as the community itself was often referred to), they are usually looking through the window of an air-conditioned vehicle enroute to some campsite along the river. Very few will give it the scantest of attentions and far fewer will wander among its ruins, giving thought to what must have been here in bygone eras.

From long before the time as a watering place for the Comanche along the San Vicente trace of their great raiding trail, Glenn Spring served prehistoric man. It is placed well for such a purpose, and as a reliable water resource has always held a special importance to any desert dweller.

It has also been a settlement, a candelilla wax factory, an army outpost, a social gathering spot and most infamously the site of a Mexican bandit raid on Cinco de Mayo of 1916. There are ruins, markers, fence posts, wire, firing pits, bits of machinery, graves and other things slowly wasting away under the relentless sun; scattered hither and yon across dozens of acres.

One of the more enduring spots from life a century ago is this dipping tank. Most likely built and first used for Army cavalry mounts and supply animals, the vat is the most complete relic to be found from those years, along with the possible exception of the James T. Lewis headstone. Even the posts for the holding pen and squeeze chute are still here, though the restraining barbed wire has by and large long since vanished.

Unless you are connected with the livestock industry of Texas or knowledgeable of what was once known as Texas Tick Fever, you are likely unaware of the great damage done to the cattle industry by these insidious parasites of the late nineteenth century. Entire herds had to be quarantined and then destroyed. Ranchers saw their life's work ruined by a tiny arachnid, and sometimes there was blood on the ground because of it.

In the early 1900s, the United States Government became active in the arsenic-based dipping of livestock to stop the spread of this deadly infection. While horses and mules are not affected by this cattle-specific disease, they could carry the ticks with them into unaffected areas. Plus, ticks carry a variety of other ailments and the US Army had strict procedures for the dipping of their mounts and supply animals.

This is an enduring statement to that policy, and the not-so-good old days of cattle ranching. So much so that USDA-employed tick force riders still patrol the counties of south Texas to keep infected animals out of our country. My grandfather was one of those riders some eighty years ago.

It was yet another way in which he was "one to ride the river with."

"Never forget that, when once God has entered into covenant with a soul, He will stand to it, till the heavens be no more."
--F.B. Meyer

On the north side of Chilicotal Mountain, near opposite Glenn Spring, sits the remains of a ranch headquarters belonging to a pioneering clan who came here early on. They were the Rice family, most notably brothers John and Fred Rice who had separate spreads in the lower Big Bend. Fred's was in the Grapevine Hills but John decided to settle at Chilicotal Spring.

He chose well, a location that had good water and yet still managed to sit high enough inside a sort of cove for protection from the winter winds. Trees of different varieties were present to provide shade and to this day the immediate area is green and lush near year round. Most of the location is grown over now but the family cemetery still stands on the high ground to the north, well cared for and tended to by descendants of those who are buried in this ground.

The photo was taken while looking in an easterly direction, over the lower elevations that trail off to Tornillo Creek, and on to the Sierra del Carmen perched along the distant horizon. Behind you are the beginning eastern slopes of the Chisos. Not too far away Glenn Spring Road runs past the almost vanished turnoff to get here.

Even in the middle of winter, one gets the sensation of what a special place this must have been to live and raise a family. John Rice was a hardworking man who had dreams, and tried his best to make those dreams into a reality. One of the enduring testaments to his legacy is Rice Tank, built by Viviano Castillo while he working for Rice.

Castillo, a noted area stone mason, finished the tank not too long before John Rice passed away. Rice was buried on the land he loved so much, in that same well-kept cemetery overlooking the spring. Beside him lie two infant children as well as the grave sites of those who labored so long and loyally for his family.

It does not matter whether they were Anglo or Hispanic, they worked and lived together in mortal life and now together they wait the coming eternal resurrection. Ironically, death is surely the most unprejudiced presence that man finds in this life. Likewise, The All Mighty that created them all will give unprejudiced judgement in what is to come, no matter skin tone, social status or last name.

So, they wait in this quiet spot for the final roll call, and one can freely admit there is not a better place in our passing world to do so.

CHAPTER FOUR

LOWER TERLINGUA CREEK AREA

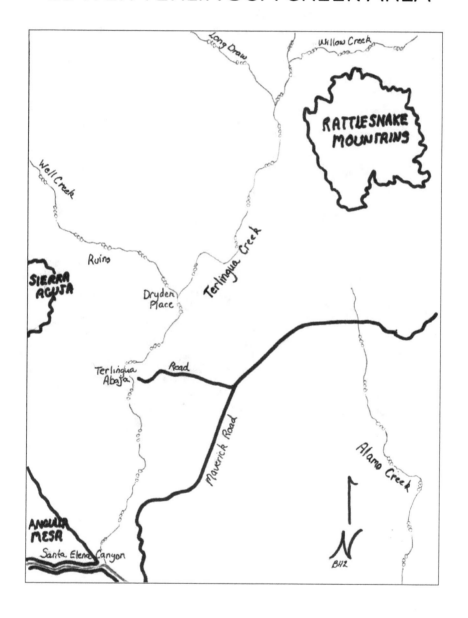

In this timeless desert I have wandered far and wide, miles upon miles on foot across some of the most inaccessible, inhospitable land found in the lower Big Bend in search of something special. Something to admire, something to ponder upon, something that brings back a memory of another time, an event, or a person now long since passed.

Those memories can be joyful, poignant, wistful, sad, even painful. But I have learned to embrace that pain, for without our pains from the past we would not be who we are today. And with much of that pain, there was usually an important lesson in life learned the hard way.

Few places bring back so many of those memories than Terlingua Creek. Our old ranch headquarters sat on high ground with it winding below us, not more than a couple of hundred feet from the house. The times I have crossed it on foot, by horseback or by vehicle easily numbers into the thousands. Yet I cannot think of a single time when something within me did not stir upon doing so. That stirring brings back those same memories and emotions, time and again.

There are times, usually late in the evening, where everything is so still and quiet that you can feel the desert itself breathing. This wild, winding, ever changing and surprising old run, some seventy miles or so in length, serves as one of this desert's main arteries to feed its singular way of living.

Without the Terlingua, the Tornillo, the Fresno and the Rio Grande collecting them all, this desert would surely die.

And so would my memories...

"What we think, or what we know, or what we believe is, in the end, of little consequence. The only consequence is what we do."

--John Ruskin

When one becomes aware of the history of a land and the accompanying personal stories of those who came to make a life in it, one seems to be able to reach through the veil of time and space and touch those long-gone souls in some special, indescribable way. Or perhaps, it is more of a case of them reaching out to touch ours.

The lower Big Bend is rife with such experiences, especially when one travels alone and unencumbered by distractions. Some years ago, while on one of these solitary sabbaticals, I made my way up Terlingua Creek to return to some childhood memories.

This photograph was taken on that journey and illustrates the very essence of three related families who came here and not only survived, but prospered. They were the Valenzuelas, the Molinars and the Francos.

Their contributions to the entire Big Bend area as a whole needs to be remembered and these ruins symbolize only the scantest of a tiny slice of what those contributions were. To this day, long-time denizens of this region recognize the three family names and associate them with peace officers, judges, public officials, career educators and other honorable pursuits.

This particular spot along Terlingua Creek was known as the Santa Rosa, headquarters for the Molinar side of the clan. The Molinar headquarters was built out of native rock and though not lived in during my lifetime, it has managed to withstand the destructive force of the desert better than most.

Behind the structure you can see how it was built close to the western bank of the Terlingua. Beyond the creek and to the middle right are the northern faces of the Rattlesnakes. Then Tule Mountain, Burro Mesa, and the Chisos themselves. No one could ever say this structure was lacking for spectacular scenery.

Look still closer at the foot of the Rattlesnakes. You can make out the huge salt cedar that marks what was once the headquarters of Felix Valenzuela, who ultimately made the supreme sacrifice while performing his duties as a duly elected constable. These families were not only related in blood but shared the same challenges, the same soil and the same water that flowed through the creek.

Like the Valenzuelas, the Molinars and Francos were involved in freighting for the mines. During the 1920s and 1930s, the Santa Rosa was important enough in the affairs of those around them to have a small grade school built on site. Children from surrounding ranches and farms received their primary education here.

The John Ruskin quote above lends itself well to these families and to this land. It brings forth many dreams in many guises, it always has. Yet by far the most important, and rarest, are those that manage to blossom into full fruition.

For the rarest breed of man is the one who not only dreams good dreams but has the inspiration, as well as the fortitude, to make them come true.

Remember that and remember these people.

"The strong do what they can, and the weak suffer what they must."
--Thucydides

These adobe ruins on the east side of Terlingua Creek, overshadowed by the profile of Santa Elena Canyon in the background, are what most people think of when they hear the name Terlingua Abaja. Those who have gone will usually park here, take a quick peek from near these ruins, and then head back to their air-conditioned vehicles as quickly as they can. Invariably they will idly speculate on how anyone could ever survive out here, or want to come in the first place.

The more adventurous sort, usually brought on by cooler weather, will cross the creek and make their way over to the Humphreys' residence. This brick and native rock ruin is the best preserved of all the dwellings present, and later served as the local school house. Then they will stroll over to the main cemetery, take a few photos and call it done. For them, that is the totality and sum of what this community once was or ever will be.

I write about Terlingua Abaja in two different chapters of my first book *Yonderings*. Furthermore, this photograph details the scene for some of the final pages of my first novel, *Destiny's Way*. With what knowledge I have of this abandoned farming community, I can assure you this: There was and still is much more present than a cursory glance could ever discern.

Its limits once stretched out in every direction; fertile fields, homes, barns and large copses of trees lined both sides of Terlingua Creek. If you happen to look even closer when wandering about, you will see bits and pieces that tell of other, far older settlements that were here. There are also unmarked graves secreted away that are at least fifty years older than anything in that main cemetery.

These bits and pieces bring forth many questions to the inquiring mind, questions that pick and nag at one's imagination every time it stumbles across the recollections of what was found. Those questions will never be answered as such forlorn, anonymous pricks of civilization are lost to the dustbins of history; as are the names, lives and reasons for being here.

But one thing is for certain, Terlingua Abaja was not the only pioneer settlement established along the lower reaches of Terlingua Creek. It was just the first one to actually survive.

Up to then, the Apache, the Comanche and the Kiowa saw to that.

"The world is charged with the grandeur of God."
--Gerald Manley Hopkins

Most everyone who ventures into Big Bend National Park for any length of time has at least one photo of Santa Elena Canyon. I know that I have more than a fair share in my personal possession, some dating back into the early 1950s or before.

What you usually see is taken from a distance and shows the very mouth of the chasm, most likely from some point downriver. Yet there are sights to behold throughout its entire length, as those who have been inside this well-known landmark can tell you. Furthermore, that statement does not even begin to cover what can be seen on and around Anguila Mesa, which makes up the northern side of the crevice and extends upriver almost all the way to Lajitas.

For those who might be interested, there once was a popular site to take photographs of the canyon from a higher point. It was located on a tiny mesita just off Maverick Road, a short spur that took you to the very edge of this elevation on the east side of Terlingua Creek. The entrance has long since been bladed under, but the remains of that track are still there if you know where to look.

The shot chosen for this essay is a little different than most. It was taken from inside the canyon looking down the Rio Grande and towards the Chisos Mountains. They sit majestically on the far horizon with Emory Peak forming the very tip of this particular royal crown of uplifts.

A short trail leads to this vantage point, not far from its end as the path is pinched into nothingness by the sheer cliff walls. Looking at the photograph closely you can see just how still the water is, there is no sign of a breeze until you look downstream near the mouth and that slight ripple in the water. It was a very warm day in the month of June, at Terlingua Abaja about an hour earlier we had recorded a temperature of 116 degrees.

With that kind of heat this particular summer stroll reminded me of a title for an old black and white movie made near the end of World War II. It was called '*A Walk In The Sun*,' a fitting five word commentary to describe this little jaunt from the very last part of Terlingua Creek and into the canyon itself.

The lack of a breeze and the reflected rays of the sun made for a near furnace like environment, a furnace in which someone had set the knob on high and then ripped it off for good measure.

Do not ever underestimate this country's ability to get hot in the summer months.

Or for that matter, any other time of the year.

"Do not go where the path may lead, go instead where there is no path and leave a trail."
--Ralph Waldo Emerson

As is so often said, a picture can be worth a thousand words. This photograph likely falls into that particular category; it was almost included in my first book *Yonderings* but did not make the final cut.

That was probably just as well, a tiny black and white space could never convey the odd feeling you get trooping across ground that looks as flat as a billiard table only to be confronted with this. It is yet another anomaly among countless others, and a perfect example of nothing being in the Big Bend quite like what it first appears.

The central subject in the frame, the Rattlesnake Mountains, are roughly divided in half by the park boundary line that zigzags haphazardly through them on a generally northeast to southwest basis. Though it might seem more proper to some to refer to this range as mere hills as far as elevation, make a mental note in doing so. The Rattlesnakes are rough, desolate and contain slides of shale and crumbly rock formations that can give way beneath you with little warning.

This is especially so along the rim for this range, which almost completely encircles the upper levels. I know it fairly well as many years ago we used to lease the adjoining Valenzuela place, which took up whatever portions of the Rattlesnakes not deeded to the park. We ran some cattle there, used it for a hunting camp and would pick up a load of candelilla wax on occasion.

The Valenzuela also served as our base of operations during some of the wild burro roundups the National Park Service attempted back in the 1960s. It is, and always has been, lousy with mountain lion. So much so that it could just as easily been named 'Catamount Heaven', much like Cow Heaven Mountain on the opposite side of the Chisos Mountains.

In this photograph you can see part of that rim on the south side of the Rattlesnakes, ample evidence of its roughness as well as why it is a favored haunt for the big cat. In that pocket concealed from the casual eye by stark shadows sits not so much as a cave as what might be best termed a hollow, worn away by erosion and time. It makes for good shelter and temporary respite from the sun on those piercingly hot days this immediate area is infamous for.

Above the hollow is a low pour off, which in turn becomes a dry run that begins at the very upper elevations for the range. After a good rain, which is not often, lingering pools of water can be found up there and around the hollow itself.

It is a convoluted, contrasting and sometimes almost otherworldly place. Yet these secluded spots containing such offbeat surprises are also why I will continue to explore this harsh, exotic land until the end of my days, path or no path.

Trail or no trail…

"Those who forget God's works are sure to fail in their own."
--Charles Spurgeon

When one glances across the desert at what is referred to as the Rattlesnake Mountains, one usually does not give them much more consideration than thinking they are aptly named.

In reality, they are nothing much more than hills; desolate, even foreboding in appearance, especially when viewed from the south across some of the most barren ground to be found in the lower Big Bend. One might further surmise that even rattlesnakes could have a hard time eking out a living there.

Yet once you venture into them, your perspective changes rapidly. For here is beauty; raw, rugged, craggy and roughhewn, but a true natural beauty all the same. More so, one can find the remnants of man's shaping hand scattered across them going back hundreds of years. This in turn leads to further inspection and in that you find sources of water in the form of springs and tinajas, the silver and gold of any such environment.

Adding to this liquid silver and gold is Terlingua Creek itself, running along the western perimeter of the range. Sometimes so close that a large boulder rolling from the cracked and timeworn rim could conceivably come to rest in the creek bed itself. The wide, far reaching run has water in it also, though often enough not very good water. But in this bleached bone environment you take what you can get and be grateful for it.

I first became acquainted with these mountains as a kid. At that time my family had possession of the old Valenzuela place, just across the fence line that serves as a northern boundary for the national park. We occasionally ventured on horseback into the Rattlesnakes over those years and in doing so I learned to not only respect them, but to also appreciate their uniqueness.

This photograph was taken just below the southwestern edge of the uplift, looking across the wide expanses consisting of Terlingua Creek, Sierra Aguja (Needle Peak), the hills surrounding Terlingua Abaja and on to the horizon and

95

Mesa de Anguila. There is a lot of history between where I was standing and the cliff faces of that mesa. However, most of what has happened here in man's struggles will never be known.

Other than by the sun, the mesa and the desert.

"Oh, do not lose heart and hope in useless weeping over the closed doors of the past. Follow Him, who has the keys."

--F.B. Meyer

On the west side of Terlingua Creek, near the boundary for the national park, are the ruins of what was once a thriving enterprise of the lower Big Bend. Known as the Dryden Place, it was a prosperous combination of ranch, farm and a brick making factory. The site even had its own cemetery.

When prowling other ruins in the lower Big Bend, pay close attention to the markings on any bricks at whatever location you are visiting. You will sometimes find the word 'Dryden' inscribed on them. In fact, there are structures still in use where bricks manufactured at the Dryden continue to do their jobs.

Many people erroneously think the kiln was located at the ranch headquarters, where this photo was taken. However, it was actually about a half a mile north from here, on the other side of Wells Creek where that dry run empties into the Terlingua.

In the frame are the remains of the headquarters itself, a rather large structure made from a mixture of rock, brick, wood and adobe. That line of bleached cottonwood tree trunks formed the foundation for the roof. Behind the ruins you can see the eastern walls of Mesa de Anguila, with the cut visible to the far left that forms the mouth of Santa Elena Canyon.

Also, to the left and beyond the lens of the camera is the cemetery, sitting about a hundred and fifty yards away. Not much has been done in many years to keep up the site and the graves are giving way to the steady march of time.

There are no cottonwoods these days at the Dryden, no fertile fields, no little cabritos in the rock shelters out back, no smoke from the kiln. Only the ruins and those dissolving graves manage to give the slightest sign of the hub bub of human activity that once occurred here every single day.

Even most of the memories of this spot have long since moved on.

"As I walked through the ruins of Tyre I heard no music nor laughter. I could not see the buildings or the gold and silver. All I saw were broken pieces of pottery and the wreck and ruin of what had once been a great city."
--J. Vernon McGee

This is certainly not one of the prettiest photos in my collection, but it and others taken during this particular outing are some of the most important among the many thousands in my possession.

The reason is they serve as a bell warning for us all, and to the truth that the road to hell is surely paved with the best of intentions.

Once upon a time, verdant fields stretched from the southeastern slopes of Sierra Aguja and almost to the mouth of Santa Elena Canyon, covering both sides of Terlingua Creek. They were the essence of a farming community commonly known as *Terlingua Abaja*. Or as Mrs. Benavidez sometimes reminds me, *Terlingua del Abajo*. She would know, her grandparents lived here. On rare occasion, you might even come across reference to it as '*Terlingua Vieja*.'

But whatever name you prefer, during its era this was one of the most successful agricultural centers in the lower Big Bend region. I have seen antique black and white photos of steam-powered tractors working these fields, giving hint of the high level of activity occurring at the time.

Terlingua Abaja was thriving in the business of supplying victuals for area mines, military camps and trading posts. It had its own school, cemeteries, church, store, post office and small cantina, along with numerous residences scattered about.

99

But a subsequent drought, combined with primitive farming techniques and overuse of water resources resulted in what you see in this photo. The decaying fingers of erosion spread rapidly, taking away the top soil and leaving little more than demanded by the now prevalent greasewood and mesquite.

When this land became part of the national park, Senior Ranger George Sholly attempted to reseed the area to hold whatever top soil remained. He even obtained an old farm tractor to help in the effort.

That bit of common sense, initiative and innate love for this land nearly cost him his job.

Since then, that terrible mistake has been realized and currently there are programs doing much of what he first envisioned all those years ago.

Finally, some eighty years after being mostly abandoned, native grasses are beginning to grow again. But the great deal of damage already done will likely take another eighty years to show some semblance of repair.

This desert gives off the most obvious of danger signs and speaks in silent eloquence of hard-won lessons to many a heartbreaking tale. One only needs to pay attention to what she is trying to tell you.

I hope the people of the present lower Big Bend are paying attention.

As should we all.

"What have you done, you there,
Weeping without cease;
Tell me, yes you, what have you done,
With all your youth?"

--Paul Verlaine

North of *Terlingua Abaja* are the ruins for what was once a large operation referred to as the Dryden Ranch. But you couldn't call it just a ranch per se, because it was far more reaching in scope than that. The Dryden was also a fairly large farm and possessed a brick kiln factory of area repute.

In this photo you see the cemetery for the ranch, which gives you an idea of how active it was over a century ago. Carefully inspecting the site, I estimated there were eleven graves.

I say 'estimated' as the graveyard sits on the edge of a low knoll and wind, sun, and rain have eroded some of these mortal testaments back to whence they came. Many of the identifying markers have rotted or disappeared with time and those still in place bear nary a name. It is a quiet, lonely place where few pass by and fewer still spend much time.

When I was a child, the Dryden was one of those agreed on locations where my family would pick up loads of candelilla wax being smuggled out of Mexico. It was way off any beaten path during those years and just inside the park boundary, with easy enough ingress and egress.

By day the cemetery is a lonesome place that brings on feelings of sadness. But at night it can be plenty spooky, cozied up to under the dark of the moon while waiting for a string of burros to come drifting in like so many wayward will-o-the-wisps.

Especially for a six-year-old boy with a very active imagination.

"The only real security that a man can have in this world is a reserve of knowledge, experience and ability."

--Henry Ford

I was on one of my solitary sabbaticals, headed from Santa Elena Canyon to the northern limit of the park just above the Dryden Place, then on to the Rattlesnakes. It had rained some hours before dawn and the greasewood had that singular fragrance that only comes after such a blessing. The weather was damp and cool, and the breeze played with the clouds above the western reaches of the Chisos, forming them into a natural collage among the peaks and vales.

Dropping off the eastern shoulders that form the high ground above Terlingua Creek, I drifted aimlessly along in a back and forth fashion through the bottoms below. You never know what you might find out here, even if you have passed through the same spot a dozen times before.

A change in shadow, season, or the slightest shift in eroding soil brings new perspective to what you would swear was not there before. Just moving twenty feet over in any one direction can bring forth a new world, for those who take the time to actually see what is around them.

The lower parts of Terlingua Creek are infamous in that. From below Hen Egg Mountain to the mouth of Santa Elena Canyon have been numerous settlements and enterprises that never really took root for one reason or another.

During the time of the Great Comanche War Trail, nearby Spanish and later Mexican settlements were utterly wiped out by hostiles. Some of these ill-fated spots dated back to the late eighteenth century, even years before the American Revolution.

Around Terlingua Abaja itself are dissolving remnants of homes, irrigation ditches, fields, farming implements, vehicles, groves of trees and an occasional gravesite, sitting quietly in a losing battle against time. It is a Rubik's cube of different eras, cultures and purposes.

One of the more modern of these past relics is shown in this photo, the partial skeleton of a Ford Model T. What was left of it was resting beside a near gone adobe wall built into the side of a small hill, forming the bank for a gulley entering the outer part of Terlingua Creek.

And yes, it is actually a Model T as the radiator cover was still laying there in that rusting heap of discarded metal. There is no better way to determine the make of a car or truck from that era than by looking at the radiator. All were different in some manner.

The venerable Model T was a true game changer in the history of the lower Big Bend, just as it was for the rest of our nation. The first roads put through this region were actually wagon tracks, and Henry Ford's masterpiece for the masses was eminently adaptable to them.

Cheap, dependable, easy to maintain and repair, and just as tough as anything that ever ran on four wheels, these cars and trucks issued in a new age of personal transportation and mobility. Most would think this to be an eyesore full of junk, but to me it was almost like a desert shrine.

A shrine to what was passing during that era as well as one to the era to come.

And to borrow that old adage; 'If only it could talk'...

"But I don't want comfort. I want God, I want poetry, I want real danger, I want freedom, I want goodness. I want sin."
--Aldous Huxley, Brave New World

These ruins sit beside the almost vanished road that once ran between Lajitas and the Dryden Place, with a spur that took off through Terlingua Abaja and ultimately to the old Sublett Store. When I was a boy, my grandfather would drive this road by dead of night, easing into the northwestern boundaries of the park to pick up loads of candelilla wax.

This spot was sometimes his destination, or served as a landmark for our longer journeys to the very edge of the river. Oftentimes he would take me along with him and it wasn't until years later that I realized he was teaching me things that a man should know.

In that I was learning from a master of the craft, because as in other things he possessed a rare gift for knowing the land and moving through it. My two hitches in the Marines and a career as a peace officer benefited immensely from those lessons, and I was not even aware of being taught.

My grandfather was a sixth generation Texan, not too far removed from the philosophy of our mutual ancestors who had squared off against Spanish lancers, the Mexican army, Yankee carpetbaggers, Comancheros, outlaws, revolutionaries, hostile Indians, environmental elements of every kind and whatever else that came along and posed a perceived threat to him and his.

He was a tick force rider, cowboy, rancher, foreman, truck driver and served two terms as a sheriff in south Texas. To hear others tell it, he never backed up or backed down from anything in his life, and his word was his law. After some sixty years of my own living on this earth, I can truthfully say he was one of the toughest men I have ever known.

Edward Benton 'Ben' English Jr. has been gone for over forty years now and like these ruins, his era has long since passed. It is now the twenty-first century and we are in a Brave New World which he would neither understand nor much agree with. Both he and these ruins were too raw, too rough, too much of their own time and the attending stark necessities of it.

In short both were what they were, without apology or explanation.

I write this not in grief for them, but for this brand-new world that we have made for ourselves. For what we have lost was of far more value to the human character and spirit than anything we may have gained in the interim.

"Only aim to do your duty, and mankind will give you credit where you fail."
--Thomas Jefferson

There are arguably two cemeteries in the abandoned community of Terlingua Abaja, with more in the general area if one knows where to look.

The lower reaches of Terlingua Creek are dotted with mostly forgotten graveyards, burial sites and solitary, lonely piles of rocks that cover the remains of a human being known only to his or her God.

As time goes by, more and more of these spots of eternal rest are found in such condition. When I was a boy there were far more markers still up, more names still legible or someone, somewhere who still knew who might lie in that sacred plot of soil. On occasion, you would be out horseback working cattle and come across one where the unknown faithful had lit a *vela votiva* in remembrance.

You'd stand up in your saddle stirrups, looking all around at miles of nothingness and wonder where they had come from and to where they had returned. A strange sort of melancholy feeling would follow, but there was also a sense of peacefulness and respect. It was as it should be, even in the desolate emptiness of the lower Big Bend someone still remembered.

These days you don't see this much anymore. It seems when more people come to a land, the less attention is paid to those who came before. Perhaps there lies an essential element that we are losing in our hectic, technologically driven lives, the grace found in showing simple respect. Respect for others, respect for ourselves, respect for the land, respect for, as Thomas Jefferson once wrote: "The Laws of Nature and of Nature's God…"

Instead we hurtle headlong into an unknown future, unmindful of the landmarks of the past and unheeding of the attending lessons to be learned from them.

This is how man's nature conspires to fool future generations and how in turn, we shall be forgotten by those who follow on.

"The ghosts of other dead men stood near me and told me each his own melancholy tale."

--Homer's 'Odyssey'

No matter where you go in the lower Big Bend, no matter how desolate it may seem or far away from present civilization, you will find the remnants of someone having been there before.

That is the difficulty with so many who come to this land. They have no grounding in the history they have made themselves a part of, nor an appreciation for their predecessors.

When you are near any source of water in this desert, such evidence becomes particularly prevalent. For every tiny mark you might find inscribed on an old map, there are literally dozens upon dozens of other places that no one ever bothered to make even such a miniscule note for. Men and women were born in this area, grew up, labored and died within those very same environs, their life stories lost to time and anonymity.

First it was the Indian, the peaceful tribes which were in turn forced out by the more warlike clans such as the Kiowa and Comanche. Then the Spaniard, the Mexican, the Tejano and later the *Norteamericano*. Each had their turn in this desert, and each in turn disappeared or morphed into something else as time went by. Those who are not native to this country must learn to adapt, no matter what their ethnic background or skin color.

Now we are here, yet who knows who will come in the future or for what purpose. But of this you can be certain, we will only be here a little while to ponder such sights and to realize that we are only the latest of so many who came before. Ruins such as these serve mute, yet brilliantly eloquent testimonies to that premise.

When you come upon such a spot, tread lightly where you step and turn not a stone. Respect what is there, for you are walking amidst dead men's dreams.

And one day, you will surely join them.

"He is immortal, not because he alone among the creatures has an inexhaustible voice, but because he has a soul, a spirit capable of compassion, and sacrifice and endurance."

--William Faulkner

One of the most popular sites at Terlingua Abaja is the rock house ruins, sitting on a low rise near the north end of this one-time farming community. You can stand at certain vantage points near the primitive campsites east of Terlingua Creek and spot the ruins quite easily, they are the most prominent of all the manmade structures in this particular area.

Some might recall this building as being the schoolhouse for the Terlingua Abaja (or Terlingua del Abajo) residents. To better understand firsthand the hardships once involved in obtaining even a basic education, I have heard that certain present-day schools bus their students down here on occasion to take a look around. Kudos to whoever came up with that particular idea.

But before it was a school, these ruins were the private residence of Joe and Sally Humphreys, who ultimately left this community in 1919. During the preceding years, Mrs. Humphreys taught the local children in her home on a de facto basis, and after the Humphreys moved away the structure was then declared as the official schoolhouse for the village.

Not long afterwards the population declined to being near nothing and the school was closed down. As far as I know, no one ever touched it after that so what you see presently is some eighty plus years of decay from the sun, the rain, the wind and the occasional vandal.

Yet through all it has endured, this crumbling rock structure is still the most complete relic of that era to be found, as all of the other community structures were made of adobe or partially dismantled for other purposes.

112

There is just something about this place, so many hopes and dreams dissolving back into the earth from where they came.

"First, she said we were to keep clear of the Sirens, who sit and sing most beautifully in a field of flowers; but she said I might hear them myself so long as no one else did."
--Homer's 'The Odyssey'

I stood on a rise on the western boundary of the national park, above Willow Creek which runs to your direct front in search of the Terlingua. The late afternoon was quiet and still, and there was not another person to be seen in any direction.

Much of my entire world as a child lay before me, bringing back old thoughts and memories, deeds both bad and good, and those who had gone on before to what waited beyond the shadowy veil. To me, this is a portrait of peace and contentment, as well as needed introspection and of knowing of at least one place in this world to belong.

This place and this land, a magnificent, desolate, singular country that had allowed me room to roam, to explore and to grow uninhibited by not much more than school, my chores and my grandmother's admonition to "*Cuidado, Bennie Howell...*" My long-suffering mother shared much the same sentiment, save for in the English language.

Everything within this frame and beyond, from here to the horizon, had started me upon my personal proving trail. This included a menagerie of lower Big Bend landmarks such as *El Solitario*, the Aqua Fria, Hen Egg Mountain, Sawmill Mountain, Leon Mountain, Terlingua Creek and the Valenzuela. Each had served as my playground, had fed my first stirrings to become a man and at certain times had been my crucible.

It all started here and I had wandered far from it, sometimes under protest. Yet even after four continents, thirty some-odd countries and many a blue sea and adventure, I always came back. In Homer's classic work *The Odyssey*, he writes of the sirens along a sea's craggy shores whose songs no man could resist. There are no craggy shores here, nor a sea, but the desert has her sirens, too.

I have heard them my entire life, calling me home again.

CHAPTER FIVE

CHISOS MOUNTAINS AREA

All days in the lower Big Bend are special for one reason or another; it is a land of extremes with all sorts of varying combinations. Each one has its own style and effect on the land, and no two are ever exactly the same.

The Chisos Mountains are likely the best example of this. The unusual shapes, the acute angles, the constant variety of formations and elevations mixed with sun, shadow, cloud, moonlight, or a canopy of stars morphs the scenery into something markedly different every few minutes.

One of the truly thoughtful things in how the National Park Service laid out the park is the variety of ways available into these mountains. You do not necessarily need to hike mile after mile, nor scramble over hill and yon to see sights that stir both the imagination as well as the spirit.

In this the park planners provided a great service to each of us; easy access to awe inspiring beauty no matter what one's physical infirmity might be. Or you can saddle up and rough it along one of the many trails that make up the Chisos system, the planners saw that need, too.

But whatever your mode of travel, do not neglect the calming of the soul that occurs by just sitting and watching. It is like viewing a motion picture in real time, though the terrain is permanently fixed the sun does move and the images constantly change with the shifting shadows. It is a masterfully orchestrated show for the ages that never ends.

Some years back, during the latter part of May, a front had moved in and settled upon the Chisos like an infant child lovingly covered by its mother. An acquaintance of mine, who is an outstanding photographer as well as human being, half-joked that he wasn't going to get any good shots because the morning was 'boring.'

I looked at him and remarked only half-jokingly: "I oughta knock the fire out of you for saying that."

He grinned back, knowing my true import and meaning. Then he grabbed his camera and took off towards the Window. That evening he extolled repeatedly on what he had found along his path.

Life is too short to have a boring morning anyplace, much less in the lower Big Bend country. This is especially true when sitting among these lofty crown jewels of Texas, sculpted so impressively by God's Own Hand.

"---O remember
In your narrowing dark hours
That more things move
Than blood in the heart"
--Louise Bogan

You are standing on the Dodson Trail, near the eastern terminus at the mouth of Juniper Canyon. It was mid-September a few years ago, and the traditional late summer rains had ordained the Chisos Mountains in all their glory.

I had spent several days up here in solitude, never saw another human being or cut recent sign of one. It was as if I was the last man left in the lower Big Bend and the feeling brought back warm memories of a childhood where I would sometimes imagine the same, both in being so isolated and in being a man.

From here you can see how the canyon moves up to the eastern slope of Casa Grande, sitting there center frame and partially obscured by an early morning cotton-ball cloud drifting across its features.

To the left and just beyond the reddish bald dome is where Boot Canyon enters the Juniper. At that point, a seldom-used trail winds around to the top of the South Rim, intersecting Boot Canyon Trail near the cabin and corrals.

The high ground on the right side of the frame is Crown Mountain, which forms the northern wall for Juniper Canyon most all the way to the head. A primitive road dead ends about midway up the gorge, the tip of a spur that branches out of the Glenn Spring/Robber's Roost area.

Many years ago, that tip turned into a trail leading all the way up the canyon and over the saddle between Casa Grande and Lost Mine Peak. These prominent landmarks, boundaries for the valley within, combine to make for a place where one would be hard pressed to see it all.

118

Then you remember this only composes a thin slice of the Chisos as a whole.

I have few other photographs in my collection that better hint of the true majesty and rugged beauty of the Chisos Mountains, and why Big Bend National Park is such a special spot in this world.

And yes, although I have considered myself a man for some time now, the photo nearly brings tears to my eyes when looking at the frame.

It makes one want to step into it and start walking forever.

"We're living in the 'information age,' but we certainly aren't living in the 'age of wisdom.' Many people who are wizards with their computers seem to be amateurs when it comes to making a success out of their lives."

–Warren Wiersbe

I have many photographs of The Window taken over the decades, back into the early 1950s not long after the park was established. But of the dozens upon dozens in my possession, this particular shot has to be one of my favorites.

Everything was just right on this early morning. Recent summer rains had moved through, adding not only vibrancy to everything living but cleansing the very atmosphere itself. It was still and quiet, the kind of sunrise where a boot slipping on stone can be heard a quarter of a mile away.

With the naked eye you could clearly pick out landmarks and places that in actuality were twenty air miles away or more. Our old ranch used to sit within view of here, and we would look backwards through The Window to where I stood now.

We had no electricity and I would stare up at the Chisos at night and see the lights twinkling through The Window, like stars that had been corralled after falling from the sky above. It just seemed to be that sort of place, even to a child.

But no matter what the season of the year or of one's life, there is always something magical when it comes to the Chisos Basin.

You know, I have stood at the front desk of the lodge and listened to irate *turistas* rant and complain about the phone service, the lack of modern 'conveniences,' that it was too hot or too cold or too far away or…Well, you get the general idea.

And without exception, the attending staff member listens and tries to make things better. They do a very good job with this sort of person, far better than I ever could.

I know that for a certainty, because meanwhile I am standing there wondering what part of the planet Clueless this one happened to beam in from.

If they would only take a deep breath and a long look around. One of the greatest shows on earth is playing to every side of them at that very moment, and a different act begins anew as each day drifts by.

But I guess that some people look, yet do not see. They hear, yet do not listen.

They touch, but they do not feel.

It is as if they have a presence but not a soul.

While they stand in the spot where even as a child I thought the stars were kept for safekeeping, after falling out of the night sky.

"When I speak of a wakeful man, I mean one who does not take the soul to be a fancy, nor heaven to be a fiction, nor hell to be a tale, but who acts among the sons of men as though these were the only substances, and all other things the shadows."

--Charles Spurgeon

AUGUST 28th, 2018

This is the story about a mountain, and a bit about a man who has seen as much or more of the Chisos as anyone I know.

Not too long ago I was visiting with my friend Bob Sholly. His father, George Sholly, was the first chief ranger for Big Bend National Park back in 1944. Bob grew up in these mountains and as a kid climbed to the top of many that most would think nigh impossible.

They say that youth is wasted on the young but in Bob's case that just might not be true, because I believe he spent every waking moment thinking about this country and the secrets it had to offer. Furthermore, he continued doing so into his adult life, sometimes going far away in body but never straying much in heart or soul.

We had been talking about different spots and places when Lost Mine Trail came up. Bob looked at me and commented, "You do realize the trail ends about a half mile from the actual peaks, don't you?"

Now folks, over the decades I have been up and down that trail more than once or twice. But it never occurred to me that gnarly, boulder-studded high ground to the northeast was actually Lost Mine Peak. Or as Bob pointed out, 'peaks', as there are two of them.

Then he went on to describe the best approach, the equipment needed, the time it would take and the effort required for the climb.

Like I said, he doesn't waste much of anything and God gave him a mind and a memory for detail that is second to none.

Bob is now at M. D. Anderson being treated for lung cancer. It is going to be a very tough battle, but he is a very tough man who has seen more than a couple hard fights.

This photograph was taken of Lost Mine Peak, near the trail's end. Studying it carefully I realized there is much in common between those peaks and the man I know as Bob Sholly. Or to be more specific, Colonel Robert H. Sholly, US Army (ret).

You see, Bob is also a highly decorated and experienced combat soldier, starting out as an infantry platoon commander in Vietnam. His many following accomplishments are far too numerous to list here, but one of the best reads about the Vietnam War is his book *Young Soldiers, Amazing Warriors*. Currently Bob is writing about his many adventures while growing up in the park.

Yes, he has a life-long habit of not wasting much, including every day he is gifted on this earth. A wakeful man indeed.

This one's for you, Bob. You are in my thoughts and my prayers.

And if anyone reading these lines is also of the Faithful, I sure would appreciate some sent his direction. I know that he and his family can really use them.

Even mountains have their moments of need.

125

"Did you ever stand on the ledges,
On the brink of the great plateau
And look from their jagged edges
On the country that lay below?"
--Bruce Kiskaddon

You are looking off the South Rim of the Chisos, gazing in a southeasterly direction to a far horizon filled with the mighty Sierra del Carmen. Below and away is the old Dodson Place, Fresno Creek, Glenn Spring, the Chilicotal, Robber's Roost, Elephant Tusk, Talley Mountain, Boquillas Canyon and a hundred other landmarks and terrain features that are visible from here.

Many times I have stood high on some mountain in the lower Big Bend, letting my mind wander as my eyes took in all they could to feed the abiding passion I possess for this land. Often enough when doing so, the words to Bruce Kiskaddon's *The Time To Decide* come to me.

Bruce Kiskaddon was a sure enough cowboy, a young man pursuing his life's calling beginning in 1898. He was one of those who saw the closing of the west in places like Arizona, New Mexico and Colorado, working as a cowhand on some of the biggest ranches then found in the American Southwest.

Later he would journey across the Pacific to ply his trade on the large cattle stations of Australia. That put him in a rarified position for a working cowboy, someone whose decades of cow knowledge and experience spanned two continents in two different hemispheres.

Kiskaddon would also serve honorably as a cavalryman in World War One, and worked in Hollywood as a wrangler and extra in many of the early westerns. It seems that no matter what he did, he just couldn't get that love for horses and cattle out of his system.

A quiet, unassuming man who ultimately worked as a bell hop in later life, Kiskaddon relived his younger years by writing some 480 poems before his death in 1950. To me he will always be the dean of cowboy poets because he didn't just talk the talk, he lived the life of a true cowboy and knew it intimately for what it really was.

His authenticity and realism sets him apart from most everyone else who has ever picked up a pen to express a thought on the matter.

To me, *The Time to Decide* is his finest work ever.

"Now Indianola, she's only a ghost,
On the jagged shoreline of the old Texas
coast;
Where the howling wild wind has raised up
its hand,
And buried her dreams in the sand..."
--Brian Burns, "Indianola"

There is a peak on the southeastern outer perimeter of the Chisos Mountains, an odd shaped formation some 5,249 feet in elevation that goes by the name of Elephant Tusk. Most anyone who has been in this region of the park knows it at least by sight if not by name, the way it is situated and its unusual profile immediately attracts the eye.

It is one of those prominent sort of landmarks the traveler almost instinctively uses to help mark his location, especially if in the lower elevations of desert to the east side of the mountain. But it wasn't always known by its present name and that is the subject for this story.

As a kid, I was a voracious reader of most any kind of book that I could lay my hands on. In my family, made up traditionally of cowboys, lawmen and pioneers, the favorite staple for literature was westerns both of fact and of fiction, and my favorite author for these was Louis L'Amour.

I believe I have read almost everything that man ever wrote, but one book in particular that stuck with me was entitled *Matagorda*. Like many of his other novels, it used an historical event for the story's background. In this case it was the near obliteration of a town in Matagorda Bay known as Indianola, which occurred in 1875.

Indianola, first known as Indian Point, was founded by German settlers in the mid-1840s. The site was chosen for its great possibilities as a port, a role that quickly saw it become the second most important of such on the Texas coast, next to Galveston. This was largely due to Indianola serving as the seaside anchor for one of three major freighting routes into Northern Mexico.

This route known as the Chihuahua Road, or the 'Cart Road' due to the large-wheeled Chihuahuan carts utilized by the Mexican *carretas*, ran from Indianola through San Antonio and points further west. It made its way into the Big Bend via Charco del Alsate (now Kokernot Springs), then through Paisano Pass and across the Rio Grande at Presidio del Norte.

At its height Indianola had over 5,000 residents, as well as a railroad to carry the vastly growing amounts of goods and freight. The port became a focal point for men with means and money, and with big dreams to make those present means and money appear as pauper's stakes. After The War Between the States, its future was as bright or brighter as any other community on the Gulf Coast.

That is until a hurricane of an estimated category three magnitude slammed into this region on September 16, 1875, with Indianola serving as the undeserving bullseye. They say the first surge in the late afternoon made twenty miles of inland prairie appear as open sea, before the tide began to slowly recede. Those who had taken shelter in the strongest structures emerged around midnight to give thanks, raising a cheer among themselves for surviving such an ordeal.

However, the true harbinger of destruction was fast approaching in the blackness of the bay. A second onslaught of sea water, calculated later as a surge between twelve to fifteen feet, fell upon the hapless townspeople in an almost biblical manner. In this nightmarish episode Indianola was literally wiped away, leaving only a half dozen buildings or so still intact. The loss of human life numbered into the hundreds.

For months the damage was vividly noticeable during an ongoing attempt to rebuild the shattered township. Indianola did come back to a certain degree, but never close to what it was prior to that single disastrous night.

A second hurricane, estimated as a category four, struck what was left of Indianola on August 20, 1886. Between the storm and an ensuing town fire, the dream of Indianola ceased to exist. What was once a major port and bustling community now lies in the offshore depths of Matagorda Bay, a final indignity brought on by the tremendous eroding forces of those two hurricanes.

The fate of Indianola serves as a truth to the old adage of "the best laid plans of mice and men," and how the course of history can be irrevocably changed by a single event. I myself have stood at the cheerless official marker for the old townsite, looking out across the bay and thinking about what it must have been like.

I have also idly wondered if any of those lost souls still have a presence, wandering about aimlessly amid those morose waters which took everything they had, including their lives. When I heard this Friday morning that Hurricane Harvey had caused a twelve-foot swell to sweep through that very spot, a chill went up my spine.

And what of that landmark in the lower Big Bend, the one now called Elephant Tusk? Well, in the late nineteenth century it bore another name, most likely in remembrance of a great tragedy that had only recently occurred.

That oddly-shaped mountain, standing forlornly in a desolate land that knows little of any kind of water, was first called 'Indianola Peak.'

"Man will have to give account for all that he saw and did not enjoy."
--Abba Arika, or 'Rab'

When one ponders upon it there is balance in this chaotic, sometimes incomprehensible world we live in. Whatever the debate or subject, or wherever we look, there are two sides to most everything. And if we but peer into ourselves and be honest, we find two sides there also.

So it is with nature in showing us stunning examples of this truth, no matter where we might go. The Chisos Basin, once known as Green Gulch, manages such an opposing scale between its two most popular landmarks, The Window and Casa Grande.

While The Window represents a great portal through which one can view the desert and mountains below to the faraway horizon, across The Basin stands Casa Grande, a superbly sculptured natural monument reaching thousands of feet higher than The Basin itself.

There is nothing else quite like Casa Grande in this region, and the uplift serves as the definitive mark of royalty for the mountains surrounding it. Even Emory Peak, though somewhat higher and impressive in its own right, does not have the majesty and captivating presence of Casa Grande.

This particular frame was taken along The Window trail, about a half mile from the pour off. To me, it captures the essence of The Basin as well as Big Bend National Park. These two opposites combine with the terrain spaced between them to create this effect, and to provide scenery that on occasion literally takes your breath away.

No matter how many times I have seen this magnificent uplift over the decades it still serves to bring forth awe, wonderment and reverence for God's Own Hand as a master sculptor.

Part of the magic of the Big Bend is that you do not have to walk far and wide across the backcountry to find yourself mesmerized, even inspired by these sorts of visual feasts.

131

In fact, you do not have to really walk at all. Pull your vehicle over to the side of the road and take a leisurely stroll measured in scant feet. Or just roll the windows down, turn off the engine and sit there soaking in all that is being offered to you.

The Basin provides near limitless opportunities for this, all you have to do is stop and enjoy.

*"Away out here they've got a name
For rain and wind and fire
The rain is Tess,
The fire's Joe
And they call the wind Mariah..."*

--Alan J. Lerner

The words to this song were running through my mind as I reached the end of Lost Mine Trail, on a huge slab of mostly bald rock. A thousand sights that supply the special moments for lifelong memories fell away from me on every side. About a mile away to my northeast sat the stark outcroppings that marked still higher ground, the two rocky knobs of Lost Mine Peak itself.

The wind was blowing hard enough to take extra care for where you had your feet placed. It was also bringing in gray, leaden clouds giving the slightest hint of moisture to the Chisos Mountains. A faint roll of thunder in the distance sounded a warning for the future possibility of lightning, and if so where I stood now was not where one wanted to be.

The three forces of nature mentioned in the lines of the ballad, those of Tess, Joe, and Mariah, were making their presence known in one guise or another.

That much needed rain would come as the sun set that evening, and continue to fall occasionally throughout the night.

The threat of wild fire would come from the attending lightning strikes as they marched across the higher elevations.

Wind, water and fire. There is nothing that Mother Nature sends to the lower Big Bend that is all good in every way.

But neither is it all bad.

For now, I would enjoy the curtain being lifted. For these coming acts, old as time itself, were still brimming with awe and inspiration in their latest performance, accompanied by a musical score echoing in my head that many have never heard.

It was the stuff those favorite lifelong memories are made of.

"The past is but the beginning of a beginning, and all that is and has been is but the twilight of the dawn."
--H. G. Wells

This is a side of the Chisos Mountains most never see, and in some ways the most spectacular. Perhaps it is because of the Rio Grande close behind me or the drastic changes in elevation, vegetation and geology from the river to the mountains themselves, a distance of not much more than five walking miles.

Or maybe it is in the individual landmarks pictured such as Punta de la Sierra, Dominguez Mountain, and Backbone Ridge while the South Rim, Crown Mountain and Elephant Tusk crowd in close from the rear.

Or maybe it is the sense of history, a history that predates any written record for people and events that have long since vanished from the face of this old and enduing land.

You see, it is my belief that one of the main forks of the Great Comanche War Trail once ran where this photograph was taken, headed further below to the long-forgotten crossing known as Paso del Chisos. Furthermore, like several other crossings that forded the Rio Grande, it was in use long before the Comanche first came to the lower Big Bend.

Paso del Chisos was said to have been nearly a half mile wide, worn down by the hooves of innumerable animals and littered with bones and castaway booty taken by the fearsome Comanche while enroute to winter in Mexico. But once the Comanche passed from the scene, the exact location was forgotten in man's memory.

I have studied old maps, transcripts and manuscripts about this place, and have put boots on the ground to retrace what I think was the most probable route. There is not only one, but rather two very good crossing points for the river below here, and even when the water is up you can plainly see the rock-bottomed shallows.

But most telling in the solving of this long-debated puzzle is the continued heavy use of this particular crossing by wild and domestic animals alike. Several very old, well-traveled paths come to a junction on the northern bank and cross over to the other side.

Man, with all of his intelligence, education and written records may forget certain places. However, the animals do not. For them such vital knowledge is passed down from generation to generation without interruption or cessation.

"When a man acts like a man, God can speak to him, and he to God. That is a declaration of dignity."
--G. Campbell Morgan

You are on the South Rim Trail about a mile from the ledge itself, in a spot where the path eases away from the edge of the uplift to clear a back slope. I had turned around to view what lay behind me, a long-serving habit to keep my orientation with the surrounding terrain and to see who, or maybe what, might be approaching. While doing so I decided to take this photograph, as the angle provides added perspective to several other landmarks.

From here you are actually looking through Boot Canyon, over the top of The Boot and on to Lost Mine Peak, framed in the far horizon. Just below the peak's summit you can see the ridge where Lost Mine Trail comes to an end on a massive slab of mostly bald rock. Behind Lost Mine Peak and out of view are Panther Mountain, Wright Mountain, Pummel Peak, and still beyond is the Panther Junction Park Headquarters.

This trip was memorable for a couple of reasons, it was the middle of summer and recent rains left everything that could grow both green and verdant. There was the feeling of the sun on my back, boot against stone, fresh mountain air in my lungs, and the sound of a thousand whispers as the breeze worked its way through the trees.

There was something else too, I was crippling along on a broken left foot.

Though I had covered this route several times before, the injured foot was slowing me down considerably. It would take most all of the daylight hours available to cover the loop from The Basin to the South Rim via Laguna Meadows Trail, then over to the Southeast Rim before returning back to The Basin through Boot Canyon and the Pinnacles.

This trip was absolutely spectacular in nature and due to my slower pace, I noticed many things I hadn't on prior journeys. Perhaps a little pain does sharpen the senses and makes you more acutely aware of what is around you. Or just as importantly, moving slower allows one to see more. I suppose there is a life's lesson in these thoughts, a moral that we too often forget when self-absorbed in personal troubles.

For no matter what challenges one may face in this life, it does have a way of balancing itself out.

*"A wandering minstrel I
A thing of shreds and patches,
Of ballads, songs and snatches,
And dreamy lullaby!"*
--William Gilbert

We launched out of The Basin early that morning, just as the sun was coming over the east side of the Chisos to bring some warmth to the chilled air of spring. Up Laguna Meadow Trail we went, moving along with shouldered packs and many a mile and mountain before us.

Past the spur for Laguna Meadow itself we branched into Blue Creek Canyon, working our way down with Emory Peak situated high behind us. The hours slipped by and then the day, night time would find us making a cold camp in a nameless wash south of Carousel Mountain.

Blue Creek Trail takes you to the foot of the Carousel and the foreman's place for the Homer Wilson Ranch. Many people erroneously refer to this as the Homer Wilson Headquarters, but in fact that was below The Window at Oak Spring.

The old headquarters, which was a two-story Sears and Roebuck prefabricated home, was moved in by Francis Rooney after he purchased parts of the earlier G4 outfit. Later, this house became the headquarters for Homer Wilson before being torn down by the National Park Service in the late 1940s.

Blue Creek Trail ends at the foreman's place, where we picked up the Dodson Trail and headed east. The Dodson was named in recognition of the Dodson family, who had a place near Fresno Creek.

The worn path we were on was this pioneer clan's life line, as no road ever went there. The long-serving sheriff for Brewster County, Ronny Dodson, is one of their descendants. His father, Bill Dodson, was raised in what is now the park and knows this area as few others do.

Blue Creek Canyon is one of those many intriguing spots one finds in the Chisos. Along its course are a variety of landscapes that reflect the awesomely rugged beauty of the lower Big Bend. The creek turns and wanders to and fro from forested uplifts, through the parched Chihuahuan Desert and finally empties into the waiting Rio Grande west of Castolon.

Those varying landscapes include a series of red rock hoodoos about a mile upcanyon from the foreman's house. Most people connect the word 'hoodoo' with Bryce Canyon in Utah, but we have a fair share of them down in the Big Bend.

This photograph, taken as the sun hung lower and the shadows grew longer, only shows a small slice of what is to be experienced in Blue Creek Canyon. Most everywhere in the immediate vicinity you see these eroding rock structures, standing like solidified sentries to some hidden sanctuary.

And we pushed on.

"A shadow never continueth in one stay, but is still gliding imperceptibly on, lengthening as it goes, and at last vanishing into darkness."
–George Horne

Along with Santa Elena Canyon and Casa Grande, the landmark known as the Window is one of the most photographed spots in Big Bend National Park. I have taken dozens of them myself, over the decades from different angles, times of days and years, and distances from up close to far away.

But this one has to be my favorite, and one of those shots when the Good Lord just seems to smile on you and everything comes together to near perfection. It was in the summertime, after a light shower and I had walked down below the lodge to take it all in.

The long dry spell this region had suffered through had finally broken and the rains had returned. When we pulled into the Basin that morning, low fog clouds still hung heavy around the surrounding peaks. Their gray, lofty bottoms rising and falling as they played with the gathering breeze that would sweep them away.

Within ten minutes or so, about a dozen photos were taken with my little Kodak digital, but this was the one that stood out.

We mortals search gropingly for true meaning in this life, and think upon what it must be like in the hereafter. Palaces of white marble, streets of gold, the singing of a choir of a thousand angels; all are images of what we try to imagine beyond the veil that separates this world from the next.

But to me at the end of days, this will be the image I will be seeking: the path leading through the Great Beyond and wandering off toward the setting sun.

"Avoid the reeking herd,
Shun the polluted flock
Live like that stoic bird
The eagle of the rock."
--Elinor Wylie

It was early March several years back during Spring Break for the college types, though you couldn't prove this once you left the roads. We were on the high lonesome to the west side of the Dodson, ascending our way from Carousel Mountain to the pass on the northern tip of the Sierra Quemada.

As you can tell from the shadows it was still early that particular morning. Quite chilly, too, though that would change quickly enough. The following dawn would find us amidst a blazing desert furnace east and below Elephant Tusk, one of those real gut checks to find out if you still have what it takes. There is always a challenge to be found in this country, in one manner or the other.

But for now, we were just enjoying the scenery, having started from The Basin on the morning before and making camp at the foot of Carousel Mountain that night. We hadn't seen another soul along Blue Creek Trail until meeting a crowd of standard-issue *turistas* at the old foreman's place for the Homer Wilson ranch. After we started up the Dodson, the world around us became vacant once again.

In the photograph we were skirting some of the high ground that blends into the Sierra Quemada, looking roughly southwest. From here you could see Mule Ears, Trap Mountain, Goat Mountain and Sierra Ponce, which is situated south of the river in Chihuahua. Most of you would know it better as the Mexican side of the uplift for Santa Elena Canyon.

We kept climbing our way to the pass, accompanied by the sound of an ALICE pack creaking, jungle boots searching for firm ground under the loose rock and the precious lilt of water sloshing inside a canteen.

It was a good day to be alive.

"Let my armies be the rocks and the trees - and the birds in the sky."
--Charlemagne

The lower Big Bend is a complex land possessing all manners of strange oddities and dichotomies that cannot all be experienced in a single lifetime, a place where you really do not know what to expect around the next turn in a canyon, or over the next piece of high ground.

Sometimes you feel as if you are walking into a world, to use the classic Robert Heinlein science-fiction title, as a wayfaring *Stranger In A Strange Land*. On occasion the sensation feels almost other-worldly, and can leave you with the exhilaration of being a twenty-first century explorer, at least for the few moments before logic takes back over.

Boot Canyon, which makes up part of the South Rim Loop Trail system, is one such spot. Moreover, there are few more intriguing landmarks found along the route than The Boot itself.

Now I have approached this point from most any direction it can be approached from, and it still leaves me with that peculiar sense described above. A solid rock monolith jutting straight up into a jeweled blue sky, and for all intents and purposes also a dead ringer caricature of an upside-down boot, complete with riding heel. The well-known landmark can be spotted from a mile and more away on the opposite side of Juniper Canyon, even though it is secluded inside the higher walls of the chasm itself.

When I first see The Boot I usually have to stop, grin to myself, and shake my head with that same recurring thought:

'Now what is that doing up there?'

"There's a long, long trail a-winding,
Into the land of my dreams;
Where the nightingales are singing,
And a white moon beams"...
--Stoddard King

Casa Grande by day is impressive, be it accented by sun and shadow or partially wrapped in low lying clouds that drift and play about its features, much like a stunningly beautiful woman who idly runs her delicate fingers through the crowning glory of her hair.

Casa Grande by night is yet another sight for the spirit, for even in darkness it stands outlined by the canopy of an infinite number of stars. Each gives off the faintest touch of light, combining with countless others in highlighting the mountain's regality.

Ah, but Casa Grande by a full moon? Such a moon in this country gives that same beautiful woman a special glow, an indescribable ethereal presence. It bathes the land in a singular luminescence in which one can literally read by, walk a rough trail securely, or just sit there in the dark and marvel at how it reshapes the world around you.

When the full moon peeks over the mountain's shoulder the resulting combination makes for a scene to behold, one that fills the viewer with an abiding wonder. It is the stuff that feeds the lover's embrace, the wanderer's sense of being and the thinker's soul. It gives life to something essential that lies deep within each of us and must be first experienced to be fully understood.

Once you do, the memory of that abiding wonderment and awe will never completely go away. No matter where you may go, no matter how many times you see a full moon again, your mind will go back to the one perched above Casa Grande.

"Bite on the bullet, old man, and don't let them think you're afraid."
--Rudyard Kipling

Standing along Elephant Tusk Trail, you are making ready to drop off into an unnamed gorge directly to your front. The trail follows along the bottom, snaking its way back and forth along the northern side of Elephant Tusk before angling away to the southeast and Talley Mountain.

If you look closely enough, you will see three men in this frame. I am the gent pulling point, scouting out the best route forward. At this juncture I was wondering why at fifty-one years old I hadn't become keen on some other more sedentary activity, like golf or tennis or motorcycle riding.

But then again, probably not. The road goes on forever and the party never ends.

Though this small canyon may not be very large or deep, it is a challenge when you have a fifty-pound pack on your back because it's rough as a cob in a few spots. The trail itself is fading away due to lack of use, overgrown and washed out at spots where it disappears for hundreds of feet at a time. No cairns are present, and you will find that being able to read a topographical map is a necessity.

This was the trip described in my book *Yonderings* that so many commented on, and details the worst jam I ever got myself into in all the decades I've prowled the lower Big Bend. Encapsulated in the chapter entitled *Thirst*, it proved to be a real gut check on the following day with no water and a hundred degree plus heat.

The biggest comeuppance in this predicament was largely due to my own overconfidence. As so often happens, we find out too late we are our own worst enemy due to laziness, complacency or using our heads for nothing more than a hat rack. It allows us to be swayed against our better judgement and me into thinking our next water cache was only about five miles further.

At the time it was but only as the buzzard flies and due to an unforeseen detour it turned out closer to thirteen, with most of the trip being like locked inside of a burning furnace with no way out but forward.

No matter how experienced you think you may be, this country is like a well camouflaged punji pit in dense jungle. Make one mistake and it can set into motion a line of falling dominos that at best will leave you feeling a bit foolish, and at worst lifeless.

One of my favorite science fiction authors, Robert A. Heinlein, once wrote a novel entitled *The Moon Is A Harsh Mistress*. Well, so is this desert. She will beguile and bewitch you, then on the slightest whim turn on you like an infuriated rattlesnake.

My grandfather used to say this desert was like being in love with a beautiful woman who is always trying to kill you. She's a comely mistress to be sure, but with strong inclinations of murderous intent.

Yet that same beautiful woman continues to beguile and bewitch.

"Oh Lord, thou knowest how busy I must be this day.
If I forget thee, do not thou forget me.
Amen."

--Jacob Astey

You are looking back into the Chisos Basin from where Laguna Meadow Trail tops out in a pass below Emory Peak. If you look closely, one can see the trail in the lower portion of the frame, zig-zagging along as it moves up in elevation.

Laguna Meadow Trail forms part of what is referred to as the South Rim Loop. Some folks claim this to be the prettiest day hike in Texas and one of the most scenic in the nation. I won't say yea or nay on that, because I know that I am hopelessly prejudiced.

As in most every other case concerning the Big Bend, there is a far greater feast for the eyes and spirit than any camera lens can ever capture. But within that limited scope one can glimpse the backside of Pulliam Bluff, Casa Grande, and just the edge of The Pinnacles with the top of Lost Mine Peak behind both.

Then there is The Basin itself and finally Emory Peak, looming over the pass as the trail skirts its western slopes. At some 7,825 feet, Emory Peak is the highest point in the Chisos. If one chooses to, another trail in this system branches off The Pinnacles and takes you to the summit.

For those with that extra drive to see more than what standing at the pass allows, there is a small knoll to the northwest you can climb easily enough. Once there, the vistas are simply spectacular in every direction.

You can spend hours by just shifting around a bit, finding another hundred points of interest both above and below. I almost always take a short break in this pass for that express purpose.

I have made this climb many times over the decades, once making the entire near fifteen-mile loop on a broken left foot. Long story and no, it wasn't as crazy as it might first sound. At that point of my life I would have crawled up here on my belly, just to see this sight one more time.

Ironically enough, that event was what led to the foot finally healing after months of stalemate. Well, that and a lot of heartfelt prayers from many others. I had already been told by the doctors I would never be able to run or walk any long distances again.

Thank you, God, for making it otherwise.

"When Earth's last picture is painted,
and the tubes are twisted and dried,
When the oldest colors have faded,
and the youngest critic has died;
We shall rest, and faith, we shall need it
---lie down for an eon or two,
Till the Master of All Good Workmen,
shall put us to work anew."
--Rudyard Kipling

The road called Black Gap running from what is now Mariscal Mine up to Glenn Spring was not always there. Furthermore, it was one of the newer tracks made prior to the National Park Service taking ownership here. Freight and ore coming out of the Mariscal was usually transported along an older road that skirted the southern fringes of Talley Mountain before linking up with the route between Glenn Spring and San Vicente.

As time passed and different owners gave different names to the mines located on the northern end of Mariscal Mountain, efforts were made to streamline their transportation costs. Thus, Black Gap Road was created but it never really helped that much.

These days the track serves to give owners of high clearance vehicles the chance to see the lower eastern side of the Chisos, as well as provide access to a few primitive camp sites. This photo is from one of those camps known as Elephant Tusk, named after the nearby peak.

It was not taken by me but rather my older son, Benjamin Levi English, a captain in the Marine Corps during those years. He was home on leave and wanted to spend some time in the lower Big Bend, in this case the Mariscal Mountain/Elephant Tusk area of the park.

You are looking to the setting sun, mostly obscured by cloud cover that in turn outlines the Punta de la Sierra, situated on the southernmost reaches of the Chisos Mountains. At the top center of the frame you can also see a full moon, trying to shine through the gathering storm.

Thunder rolled across the arroyos and flats, and the smell of rain was in the air.

Then, just as he snapped the shot, it began to sprinkle.

"I sat in the orchard and thought with sweet comfort and peace of my God, in solitude my company, my Friend and Comforter." --Henry Martyn, writing his last words

I had been on the move for three days; three days of blissful solitude in which I had not seen another human being, or even the footprint of one. It was late September and the rains had come as they usually do this time of year. I was prowling the Dodson Trail and Juniper Canyon areas at just the right time; the land was so green and alive everywhere you looked.

This shot was taken below the Dodson and down Fresno Creek a bit. I had stopped for lunch, dropping my pack and pulling off my boots to let my feet air out and change my double socks. The meal had been primitive by most folk's standards, but satisfying. I lay there half reclined, the warm sun and full belly making for a lazy, contented feeling that is hard to find in the so-called 'civilized' parts of this world.

And the view! A narrow rill of water drifting through multi-hued rock, contrasted by the verdancy of desert plants, while the South Rim of the Chisos loomed high on the horizon. I have been atop there many times yet one never fully sees its majesty until you stare up from thousands of feet below. The craggy, time worn face of the rim was framed by the brilliantly blue sky, while occasional puffs of white clouds drifted by like small pieces of fluffy cotton balls.

True contentment is found in the most basic of things in our lives, things that also fall under the definition of being most precious. Yet it seems they are so neglected in the rush about, mad dash of the topsy-turvy world we live in, a world where those precious things are often so few and far between.

That time and that scene will always be precious in my memory, ready for a replay when thinking of those last words of Henry Marten.

Everybody dies, but far fewer die well.

161

"We cannot help reflecting, that there is a ship in which we are all embarked; there is a troubled sea on which we all sail; there are storms by which we are all frequently overtaken; and there is a haven which we all desire to behold and enter."

--George Horne

There are so many special places in the lower Big Bend, all for different reasons. It is like exploring a kaleidoscope of different landscapes that constantly change as you make your way through this land. No two spots are the same, singular scenes in a singular country.

It is hard to describe the religious effect that comes upon oneself when alone in such wondrous works. I have found myself closer to God in this land than in any church, and I have been in a bunch of those. It becomes obvious why so many prophets of the Bible found their Lord in the desert and mountains of the Holy Land. It is something I try mightily to convey to others; I can only hope I am successful in doing so to some small degree.

One of my favorite places to wander about is where this photo was taken, Juniper Canyon. In a region of extremes, it is a rather temperate place, usually not too hot in the summertime. When winter comes you can find protection from the chilly winds of the north. It is also one of the more remote sites in the park by vehicle, nearly twenty miles from pavement via primitive tracks that once saw the wheels of wagons.

Squarely in the frame is Crown Mountain, sitting much like its namesake amid so many other peaks that make up the Chisos. To the very left is the edge of Casa Grande and more to the center a hawk in midflight, riding the invisible winds that in a single moment can take him where no man has ever gone.

162

From this point one can work his way up the bottom of the chasm to Juniper Canyon Trail, zig-zagging to higher elevations to connect with the Boot Canyon route as well as the network of paths above. Or, if need be, push all the way to the saddle along the shoulder of Casa Grande, where Lost Mine Trail runs.

Or you can double back along some long-abandoned wagon roads and trails that lead off in the direction of Robber's Roost and Glenn Spring. Juniper Canyon is a place to suit one's mood and calling, and often enough there is no one else around to spoil your need for isolation.

Many years ago, long before there was a park, many of these trails were used by the first ranchers. Before them were the Apache, who utilized the routes to make their last stand against those encroaching upon them; be they Spanish, Comanche, Kiowa, Mexican or *Norteamericano*.

Less than two centuries prior, the Apache had taken their turn by pushing still other tribes out of this same area, using some of these same trails. Who knows what happened before then, or of the other paths that once led through here.

To me there is something sad when I come across the remnants of a forgotten trail. I tend to think of the likewise forgotten men who walked along them, all in their own era and for their own purpose.

"We gotta be free---
The eagle and me."
--Edgar Y. Harburg

There is so much in the lower Big Bend still to be seen, and I have been into the Basin and surrounding locales dozens upon dozens of times in all seasons and weather. Even after nearly sixty years of wandering this country I know I will never be able to cover it all, and prefer to concentrate on those places that are new for me.

But when I do venture into the crown jewels of our Lone Star State, I often have to contend with at least the urge to take Lost Mine Trail. While each path in the Chisos Mountains system has something special to offer, few have as much in scenery as this one.

Once at the terminus for the trail, the world drops away in every direction and your eyes see so much of God's Creation surrounding you. Moving along the uppermost ridge you can see Pummel Peak, Pine Canyon, Juniper Canyon, Boot Canyon, Hayes Ridge, Crown Mountain, Elephant Tusk, and just the tip of Emory Peak.

These are the landmarks in the Chisos Mountains themselves, but look beyond to the horizons and admire the mighty Sierra del Carmen to the east, and *El Solitario* to the west, and a lot of country in between.

It is one of those places in this world where you feel closest to being an eagle, with two feet still on the ground. This photograph was taken while still moving up the trail, some distance away before it tops out.

In it you are looking roughly due west between the back side of Casa Grande and Vernon Bailey Peak, as well as over the northern part of Burro Mesa with Maverick and Cigar Mountain behind.

Directly below and in the lower center is the park road leading into The Basin, snaking its way up to crest at the foot of Casa Grande before dropping into the bowl itself. Almost dead center is Carter Peak, forming the southern wall for the crevice known as The Window, which serves as the outlet for The Basin watershed.

From there to the horizon is just miles and miles of Chihuahuan Desert; harsh, unforgiving country that the exploring Spanish named *El Despoblado*, meaning 'the deserted.'

That was four hundred years ago, yet in some enclaves and stretches the name still fits.

167

"It is painful to remember how much light may be shining around us on every side, without finding an entrance into the heart."
--Charles Bridges

I don't spend much time in The Chisos anymore, leastwise not as much as I used to. These days those mountains seem to be overrun with people, especially in The Basin area and along the western slopes. Not that I have anything against that, or against folks in general. But to me the best parts of the lower Big Bend are those where the people are fewest. Where there is time and lack of distractions to think, to ponder, to remember and to imagine, and to let this land speak to you as only it knows how.

But when I do get the urge for the higher country, I tend to frequent the eastern ridges of this range running from the tip of Punta de la Sierra up to Juniper Canyon. These are the spots where one does not go for an afternoon stroll, or even an overnight campout. Some of the base camps I prefer can take a half day to reach from home, so when going I prefer to stay awhile.

The attached photograph was taken on a late afternoon some years back. I had made a big loop around the backside of Tortuga Mountain, past the old Dodson homestead, down the Fresno and back up to Dodson Trail before calling it a day. As I reached my base camp I turned and looked toward Chilicotal Mountain and the Sierra del Carmen.

This is what I saw.

I have heard that for many the sense of being completely alone can be uncomfortable, even somewhat frightening after a length of time. That is a sensation I have never experienced, for me it is more akin to a great uplifting of the spirit where I feel most at ease with the world around me. During this trip I had not seen another human being, or fresh sign of one, since turning off Glenn Spring Road four days before. The ensuing feeling can best be described as exhilarating.

168

Perhaps that is because I am so easily distracted by my surroundings and the need to go and see, or of the thoughts that I otherwise would not have time to think through, to be missing human company. For wandering about without restraint and able to go wherever I so please has to be one of the greatest thrills in my life, it always has been and likely always will be.

For centuries there has been a long-standing controversy of nurture versus nature in how a child grows and matures. I do not honestly know the answer to that question, but I do know this:

I have been blessed in both, because both were riding with me free and easy on this particular day.

170

"Kill reverence and you've killed the hero in man."

--Ayn Rand

When Bob Sholly was a little boy, he took his even smaller brother Dan and climbed to the top of Casa Grande, the peak shown in this photo. Standing at the top of the precipice he shouted down to his parents far below, "Hey, look at me! I'm up here!"

His parents, listening outside their government housing in the Chisos Basin, were first at a loss as to where their two sons had gotten off to. Bob kept hollering until they finally looked up and saw he and Dan standing upon high, proud as little peacocks.

You can well imagine the erupting pandemonium that followed that realization.

And so it went in Bob's growing years. His father, George, was the first senior ranger for Big Bend National Park when it opened in 1944. There was much that needed doing and scouted out in such a vast area, and Bob knocked out his dad's tracks all over that country in one adventure after another.

One time when Bob was about fourteen, his dad was demolishing one of the many candelilla wax camps found on park land near the river. During the activity Bob wandered up to some high ground, making for a fine target. He was at first a bit perplexed at the dust kicking up in his immediate vicinity and the sound of a rifle firing. It was at that precise moment that Bob received some very useful fatherly advice:

"Get down, you idiot!"

This marked the first occasion that Bob Sholly came under hostile fire, but it was far from the last.

Years later I was to meet Bob and we became friends, I suppose because we had some things in common. We had both been raised kind of wild and free, and both had joined the military when we were barely old enough to think

171

upon ourselves as men. We both enjoyed a good book, good conversation and felt blessed in how we had lived life.

But most of all we shared an enduring passion for the land that was always 'home' to us, the lower reaches of an awe inspiring, near magical place known as the Big Bend.

Bob knew more about the Chisos Mountains than most any other person I've known. We'd sit for hours swapping stories and information about parts of that country that one of us had seen but the other hadn't. As a board member for the Big Bend Natural History Association, I was proud to have Bob as our 'Veteran Artist in Residence' in 2017.

You see, he was also a published author and wrote one of the finest volumes I've ever read about Army infantry in Vietnam: *Young Soldiers, Amazing Warriors*. Anyone that was ever a grunt, or served in Vietnam, or wants to truly understand what war really is, needs to read that book.

On Saturday, January 19th, 2019, at about 0638, Colonel Robert H. 'Bob' Sholly, US Army (Ret), holder of the Silver Star, Bronze Star with three oak leaf clusters, the Combat Infantryman's Badge, Ranger Tab, Jump Wings, inductee of the US Army's OCS Hall of Fame, and beyond all that a human being extraordinaire, died after a long, bitter conflict with yet another enemy called cancer.

Like any other battle he ever fought, Bob never gave up and he never gave in. Because that is the stuff that real heroes are made of.

And as long as I live on this earth and see God's Handiwork upon it, I will look up to the highest reaches of Casa Grande with those words in my mind:

"Hey, look at me! I'm up here!"

You always were, Bob, and you always will be.

I'll see you on the other side.

CHAPTER SIX

ALTO RELEX AREA

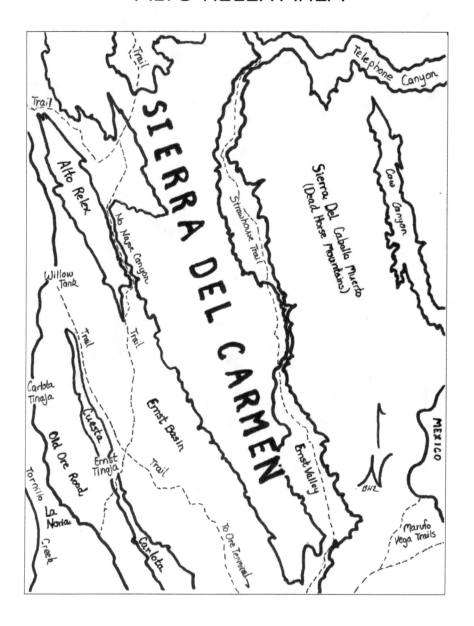

For better or for worse, the world at large has discovered the Big Bend. This fact is obvious when studying the number of visitors, the increasing number of vehicles on its highways and byways, or when looking in any direction between Nine Point Mesa and Lajitas.

What is more, so many of those who come to 'get away from it all' seem to have the distressing habit of bringing their 'with all' with them.

Yet there are still large, mostly untraveled spaces that run through ranchlands, natural preserves, and the state and national parks we have been blessed with. Each in turn represents something of what this country once was, and just how lonesome and out of the way it used to be.

The park area east of Alto Relex is one of these places. With the utilization of a cut I call 'No Name Canyon' you can move north from Rio Grande Village up to the collapsed ore terminal, follow what was once the real 'Ore Road,' and enter Ernst Basin.

At the northern end of Ernst Basin, the low ground narrows and you come to the bottom side of No Name Canyon. This chasm serves as a natural chokepoint for anyone moving along a north-south axis, and who wants to stay east of the Cuesta Carlota.

Once clear of the canyon you can either pass through the saddle just beyond Alto Relex and into the valley below, or continue north through a series of small cuts until teeing into Telephone Canyon Trail.

If you choose the saddle and ease past the old dam, you can drift along in a northerly direction all the way to Dagger Flat. Most don't know it, but the upper tip of Dagger Flat actually becomes the entrance for Devil's Den.

This is a long, arduous trek that requires knowledge, stamina, and a couple of water caches for safety's sake. It is also not recommended during the warmer months; I have seen it well over a hundred degrees through here even in mid-October.

But if you have a strong longing for the lonesome country, this is a good place to be.

"There comes a time in every man's life and I've had many of them."

--Casey Stengel

Hardly anyone takes the Telephone Canyon Trail when the weather is mild, and nobody ventures there during the hot and dry months. I suppose that's why I never laid an eye on another soul during this entire trip.

But if you want to get away from people and travel the path less followed, this is one of those paths you seek. The trailhead on the park side starts just off the Old Ore Road, along the northern tip of Alto Relex. It's one of those tricky ones, the kind that begins easy and well-defined enough yet changes character dramatically within only a couple of hundred yards.

From that point on the trail curves to and fro, wandering among nameless hills, canyons, crevices and creek beds; as if not quite sure where it really wants to go.

There are also some fairly unstable parts to negotiate. I took the hardest spill I've had in many a year climbing out of an arroyo near where this photo was taken. Yet that bruising of both pride and body was more than worth the trouble, and the photo shows why. You are looking roughly due south, that road-like feature in the middle of the shot is actually the dry creek bed that uses this country for its watershed, and will ultimately run through Ernst Canyon before dumping into the Tornillo.

The rugged escarpment to the right is the southern part of Alto Relex, and everything in between and to the east has not a name until you reach the Dead Horse Mountains. Those souls who once lived here and had their personal references for a particular spot have long since passed, and the knowledge of those names and the reasons for them died alongside.

Not a road ran nearby for miles, and not a sign or track of another human being was to be seen.

Nothing but the desert and its age-old inhabitants, unperturbed by a manmade twenty-first century world out there beyond.

It was definitely 'over on the lonesome side.'

And I find myself praying this unique slice of the Lone Star state, known as the lower Big Bend, will always have a lonesome side to it.

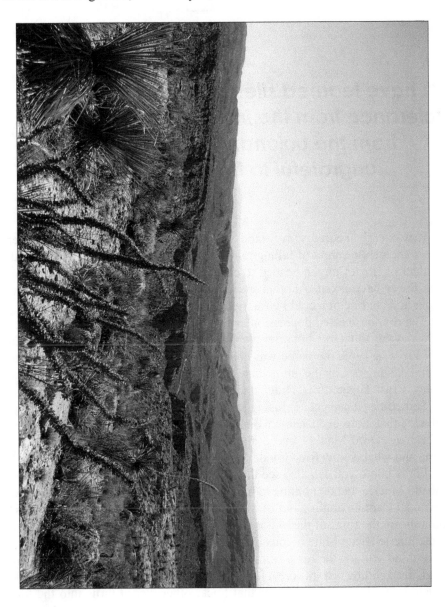

"I have learned silence from the talkative, tolerance from the intolerant, and kindness from the unkind; yet strange, I am ungrateful to those teachers."
--Khalil Gibran

It was early February in a land which sometimes seems to have never known the gentle caress of falling rain. I was working my way over the south shoulder of Ernst Canyon headed to camp, along a trail that few know of and even fewer have taken. Another evening was coming as the shadows grew longer and the bite of a cold February night was first being felt.

The dry, desiccated depression sweeping across in front of you was once known as the Valverde, but after the unsolved murder of local leading citizen Max Ernst in 1908, the name was changed to Ernst Basin. This happened to several landmarks in the immediate area and is why you now have Ernst Valley, Ernst Tinaja, Ernst Ridge and the two locations already mentioned.

Sometimes it can get confusing for those just starting to learn this country. Folks at that time even named the spot where Ernst was shot down from ambush as 'Dead Man's Curve,' along the old road between present day La Noria and what is now Rio Grande Village.

In the photo you can also see the near foothills that obscure the Sierra del Caballo Muerto, but do nothing to hide the majesty of the upper reaches of the Sierra del Carmen angling out of Mexico. Nestled just the other side of these foothills are the ruins of the old ore terminal, which used to bring raw ore out of the Puerto Rican Mine in tons by the hour.

Behind you are the remains of a primitive track spurring off the Old Ore Road, dead ending near the crest for the Cuesta Carlota. I have never been able to determine the real purpose for that track, other than it turns into the trail from where I snapped this shot. From here the path gets much rougher as it wanders off the high ground into Ernst Basin below.

178

Once in the valley you are free to roam to the east, north and south, though 'free' is a relative term in this case. You are facing some of the most rugged, desolate and unforgiving country you can find in the lower Big Bend, or anyplace else for that matter. Water, and your individual ability to navigate through this rough terrain are the very real limiting factors.

I had covered over eighteen miles on foot this day, and it wasn't my first visit into this seldom seen or heard of area of the park. Yet I still felt like one of the proverbial three blind men, trying to describe an elephant in regards to what is actually here.

In sum, it is a place for a man to go to be left alone in his thoughts.

And to who, and what, he really is.

"Discovery consists of seeing what everybody has seen and thinking what nobody has thought."
-- Albert Szent-Györgyi

As you are crawling along the Old Ore Road, between La Noria and Willow Tank, the track makes a couple of sharp turns as it negotiates what appears to be a bone-dry wash running from Alto Relex into Tornillo Creek.

But first appearances can be deceiving. If you will park your vehicle in the run and wander off downstream, within a couple of hundred yards you will come upon a series of tinajas that manage to contain water in the driest of seasons.

This spot is known as Carlota Tinaja, and though I do not know who Carlota was (Mexican for 'Charlotte') the high ridge that runs to your southeast just happens to be named Cuesta Carlota. Ernst Canyon splits that ridge in two.

In the photograph you can see one of these tinajas, and this was during a very dry part of a dry year.

Note I said a dry year. Many of the uninitiated tend to refer to such a period of seasons as a 'drought.' Like the words 'love,' 'beautiful,' and 'hero,' the term is used far more often than actual circumstances might dictate or allow.

The way to tell the difference is when the greasewood and mesquite start dying. When you see that occurring, then you know you are in a sure enough drought.

These tinajas are well hidden, and this is one of the reasons they are able to retain copious amounts of water. For example, as the road winds around in two different spots it is only about fifty yards away from these tinajas. But any occupant inside a vehicle would be clueless as to that much water being so close by.

You have to get out on foot and walk the area through, really seeing what is there rather than what so many others only skim over with a single glance.

That is discovery.
And that is the way of the desert.

"What is the difference between a squirrel in a cage who only makes his prison go round the faster by his swift race, and the man who lives toilsome days for transitory objects which he may never attain?"
--Alexander Maclaren

As the decades pass and so many appear to have discovered the lower Big Bend, I find myself pushing further into the more lonesome places, the places that few have heard of and far fewer have journeyed to.

Some of these spots are located above No Name Canyon, consisting of a series of smaller cuts and crevices leading out north to Telephone Canyon as well as easterly into the Dead Horse Mountains. Together they form the upper watershed for the large wash that runs through Ernst Canyon and then into Tornillo Creek just south of La Noria.

Each of these gorges, whether large or small, have their own individual look and 'feel' to them, for lack of a better word. The accompanying frame illustrates the opening for one of these that has to contain the largest number of black rock squirrels I've ever seen.

This small cut is a made to order refuge for them. The vertical walls are fractured in haphazard fashion while also being pierced by hundreds of naturally occurring holes set at every angle imaginable. These holes measure from just an inch or so wide to a foot or more in diameter. Due to the fracturing as well as the presence of these cavities, some portions of the walls have either already partially collapsed or appear about to.

This particular jaunt was occurring in mid-October, but the temperature was still well over a hundred by early afternoon. Combined with the lack of any sort of breeze inside the cut, the environment would be judged as uncomfortably hot for most any creature.

182

Yet even in this heat and with the obvious instability of their surroundings, those furry little bundles of energy never seemed to balk in the least at using both to their fullest advantage. Darting back and forth with phenomenal speed and agility, in one hole and out the other, they put on a demonstration that no gathering of circus clowns or gymnastic team could ever hope to compare to.

One could spend an entire day and then some just watching their continual antics, so frettingly curious but still fearful of the seldom-experienced visit by man. Other than the effort to get here, the admission to this wonderfully choreographed show is free.

However, with that free admission comes a warning in picking one's seat for the performance.

Because where there are rock squirrels, there will be rattlers too.

*"We can only pay our debt to the past by
putting the future in debt to ourselves."*
--John Buchan

If you are driving along the highway to Boquillas Canyon from Rio Grande Village (once known as Boquillas, Texas), you will find a National Park Service interpretive display beside the road.

It explains in brief about the overhead ore tramway that once ran from the Puerto Rico mines in Mexico to a terminal some miles north of the marker. You can still see the two cables that stretched on for miles, hauling tons of raw ore each hour in large aerial buckets. The roadway was actually paved over these steel coils, signifying its half-buried past in literal fashion.

There were actually two tramway systems that were built during a period from about 1909 until 1918 or so, the dates are approximate because of temporary cessations in operations brought on by business reorganizations, the rise and fall of profit margins, and area unrest.

What is known was the older, shorter tramway was replaced in 1914 by a greatly improved version. Some six miles long, the new tramway connected the Mexican mines to an ore terminal constructed roughly southeast of Ernst Basin.

In this photograph one can see what was is left of this terminal, as well as one of the buckets that carried the raw ore to the location. When the tramway ceased operation, the line was abandoned and left to fend for itself in the quietude of the Chihuahuan Desert.

From the jumbled heap of wood timbers, steel cable and debris, it is hard to imagine this structure once stood some three stories high. From here the ore was transported by wagon and later truck all the way to the railway in Marathon, and sent on from there to refinery plants.

Behind what is left of the terminal, hidden from view, are the ruins of the first cable support tower. These towers were spaced at varying distances from each other, depending on the terrain and load stress put upon them. They were

185

built well enough that even a hundred years later a few of the structures still stand. At each tower you will find the same two steel cables present, frozen in time in their journey toward Mexico.

On this trip to the terminal, my approach was made deliberately from the north. Most folks who come here utilize the trails winding in from the south, but I wanted to walk out the long-abandoned roads used by the trucks and wagons to pick up their payloads. A great deal of effort was put into these routes due to their intrinsic need.

Like the tramway itself, I found that time had taken its toll on these also. Unused and unrepaired for many decades, some parts of the roads are now long gone; the victims of wind, sun, rains and erosion.

Given enough time, the desert always seems to reclaim her own.

*"We are the music-makers,
And are the dreamers of dreams;
Wandering by lone sea breakers,
And sitting by desolate streams"...*
                    --Arthur O'Shaughnessey

There is a crevice that runs the length of the eastern side of Alto Relex, a place where eons of floodwaters and erosion have created a passageway from the backside of Telephone Canyon down through here and then on to Ernst Canyon, and finally into Tornillo Creek.

Not many people come to this place, it's usually too hot, too dry, too desolate or too far to hike. Most of the area east of Alto Relex and on to the river is that way, so much so that many of the landmarks located between these two boundaries have no names to go by.

For myself I call this chasm No Name Canyon, and it is one of my favorite spots to wander around and take in the view. The scenery varies from interesting to spectacular, as the cut makes several abrupt turns and bends while making its way along.

Part of this attraction is due to being paired with Alto Relex, the imposing uplift that forms the west wall for the canyon. The rugged heights and sheer bluffs that make up much of Alto Relex brings to mind the tales of Masada, the legendary fortress where badly outnumbered Israelite rebels made their stand against the Roman Empire around 73 A.D.

This photograph shows the upper entrance to the crevice and unless you are familiar with the area or viewed it on a topographical map, you might be fooled by the casual glance into thinking there was no crevice at all.

But the surrounding watershed formed by the southern slopes of Telephone Canyon, as well as the desolate reaches between Alto Relex and the Dead Horse Mountains, has to drain some place. This narrow opening, partially hidden by huge slabs of solid upright stone, is that spot.

From its entrance No Name Canyon twists and turns like a frightened angel while charting its course toward Ernst Basin, angling back and forth among high walls, otherworldly overhangs and craggy openings. Though no real surface water is present, there is still that inviting shade no matter the time or season.

When there is water, you don't want to be anywhere inside because it comes roaring through the canyon, sounding and moving like a runaway freight train on a downhill rail. Few sights can be as exciting and fearsome as the power of a major flash flood contained within these walls.

You can always tell when a big one is coming; you can hear the rumble echoing off the cliffs as the force of water overturns hundreds of large rocks and small boulders.

Only the desert could make such a precious, life-giving resource so potentially deadly to the unwary.

"Nothing would give up life:
Even the dirt kept breathing a small breath."
--Theodore Roethke

It was late in the evening of a past winter when this photograph was taken. I had just topped out on the Cuesta Carlota, working my way along a trail that runs parallel with the south rim of Ernst Canyon. This was the view that greeted me when I looked to the northwest.

From here you can see Lone Mountain at the left of the frame. As your eyes move across the horizon you find Grapevine Hills and the Rosillos, as well as the tips of peaks and mountains appreciably farther away, their blueness contrasting against the desert sky.

Mostly concealed in a thousand shadowy crags between those far blue reaches and where I stood are spots like Banta Shut-in, Carlota Tinaja, Rice's Canyon (known now as Estufa Canyon) and Hannold Draw as well as a massive expanse of rough, cacti-strewn hard country in between.

Meandering through the middle of all is Tornillo Creek, which with the Terlingua as well as the Fresno form the three major arteries for this moisture-starved land. They in turn flow into the Rio Grande, twisting and turning its way through canyon and gorge before finally completing the vast sweep that gives this region its name: The Big Bend.

In my writing I sometimes refer to this country as 'the land of broken dreams' because that is exactly what it is, a slowly eroding depository of man's efforts and schemes to extract some measure or form of treasure from these environs. Treasure of coin, treasure of security, treasure of heart.

But this desert is likely the harshest of all mistresses, and for each success a hundred failures occurred that have been lost to the hoary memory thief of anonymity. What we do know tells us of true irony as the story often ended with the taking of the challenger's coin, security and heart, and sometimes their lives.

Yet to this very day they still come.

189

"Nobody cares to meddle with a man who can gather a clan of brave sons about him."
--Charles Spurgeon

There are some places where a camera seems next to useless, that the very idea of capturing nature's majesty and rugged beauty through a lens is near laughable. I traveled the world over in my younger years trying to do just that, but there is no spot on earth where this becomes more pointless for me personally than in the Big Bend country of Texas.

A photograph, no matter how stunning it may be, can never accurately express the sheer size or depth of an object, or of the surrounding countryside outside of the frame that serves as such a stupendous back drop.

More so, it cannot convey the call of a mockingbird, the buzz of the cicada, the breeze in your face and the hard, rocky soil under your feet. Nor can it give forth the smell of greasewood after a shower, or the sense of the hot sun upon your back as sweat trickles down your face.

For all practical purposes, a camera shot is only the weakest of visual facsimiles, and does pitifully little else in regard to the other senses.

This photo brought this all to mind while rummaging through my collection. You are looking at the western pour off for Alto Relex, that in turn overlooks Old Ore Road and Tornillo Creek basin beyond. It was a beautifully clear day, the kind when you can look at a mountain twenty miles away and feel that you can almost reach out and touch it.

We were there as a family. You can see my sons, Benjamin Levi and Ethan L'Amour, standing in the lower right part of the photograph, at the very bottom of the pour off. With the two of them in frame, the viewer can get at least some idea of the scale for this very small part of Alto Relex.

It was a good day to be alive and one of those precious ones when my sons were home from faraway places. Some months prior, Levi had graduated from Annapolis and been commissioned as a second lieutenant in the Marine Corps.

Ethan would do the same less than a year and a half later, becoming an ensign in the Navy.

Duty would be calling again soon enough and send them into harm's way at different points on the globe.

But for now, they clambered carefree on the same ground where some five generations of my family had done before. Some day in the future, their descendants will do the same.

Perhaps in all its lacking that is what a photograph does best, it bring back the memories.

"Permanence, perseverance and persistence in spite of all obstacles, discouragements, and impossibilities: It is this, that in all things distinguishes the strong soul from the weak."
--Thomas Carlyle

This was taken as evening was falling on a brisk winter day, looking across the McKinney Hills to Alto Relex on the horizon. I was making my way back to a base camp at the head of Telephone Canyon Trail, having spent much of the afternoon looping along the remnants of a road now rotting away in near anonymity.

Many folks are aware of the Old Ore Road on the eastern side of Big Bend National Park. But they usually don't know of the sister road running roughly parallel. This one carried more raw ore during the heyday of mining operations in this country than travelers of the named 'Old Ore Road' ever thought possible.

Of a later date than the prior route, it quickly fell into disrepair after the mines shut down and the National Park Service took over. In another twenty to thirty years you might be hard pressed to find any part of it remaining, save for some of the attending rock foundations constructed to handle the heavy loads.

This once improved track joins the Old Ore Road on the west side of Alto Relex, near Willow Tank, after coursing through Ernst Basin from the ore terminal. Just north of Alto Relex it angles off again, staying closer to the Dead Horse Mountains before the two become one again about a mile and a half south of Javelina Creek. Where it turns off at Alto Relex is easy enough to find, a short portion serves as the entrance to the primitive camp site for Telephone Canyon Trail.

Alto Relex itself has always fascinated me, even the name has confused many as the origin is somewhat obscure. Most probably 'relex' is yet another cartographer error for the Mexican word *relej* or *releje,* which can mean a talus or slope. Those with even a rudimentary knowledge of the language also know that *alto* can translate into tall or high.

The uplift is impressive and you never know how much so until you have completely circled it, or gotten in close and looked up. Old Ore Road runs fairly close by on the western side, allowing the casual passerby a glimmer as to just how big and roughhewn it actually is. There are only two basic ways to get to the top and neither are easy, these approaches are along uneven, sometimes tricky ridges leading in from either end of the escarpment.

To me, this lower Big Bend version of Masada marks a physical boundary line that runs roughly north to south. Most areas to the west are fairly well known and traveled, and oftentimes have a fair amount of people about. But to the east, from the park's northern boundary line down to nearly the Rio Grande, you'll hardly find anyone at any time.

Keep that in mind if you ever consider challenging this area of the park. Because whatever you get yourself into, you had better be prepared to get yourself out of it.

Alone.

CHAPTER SEVEN

LAJITAS AREA

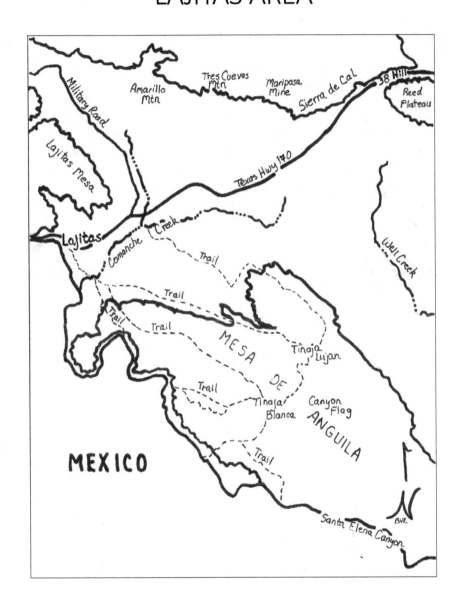

To those who desire to learn the real history of Lajitas, I would advise the reading of my first book 'Yonderings.' By and large I grew up there, my grandparents ran the Lajitas Trading Post for many of those years.

If home is truly where the heart is, the Lajitas I knew as a small boy will always be home to me. However, in reality that place of the heart no longer exists and hasn't in some time.

Known before as San Carlos Crossing or Comanche Crossing, Lajitas was one of the three main branches of the Comanche War Trail as it crossed over the river and into Mexico. This crossing, though named after the Comanche, was most likely in use hundreds of years before the first of those fearsome raiders ever sat astride of a horse.

Yet the name carries on in different guises through the twenty-first century, including the large dry wash running below Lajitas that is traditionally known as Comanche Creek. This is where the war trail came in from the east, described during those days as being almost a quarter of a mile in width.

As far as I know, no archaeological digs were ever conducted before this area was filled in and reshaped into a golf course for well-to-do tourists. We as the inheritors of this historical debacle will likely never know what exactly was lost there.

Yes, Lajitas will always be my childhood home, the place where memories of the heart reside. However, I don't go back any more, other than for book research or use as a starting point for a hiking trip.

Everything and everybody I ever knew in Lajitas is gone now; the victims of time, circumstance, and a bulldozer's blade.

Call it 'progress' if you will, but it just hurts too much to see the results.

"The Future...something which everyone reaches at the rate of sixty minutes an hour, whatever he does, whoever he is."
--C.S. Lewis

You are standing on an old smuggler's trail along the western shoulder of Anguila Mesa, looking in a northerly direction toward Lajitas and beyond. On the horizon stands Lajitas Mesa, rising from the surrounding desert. It serves as a distinctive landmark from twenty miles out and more, if you have the right vantage point.

Near mid-frame between higher ground on either side is Comanche Creek, emptying into the Rio Grande to the extreme left beyond camera lens. This is the general area where the San Carlos Crossing branch of the Comanche War Trail passed through. So much of historical value, dating back to pre-Columbian times, has been lost here. Anguila Mesa is the best place to see an overview of what has happened.

Of the hundreds of thousands of people who visit the lower Big Bend each year, only a handful have ever heard of Anguila Mesa. Of those, only a minuscule tenth of a percent have actually put boots on the ground that makes for the uplift. The same came be said for those who have lived in this region for decades, or their entire lives.

Even those who come usually have no idea that the original purpose of this hiking trail was as a smuggler's route in and out of Mexico. It carried human captives, guns, stolen livestock, bootleg liquor, candelilla wax and illegal drugs, among other things.

The mesa figured large into my own life early on. When my grandparents ran the trading post in Lajitas we bought candelilla wax smuggled out of Chihuahua, and this was one of the ways used to bring in the loads.

Due to the continual smuggling as well as occasional gunfire, the mesa was forbidden territory for me as a child to explore. Of course, those two extra ingredients made it even more naturally magnetic to my overactive five-year-old imagination. It was so massive, so desolate, so rugged and mysterious; full of area legend and lore.

About every trail on, around or through Anguila Mesa was originally a smuggler's path. For anyone reading these lines, please take this to heart: there is no harder work on earth than in the gathering, processing and transporting of candelilla wax.

We called the practitioners of this peculiar trade 'wax men.' The Mexican government and their representatives who patrolled the opposing mountains, mesas and canyons had a different name for them---'banditos.'

Be that as it may they were not anything like the Hollywood version wearing large sombreros, riding fine horses and armed to the teeth. They were small, sunburned, sometimes gaunt men in stature making their way on foot, leading their burro trains through the merciless Chihuahuan Desert.

I often think of those men when hiking through these places, purified by the elements and barbed wire tough. Much like the original Lajitas they are gone now, removed from the scene by a future they would have not understood or likely want to be a part of.

Vaya con Dios, esos hombres de mi memorias.

"How green was my Valley then, and the Valley of them that have gone."
--Richard Llewellyn

It may not look like much; the sun-bleached skeleton of a primitive road from long ago, devolving into a trail used by few who know anything of its original purpose.

But during the border troubles of a hundred years ago it held real importance in the affairs of many purposeful and important men, men who would grow even more so as time and attending world events unfolded.

For this was the Military Road, winding its way north out of Lajitas before joining with the route used by the Marfa-Mariposa Mines that transported raw ore to the nearest railway.

The track dropped into Fresno Canyon near where Buena Suerte would later be established, and ran up to the head of the canyon before topping out and arrowing for San Jacinto Mountain. From there it followed along Alamito Creek until ending at what was later known as Fort D. A. Russell, on the southern outskirts of Marfa.

When I was a kid, it hadn't been used much since Lajitas was regarrisoned briefly following the attack on Pearl Harbor. Falling into general disuse but still bearing the name, it served as a route for area ranchers such as my family. We used the road to reach properties along the way, though at that time it was impassable for any vehicle once you were above the Smith Place.

Its presence made for a pathway through the greatest playground and natural mentor any small boy could have. There are the remnants of a hundred adventures in a dozen different locales embedded in those ruts, and as I look back now in my sixtieth year the life-long value of those lessons become more and more clear.

Of all the roads I have traveled, it still has a pull on my spirit that cannot be fully explained or understood. Perhaps in itself that best illustrates what it really means to me.

There are no green valleys in the lower Big Bend, at least upon the land that my family lived and worked. But green can be far more than a mere color and in my mind are so many rich, verdant memories of times and loved ones long past.

"Follow your bliss."
--Joseph Campbell

You are standing on Anguila Mesa, looking southeasterly to Santa Elena Canyon and the Sierra Ponce. In the lower right part of the frame is the river and its accompanying ribbon of green showing the way to upper parts of Santa Elena Canyon. That is likely the only lush shade of green you'll see involving this uplift.

In my first book *Yonderings*, I write about this area in the chapter entitled *Perfect Place for A Pterodactyl Farm*. The name came to me many years ago after thumbing through a comic book where World War One biplanes were dogfighting with winged dinosaurs. If there were any such creatures still around in 1963, I calculated the perfect place for them was atop Anguila Mesa.

I was five years old then, riding an old jenny around Lajitas like some sort of half-wild Comanche. There's a reason why wise grandparents put their grandchildren on such animals, as the jenny possesses far more sense than does the child. This was especially true in my case, and there are those who would argue that not much has changed since then.

Those were free and easy times and I pretty much had the run of the place, save for being under strict orders to stay away from the mesa. The concept of being tempted by forbidden fruit thus first made its presence in my usually fermenting mind.

After entering the age when I considered myself a man, I have since made several journeys to that mesa. In fact, it has become one of my favorite places to go in the lower Big Bend. It must have something to do with that forbidden fruit hanging low enough to finally reach.

But that does not mean it is easy to grasp, as there is nothing easy about Anguila Mesa. So far, I have ascended it on four different routes, each time becoming more appreciative and respectful of those who came before to this dry, harsh, merciless slab of rock.

Many people raft this part of Big Bend National Park, pushing off near Lajitas and going all the way through the mouth of Santa Elena Canyon. I prefer to take a slightly different tack by hiking along the banks of the river. Or, when need be, climbing out to what may lay above when blocked below.

Walking it out, you see so many things that cannot be observed by floating along in a raft. This section of the Rio Grande, though few realize it, is dotted with dozens of ruins on both sides, remains of habitations going back at least a hundred and fifty years. Most have never been noted on any map, but they once mattered greatly to those who lived in them. When exploring these sites, one becomes thoughtful of those born here, and who lived and died in such a meager, isolated circumstance.

By and large not a word was ever written about them. Their stories have been lost to the ever-encroaching desert, much like the dwellings that once sheltered them in this desolate land.

And now they lie in forgotten shallow graves, scattered like windblown tumbleweeds across the barren landscape.

"To ride, shoot straight and speak the truth,
This is the ancient law of youth,
Old times are past, old days are done,
But the law runs true my little son."
--Charles T. Davis

This is about a canyon and two of the stories linked to it as my mind wanders to this particular spot. One is mostly forgotten history, a time and place now lingering in the memories of only a handful. The other story is still playing through, and I hope it will continue to do so far off into the future.

The canyon has no name, it runs only a relatively short distance and is no more craggy or desolate or inhospitable than many others along both sides of the Rio Grande, where it empties into. Owing to the lack of a better descriptor we call it 'Smuggler's Canyon,' for that is what it has been used for as long as anybody can remember.

It lies along the western side of Anguila Mesa, which forms above the cliffs to the left side of the chasm. Behind you is Lajitas, sitting over a steep, rock strewn slope to the rear and downhill from there. At one time there was no reason for Smuggler's Canyon until the Comanche had gone away, and civilization started making its presence felt in this heretofore wild country.

In response to that inconvenience, the route through this passage was born. If you look closely, you can see where one trail ran to the left of the bottom while a far more well-defined path works up the other side. One can only imagine how many burros and other pack animals have passed through here. However, I imagine that very little of that traffic was in any way strictly legal in nature.

That's one story.

The second concerns the photograph itself, taken when my younger son and I were on one of our frequent prowls together. Ethan L'Amour, as well as his older brother Benjamin Levi, have been with me on so many such forays that I have long since lost count.

But I have a memory of each one, as each one is precious to me. As boys they could have cared less about Six Flags, Fiesta Texas, Disneyland, or any place else. They always wanted to go to the Big Bend.

When they were only five or six, each learned the short introductory poem for this particular commentary. Levi ended up as a captain in the Marine Corps, flying Harriers. Ethan is a lieutenant in the Navy, skippering a Mark VI patrol boat best described as a modern recast of the World War II-era PT.

Lieutenant English, USN, is enroute for the Persian Gulf as I write this. He has always excelled at anything he ever attempted, his crew and boat are as ready as they could ever be. I am so very proud of him.

Decades ago, there was another Navy lieutenant who said; "Ask not what your country can do for you---ask what you can do for your country."

My sons learned that, too. They live by it.

As for me, I have sent my country the best I've got.

God speed, my sons.

"The magician Merlin had a strange laugh, and it was heard when nobody else was laughing----He laughed because he knew what was coming next."
--Robertson Davies

I had been working my way along the eastern side of Anguila Mesa, moving along an old smuggler's trail that ultimately climbed up the shoulder of the uplift past Tinaja Lujan and beyond.

When I reached the split where yet another path looped back to Comanche Spring, some vague remembrance caused me to guide upon a pair of diminutive caves too small for a normal-sized man to shimmy into.

Climbing out of the dry run I scrambled up to the base of the vertical wall ahead, still below the paired holes but now high enough where I could see a heretofore hidden tinaja to my right. More tiny bits and pieces of something heard as a child flittered through my mind.

It was obvious the area had once been a camp of sorts, and most probably having to do with the candelilla business. During those years Anguila Mesa was a hotbed for such activity, which in turn stretched back for some thirty years or more before my immediate family arrived in Lajitas.

As the National Park Service increased its efforts to stop the transportation of candelilla wax across federal land, the smugglers shifted their routes to the most inaccessible and desolate parts of the park. That included Anguila Mesa.

Old tins of sardines, rusted cans and assorted rubbish dotted the general area where I surveyed what was around me. Likely most of these articles ultimately ended up in the arroyo below, as there were remains still visible along the edge of the outcropping.

But it was away from the edge where I found the boot soles.

The first one was sole up to the sun and it had been there a long time. The metal tacks for the heel were still in place, and the repaired heel itself had been made from a tire tread pattern at least sixty years old or better.

Scouting about, I found the other sole not more than fifty feet away. A matching pair of boot soles with no uppers whatsoever. Evidently the rodents had completely eaten the leather away, leaving the bottoms intact as the rubber did not agree with their digestive tracts.

Yet the big mystery remained: What had occurred to make a man pull off a pair of Mexican-made and repaired boots, and just leave them in the open? Did he buy a new pair at the trading post at Lajitas and decide to put them on here, throwing the old ones away?

Not a likely spot to break in a new pair of store-bought boots, and not something these sort of men would simply cast away if there was any possible use remaining in them.

So?

I prowled up and down the outcropping until running out of time. The sun was starting to sit low and I still had six and a half miles on foot back to the highway.

And what of this predicament my long-ago predecessor might have found himself in?

To him I say a sincere "*Buena suerte, amigo.*"

...About sixty-five years too late.

213

> *"It is better to know some of the questions than all of the answers."*
>
> **--James Thurber**

This was taken on the backside of Anguila Mesa, where a large arroyo from Mexico runs into the Rio Grande about three miles south of Lajitas. As one can discern from the photograph, there are few other places better suited in the lower Big Bend to cross the river than at this one spot.

I do not know the name of this arroyo, but I can tell you that its watershed runs all the way to the northern side of a large mountain shadowing San Carlos, Chihuahua. I also know that it has been a favored locale for smuggling since before the beginning of the twentieth century.

When one crosses the river here he basically has three routes to take him to Lajitas: follow the river up, move downstream until turning north along Aguila Mesa's southwestern cliffs, or follow those same cliffs southeasterly before climbing up the mesa and exiting near present-day Lajitas Airport.

Out of camera frame are some rock ruins denoting that somebody once lived on this high ground, for what purpose is best left to the imagination. The site was never on any map that I am aware of, but neither are the dozens of others dotting this particular area along the Texas side of the Rio Grande.

That history was made here is of no doubt, a history that if known would make for a far better understanding of life in the lower Big Bend a hundred years ago and more. San Carlos, about eight miles away by buzzard miles, was established before our own American Revolution was fought. That much we do know.

But as for the rest, *quién sabes?*

Smugglers, outlaws and bandits were not keen about keeping detailed notes of their activities. The smart ones realized early on the less they drew attention to themselves, the likelier for a longer stay this side of graveyard dirt.

For those nameless others who tried to eke out a living in honest fashion from this harsh land, they were either not educated enough or did not possess the time needed to keep any sort of written record of their day by day struggles.

So, all that one is left with are some piles of rocks, a likely overlook, and a smuggler's interstate below.

As well as one's own musings…

"Make my steps firm. Oh, how we often stagger along! We do what is right, but we quiver and shake while we are doing it."
--Charles Spurgeon

Not too long ago I was contacted by former Brewster County Sheriff Carl C. Williams concerning a half-century-plus unsolved death outside Lajitas. This case, culminating in a horrendous crime scene straight out of a Stephen King novel, was sensational enough to be covered by The New York Times in July of 1965. The female victim became known as The Lady In Chartreuse.

For those not familiar with the name, Carl C. Williams was a long time peace officer of the Big Bend, born and bred to this country. His is a well-lived life filled with loyal and faithful service to his fellow humankind. I grew up on stories of that life, as did other young boys who ultimately became peace officers themselves.

More so the sheriff had been *muy bueno amigos* with my grandfather, himself a former sheriff in Zavala County. That particular Ben English had acted as special deputy for Sheriff Williams when called upon, and the two shared many an adventure on both sides of the river. It was my grandfather who notified Sheriff Williams of the partially devoured human remains and led him to the gruesome spot.

No killer was ever identified, in fact neither was the victim. These wretched circumstances, along with others pertaining to the unsolved case, stayed in the minds and hearts of those involved in the investigation. Carl C. Williams, now in his mid-eighties, is the last of these lawmen still alive.

That was when I entered the picture. Recently Sheriff Williams had traveled to Lajitas in an attempt to locate the soul-haunting site. But with the many intervening decades and changes to the surrounding area, he had found himself unable to do so.

To lose the location of the scene itself would be the final blow, and even the consulted DPS records were a good two miles off. Carl asked me to try to re-establish the location, and to me that was a matter of personal honor in regards to my grandfather as well as his good friend from many years past. Plus, there was still enough of a peace officer residing inside me to spur my way through this task.

So, with some old photos in the sheriff's possession, as well as helpful memories supplied by my Tia Maggie, I saddled up my pack and ventured into the desert. On a low hill among many others, the improvised marker and broken *veladores* left by those who prayed for an anonymous young woman, were found fairly quickly.

After taking photographs and making field notes as well as grid coordinate calculations, I said a short prayer myself and pushed on toward Anguila Mesa, in the direction of Tinaja Lujan. I had a driving need for solitude at this point, and to be as far away as possible from all human ugliness and tragedy.

Hours later, I came to a juncture where good sense and lack of remaining daylight hours warned me to go no farther. Resting on a rocky knoll and eating a late lunch, I gazed across time and space all the way back to the western face of the Fresno.

Sitting there I thought of what I had left behind me, and of man's unending inhumanity to his fellow man. Or in this case, a young woman known only to God.

I began mentally leafing through what I had seen as a child growing up in this country, as well as two hitches in the Marine Corps, a career in the Texas Highway Patrol, and my life as a whole. Gains and losses, griefs and ecstasies, glories and terrors.

Spurgeon's words came to me in my self-imposed solitude: "We do what is right, but we quiver and shake while we are doing it."

Make my steps firm, Lord.

That's all I ask.

"In three words I can sum up everything I've learned about life: it goes on."
--Robert Frost

It is said that time is like a river, flowing into the seas of eternity. The river never remains the same as it courses along due to the constantly changing flow. Dip your cup into the waters one moment and drink. When you do so again, it is different water and thus a different river.

More than one river flows in this story; both the river of moments and memories, and the muddy waters of the Rio Grande carving through the lower Big Bend and on to the Gulf of Mexico. Commanding a high ground view and perspective above both is a place out of time, a spot central to my childhood as well as the lives of so many others.

This venerable adobe and wood structure has signified Lajitas for nearly as long as the locale has had that name. The crossing below has been known prior as Comanche Crossing, San Carlos Crossing, and likely a dozen other names in human tongues long since lost.

It is the Lajitas Trading Post, once the defining man-made symbol of a way of life central to this land and both rivers described. Now it is only a prostituted shell of itself in the form of a golf pro shop. Yet it still stands, alone and defiant in those moving waters of time.

Likely one of the greatest travesties ever to occur in the lower Big Bend is what has happened to Lajitas. Doubly so because the boundary lines for the national park as well as the limits of the state park run almost right up to it. Of all the places you can name with historical significance to this country; very few possess the long, involved, rich, multi-cultural story of Lajitas.

It is now all gone; irretrievably lost to the blade of the bulldozer, the hundreds of tons of fill dirt forming out-of-place golf greens, and the lack of knowledge, foresight and respect of its successive owners. As far as I know not one single archaeological dig ever occurred here, the ground zero site of man's existence for as long as he has been in this region.

Now, about the photographs:

The first photograph is of myself at four years of age, I am standing on the front porch of the trading post in 1962. It was Christmas time, evident by the closed doors to the store customarily open except in cold weather, and my new clothes and the brace of shiny cap pistols hanging on my hips.

The photo was taken by my grandmother, whose partial shadow you can see at the bottom of the frame. It was unusual for her to shoot in color, which lends some importance to this particular event. When I look at this photo and think back I have to smile, so much of who we were as a small child ties directly into who we became later in life.

The second photo was taken fifty-three years later, also close to Christmas time. It had been a while since I had visited the site and was shocked at what I found. Nearly everything I remembered was gone or near unrecognizable. I wandered about almost aimlessly, trying to connect with that four-year-old boy standing on the front porch.

Finally, around the rear of the building masked by cast away junk, I found one of the original windows still performing its set task from when the store was first built.

Then it came to me where all those memories and that four-year boy had gone off to, and just how far that river of time had floated me down stream. Childhood memories can be castaways, too.

I write this with no malice or anger to anyone, but only with a great sadness in my heart as to what has transpired in Lajitas even in my own lifetime.

And the waters of both rivers continue to flow.

223

CHAPTER EIGHT

MARISCAL MOUNTAIN AREA

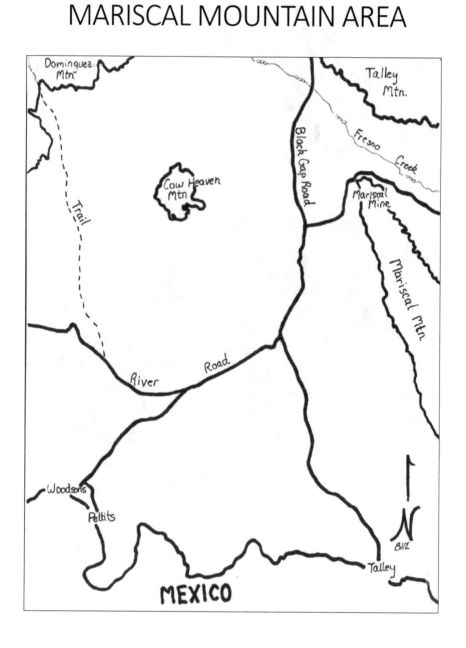

The area of Big Bend National Park surrounding Mariscal Mountain is explored but rarely, even by those who venture beyond the paved roads or take other routes more primitive. Arguably it is the most unvisited section of the park that still provides folks with some sort of vehicular access.

By and large it is usually seen by those headed for the river camps or who want to drive what the park service calls River Road, coursing between Castolon and the Tornillo Creek Bridge west of Boquillas.

But to 'see' is not to experience, especially while bouncing along with one's air conditioning and satellite radio turned up full blast. This desert literally radiates with history, while in contrast people pass through as quickly as they can. Often enough just to say they have been there.

There is nothing wrong intrinsically in that, other than the shame of missing so much in a place where the unexpected is nigh the norm. I have explored this country many times on foot, each time leaving with the irony of having learned more but believing I know less.

I suppose many would find frustration in that dichotomy. However, in the present world we live in there is some solace in such a realization.

After all, inner peace is not found at breakneck speed.

"This age does not generally sin in the direction of being too excited concerning divine things."

--Charles Spurgeon

I named it 'God's Own Marble.'

That might be bordering on sacrilegious to a few but since I had a Baptist preacher with me, along with a lifelong friend who has always been strong for the Lord, I considered myself on fairly sure theological footing by doing so.

We were on a four-day expedition along the outer reaches of the east side of the Chisos, while at the same time commemorating the twelfth birthday of Chris Johnson's eldest son Elijah.

When Elijah was asked months before what he wanted for his birthday present, my phone rang. Elijah wanted to come to the lower Big Bend and Brother Chris was inquiring if I could guide. It didn't take long for me to say yes, honors like that from a near twelve-year-old don't come around often.

Shortly thereafter, Steven Williams' phone was also ringing. I needed another experienced hand and you could look a long time before finding a better one. We have been friends for nearly a half century now and he has never come up short, no matter what the situation. A good man in good times, and a better one when things get a mite tough in rugged country.

So here we were now, miles from any road of any sort going through a nameless cut along a rocky ridge northwest of Cow Heaven Mountain. We just happened to turn left instead of right, looked down, and there it was.

One of those moments of awe and wonder that one can only experience in the lower Big Bend, along a path less traveled.

And everyone, from twelve years of age minus one day to sixty-one and counting felt pure glory in their hearts, and then the grins appeared.

Not one of us had a single clue as to how that solid rock sphere had been created, shaped and deposited along this craggy, insignificant finger angling

226

into a steeply eroded arroyo. The ravine was only one among dozens of others running in every direction, forming a natural maze to challenge the body and bewilder the mind.

But we were blessed with the opportunity, no doubt about that.

Maybe, just maybe because at the same time, God was grinning down on us. Letting these four mortal wanderers find in the midst of the Chihuahuan Desert…

His Own Marble.

"I therefore claim to show, not how men think in myths, but how myths operate in men's minds without their being aware of the fact."
--Claude Levi-Srauss

It was late in the evening as we eased along the ancient path. It had been there so long the repeated pounding of countless feet had literally sunk the track into the surrounding field of small rocks.

This starkly etched *sendero*, in conjunction with several similar ones, angled in at different points spreading out to the north, all converging at a crossing along the Rio Grande that ran below us. We were on the hunt for a long-vanished part of historical lore, the Paso del Chisos branch for the Comanche War Trail.

As most who have knowledge of the raiding route can tell you, originally there were three major crossings for the Comanche moving through the Big Bend. These were at present day Presidio, Lajitas and San Vicente. Along these routes fortunes in stolen livestock, trade goods and human captives were herded across in both directions by these superbly mounted buccaneers of the Southwest.

Truth be known, the crossings had been in use for a long time before the Comanche first came to Texas in the mid-1700s. Furthermore, they would be utilized long after the Comanches were killed off or relegated to a reservation. Commerce routes are commerce routes, no matter the cargo or the finer points of the legality involved.

In an attempt to stem the hostile incursions into Northern Mexico, Spanish authorities built three forts, or *presidios* near those locations. Of limited effectiveness overall, the one at San Vicente was deemed enough of a nuisance for the raiders to seek another way through.

229

Thus the Paso del Chisos came into being. At one time it was rumored to be nearly a half mile wide, littered with cast off stolen belongings as well as the bleaching bones of man and beast alike. But unlike the other branches, the exact location quickly vanished from memory. Several claimed to have located the 'lost' crossing, and some discoveries have been quite plausible. Others, not so much.

Thing is, hardly anyone considered where the animals of the area still choose to ford the river. Theirs is the hard-wired memory of survival over countless generations, finely calibrated by their ancestors who once crossed the river too.

Thus, these well-worn trails are still being used by wild and domesticated alike, all converging in masse at one spot.

And that is how we believe we may have found what man himself had long forgotten.

231

> *"A slender acquaintance with the world must convince every man that actions, not words, are the true criterion of the attachment of friends."*
> **--George Washington**

Steve Williams is one of the chosen few I take along on some of my prowls. He's known me long enough to still kid me about speaking English with a Mexican accent when I started school in Fort Stockton. We have been good friends ever since. My grandfather would have said that 'He'll do to ride the river with,' and that was why he was with me now.

Since just after sunup we had worked our way across the flats west of the Mariscal, and into the foothills that brace against the southern and western slopes of Cow Heaven Mountain.

When compared to the other lofty uplifts present, this particular landmark doesn't look like much in comparison. However, looks can be deceiving, and on this end it's as rough as a chewed up Indian corn cob. A series of rugged arroyos and low jagged ridges corkscrew haphazardly in every which way, and there is no quick or easy path through.

I have heard tell from old timers the name was actually a cartographer's misspelling. It was supposed to be Cow *Haven* Mountain, due to the difficulty of flushing cattle out of this natural labyrinth during roundups. Invariably the ranch hands of that time would have to make several passes to assure the job was properly done.

Yet there is a flipside to such a jumbled maze of rock, dirt, cactus and other obstacles; the wondrous and somewhat weird artifacts you find along your improvised route. While I was fixated on a rock monolith in the distance, rising from the desert floor like some sort of otherworldly apparition, Steve was watching for what laid closer in.

This was the 'what' that caught his eye.

Don't ask me what it is exactly, or how it was formed as I have no idea. Much like the land that gave birth to it, this oddly shaped rock presents itself as a puzzle placed within an enigma, and giftwrapped with innumerable mysteries.

We paused, puzzled and after a few moments more began to grin. Then we moved on.

234

"We are the children of our landscape; it dictates behavior and even thought in the measure to which we are responsible to it."
--Lawrence George Durrell

Of all the mines situated in the lower parts of the Big Bend, what is now known as the Mariscal was surely the most isolated and challenging to those who came seeking their fortunes.

Known at different times as the Lindsay, the Ellis, the Texas Almaden and finally the Mariscal it was actually Martin Solis, a member of the Solis ranching family, who first found cinnabar on the northern end of Mariscal Mountain in 1900.

From that point forward there were drastic ebbs and flows in the mining activities here coupled with numerous civil suits, bankruptcies and legal intrigues that gave the mine a notoriety as well as a checkered past unmatched by any other in the region. Before it was finally shuttered for the last time around 1944, numerous owners and investors had been called before various courts in regards to the operations as well as proper ownership.

But still they came seeking the proverbial pot of gold at the end of the rainbow; planning, building, enlarging, upgrading and dreaming of that one big spike in cinnabar prices. The one that would pay off handsomely for all of the hard work and sacrifices put into this implacable, unyielding, stubborn beyond belief desert land.

Even the workers and supervisors were a breed apart. Most all were Mexican, and many had fought in the Great Mexican Revolution from 1910 to 1920. The blacksmith was said to have been a well-regarded horse farrier for the Federales while the storekeeper had been a major in the Villistas.

They too came here in search of something worthwhile, leaving a war torn homeland and their own checkered pasts behind them. Ironically, each ultimately decided they had more in common with the other than what remained of their previous animosities.

The remnants of their dreams as well as those of others still remain in this desert, where man now comes to discover lessons learned among the ruins of a rapidly receding past. We walk, we see, we wonder at what all occurred here not that long ago.

It is then we begin to understand that we stand on the shoulders of those who came before. Good, bad, or indifferent in action and spirit, each carried with them an innate resourcefulness that few seem capable of in our modern times.

Assuredly they were hard men, but just as assuredly real men.

"I shall tell you a great secret, my friend. Do not wait for the final judgment. It takes place every day."

--Albert Camus

The shadows of early evening were beginning to stretch out across the desert as Steve and I made our way down an unnamed dry draw. We were still some miles from base camp, he would later figure we had covered a total of between seventeen and eighteen miles on foot this day.

Having started on the west side of the Mariscal, we had crossed over to the southern reaches of Cow Heaven Mountain. Forging our way along the small, knifelike ridges and constantly twisting gullies, we pushed west and on to higher ground. Before us stood the craggy peaks of the Sierra de la Punta, reaching up into an incredibly blue sky.

Near where the jumbled ravines ended along the southwestern borders of Cow Heaven Mountain, we turned north and nooned in an abandoned mountain lion lair, making use of the scant shade much like the big cat had done. I glassed for likely routes leading northward, selecting a near solid rock run that spilled off the western shoulder of the mountain.

Snaking our way to the entry point we moved up toward the crest, having to needle our way through a part so narrow that at a hundred feet away it looked completely impassable. Clearing it, we stepped into an unlikely small flat on top. After eyeballing the area now presented below us, we started down the other side through jumbled boulders, loose dirt and cacti of all shapes and varieties.

Following the ravine around and through a space where eons of flash floods had forced their way through the free-standing wall of a black granite ridge, we stepped into open desert again and began angling our way back to a hot meal and a good night's sleep still a good distance away.

238

I turned around and took this photograph as we did so. Backbone Ridge to the left, Elephant Tusk front and center, and the blueish South Rim of the Chisos looming on the horizon above all. Not a word was said between us as I did so.

No need to, we were both thinking the same thing.

It felt good, even glorious, just being alive today.

240

"The world is a very poor critic of my Christianity, but it is a very sufficient one of my conduct."
--Alexander Maclaren

It was coming on evening time in early November, near the spot where Fresno Creek crowds hard against the bleached rock of the Mariscal and separates it from the reddish-brown formations of Talley Mountain. I was on the hunt for a cemetery dating back to almost the beginning of the twentieth century, used by the miners who dug for cinnabar here.

Though a hundred years and twenty might be nothing more than the proverbial blink of the eye for Father Time, it can be far different for the remains and markers of those interred in such a place. People move away, memories fade, and what written records made are lost to decay and disinterest.

Those same remains and markers also fade and decay, as the desert encroaches in its patient pace to reclaim what began as its own. It is as if the land takes its own peculiar, perhaps even unbalanced joy in doing so where man worked the hardest and grieved the most. Finding such spots can be a challenging process, particularly when not noted on any map and the information dealing with it is often incomplete in detail, or near completely wrong.

A note to the fellow journeyer with an eye for the written word, just because it is found in a book does not make it in fact necessarily so. This seems especially true for the lesser known history and locales of the lower Big Bend.

And so it was in this case, the description found in a book was only correct as far as on what end of a mountain the cemetery lay. Everything else was either imagination, the repeating of other bad information or a nigh useless understanding for terrain.

But with the assistance of long-time friends and fellow seekers Steven Williams and Brother Chris Johnson, along with Chris's twelve-year-old son

Elijah, we combed the general surroundings until we found what we were looking for.

As best as we could tell there were eleven graves containing the mortal remnants of those now known only to God. Most of the markers had either fallen down or rotted away, with no legible names or dates to go by. It was a rather quiet and forlorn place, woeful in the obvious that it had been a long time since the warmth of any human hand had reached out to those lying below.

So, we reached out in our own way; restacking dislocated stones, re-erecting the salvageable wooden crosses, and taking photographs to document the site. Knowing full well those same stones will become dislocated again, and those wooden crosses would ultimately rot away into nothingness.

But we felt the need to render a certain respect to these nameless eleven; somewhere, sometime there was someone who cared for them, even loved them. Most likely they are also dead and mostly forgotten by now.

Besides, there is an old Mexican saying that goes: *"Mañana a mi me toca."*

And that time can come sooner than any of us would care to think about.

*"I must go down to the seas again,
For the call of the running tide;
Is a wild call and a clear call,
That may not be denied."*
--John Masefield

I was answering my own call yet again, the siren song that has echoed through my mind for as far back as I can remember. While Masefield spoke of the siren song of the sea, mine was of the desert. At first glance as polarized as any two places might be, the sea and the desert are more alike in many ways than they could ever be different.

My officially noted purpose for the trip was research for an upcoming historical novel. But truth be known it was all to answer the call, to get as far away from the noise, confusion, and perpetual spiritual bombardment that so-called 'civilization' seems to foist on us all. Steve Williams had been fighting the same war, so we saddled up together and headed for the lonesome country west of the Mariscal.

There we slept under the stars, with no tent and precious little more present than needed to subsist upon. We were up at dawn and often not back to camp until way after dark, eating cold rations by flashlight due to spending too much time in one out of the way spot or another.

On this day we were making a big loop around Cow Heaven Mountain and were about halfway along. In fact, we had just left our nooning site on that low ridge to the front, dining in a hollowed-out overhang that had served as an observation point for a mountain lion.

While sampling the cuisine, we noticed what appeared to be a road of gold shining in the bright sunlight, going up the shoulder of Cow Heaven Mountain. Since we were looking for a crossover route to complete our loop, the decision was made to investigate. Moving our way up, I looked to our west and took this photograph.

Pictured before you along the horizon is Punta de la Sierra, which you might think upon as being the very southern tip of the Chisos Mountain Range. On this side of the sierra runs Dominguez Trail, angled along a roughly north-south axis leading up to the ruins that give the trail its name.

Wild country there, all the way from Cow Heaven Mountain up to the south rim of the Chisos. I don't know of any cow that would consider this a proper place to spend one's afterlife, but I know that I do.

The 'golden road' turned out to be a dry wash of solid rock over two hundred yards long, winding its way off the higher elevations while also forming a pass to the northern side. At the bottom of the frame, you can see where the solid rock part of it ends.

And these are the sort of memories that no road of solid gold bricks could ever buy.

"The New Frontier of which I speak is not a set of promises---it is a set of challenges. It sums up not what I intend to offer the American people, but what I intend to ask of them."
--John F. Kennedy

We were moving up Fresno Creek, shadowing the traces of an old wagon road that had been there for over a century now, running north from the Mariscal Mines. I seek out these disappearing routes and trails because there was a time and a purpose for them, but one never really pieces together their story until you walk them out.

And so we ambled along; studying, considering and seeking out what had been at one time. Along the way we found crumbling ruins, mine diggings, pieces of antique cars, rusting strands of barbed wire, an earthen dike, and a solitary, hastily dug grave emplaced in a barren flat where hardly anything grows.

Who lies there remains a mystery, much like so many other final places of rest found in this country. It is a harsh land and these markers serve as a warning to those who journey into its environs.

It was shortly before mid-day when Brother Chris said there was something ahead. At a rawboned six-foot-seven and of a good eye, he holds an advantage over the rest of us who roam through our lives at nearly a foot below. Our little group shifted course and guided toward the spot, swinging wide of each other as to not miss anything in the approach.

What Chris had spotted was the remnants of some sort of water well. Or more exactly, the plural. There were at least three shafts present along with a slowly corroding steel water tank, the foundation for a long-departed wind mill and the carefully made rock structure shown in this photograph. Its purpose had been to support the tank.

Whoever chose the location was of a canny nature and knew how the desert secreted its most valuable resource. The head of Fresno Creek lies directly below the South Rim of the Chisos, so when it rains the normally dry run can carry a great deal of water. The builder here knew that, and he also knew that one of the best places to tap into that treasure was where the creek came to a choke point with rocky uplifts on either side. His wells were set near one of them, where the creek bed ran close to higher ground.

After scouting around a bit, our party formed up again and started on to the north. There was a lot to see that we had never seen before and we were burning daylight. As we did so, I took one more look behind me and thought of that lonely grave less than a mile away. There were so many possibilities as to what had happened to its unknown resident.

Did he know about the water here? Was he trying to reach the wells and fell short?

Quién sabes?

Old frontier or new, there are no promises in this desert.

Only challenges.

CHAPTER NINE

TORNILLO BASIN AREA

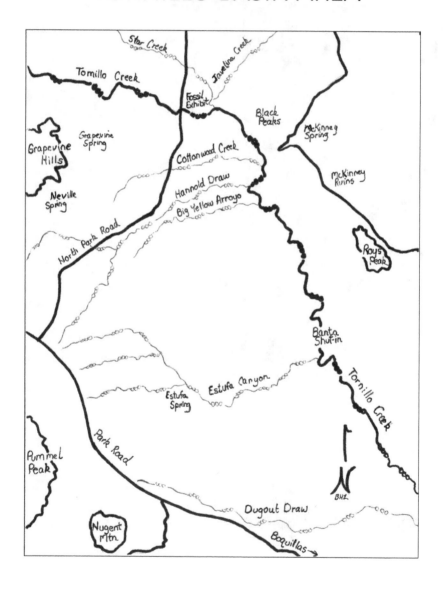

Like any other, the Chihuahuan Desert permeating the lower Big Bend region is one of a hard environment, survived only by equally hardy creatures and plants.

Those termed as creatures would surely include the species of man, especially those who came early on. With the availability of water being one of the prime ingredients in this continual struggle, an inordinate amount of past human activity is found in the Tornillo Basin.

Life was never easy in the lower Big Bend, and ample evidence of this never-ending battle abounds. Ruins, shelters, dikes, diggings, rusting barbed wire, worn trails and gravesites of all sizes are present here, all in numbers that would shock the average passerby who only views the Tornillo from afar.

One of my favorite authors, Louis L'Amour, wrote a series of short stories that were ultimately compiled and entitled 'The Strong Shall Live.' Coincidentally enough L'Amour spent some time in the lower Big Bend, and wrote some of his short stories using this singular land as a backdrop.

"The Strong Shall Live." Anyone who knows anything about the history of this country would agree those few words pretty much sums that history up.

And that sometimes being strong was still not enough.

"Give us all the blessing, but do let thine own purposes be accomplished, and thine own glory come of it, and we shall be well content, though we should be forgotten and unknown."

–Charles Spurgeon

I have written before of the many burial grounds dotting the landscape of the lower Big Bend, some extending back at least three hundred years and more.

They can be found by written references, topographical maps and sometimes still by word of mouth. On occasion the journeyer will simply stumble across one in the unlikeliest places, while others never will be found. So much has been lost in the topsy-turvy chain of history of this area that a complete record will never be obtained.

A few have a special aura to them: wrapped in difficulty of locating, lack of names and dates, and a real question as to why they were placed there to begin with. Such an elusive, mysterious spot naturally leads to speculations, then stories that ultimately take on the substance of legend.

Such is as in what is known as either *El Panteon de las Tres Negritas* or 'The Black Peaks Graves.' Even over the past ten years or so, there has been some discussion as to whether they still existed due to time, lack of maintenance and exposure. Many have looked for this spot without success, even after multiple attempts.

More so, a lack of written record with details such as names, dates and circumstances has led to numerous stories as to the who and why for these graves. Some have claimed they were a family wiped out by marauding Apaches, or died during the Spanish Flu epidemic of a century before. Others have said they were victims of an ill-fated attempt to cross the nearby Tornillo Creek during a flash flood.

The truth is this resting place was the graveyard, or *panteon*, for a nearby village. Likely made up entirely by Mexican immigrants, they could have been refugees from the Great Mexican Revolution, the Cristeros War or some other calamity involving bouts of famine or pestilence that so often swept their unhappy homeland.

Like the cemetery, the village itself is an enigma. As far as I know there is no historical account of it ever being there. No words in a book, no marks on a map, no oral history; nothing more than the crumbling ruins and castaway relics of a people who evidently both lived and died in anonymity.

That, and the unmarked, decaying graves on a barren hillside whose very existence has been called into question numerous times.

Eight graves, perhaps nine, known only to their God.

They are not the only ones.

"There is nothing permanent except change."

--Heraclitus

If this photograph first appeals to you as some sort of prehistoric or even otherworldly setting for a 1950s science fiction movie, you would not be far from wrong.

What you are seeing is referred to in the geological sense as the Black Peaks Formation, which has been dated back to the late Cretaceous Period of some sixty-six and a half million years ago.

The three peaks, also known informally as the *Tres Negritas* can be seen upper center right in the frame, with the largest in the middle. Large is a relative term in this particular example. As you can tell from the surrounding terrain, they are not very big as far as physical size.

However, they are very big is in the realms of regional history, both from the time that dinosaurs roamed this ground to the scattered remains of ranches and settlements lining both banks of nearby Tornillo Creek.

Fossils for the *Bravoceratops Polyphemus* (a derivative of the triceratops) and the pterosaur *Quetzalcoatlus*, the largest flying creature ever discovered, were excavated not far from here. Adding to those are numerous varieties of ancient crocodiles, turtles, fish and extinct species of mammals.

Rock examples of different ages abound, including those referred to as 'cannonball concretions' seen in the photo's foreground. An outdoor exhibit celebrating these finds is situated along the Persimmon Gap park road, about two miles from the peaks themselves.

But when you simply park your vehicle and walk up the low knoll that makes for an overlook, there is no way to fully appreciate what is out here. From a distance the Tornillo flats and surrounding hills appear barren, lifeless and dull, not worth much more than an obligatory bob of the head before driving off to the Chisos Basin or Santa Elena Canyon.

Much like the rest of the Big Bend, it is not until you actually saddle up and begin prowling on foot that it begins to begrudgingly reveal its secrets. Not only the ruins, the springs, the tinajas and the stark natural beauty itself, but also the mostly obscure yet amazingly abundant wildlife activity.

In one day alone I came across packs of javelina, magnificent muley bucks in velvet, the very recent sign of a good-sized bull elk (hoof prints some four inches long) and the biggest black bear I've seen in the wild in many a year.

And all the while you are walking through the open bowels of an ancient land that has gone from inland sea to coastal marshlands, and from raging volcanos to a dry and decaying desert.

And it is still changing, if ever so slowly.

Every single day.

"The day was hot, the wind was dry, and mesquite barred the way,
The maguey and the cactus tried to drain our lives away;
We came up to a ranch house a' dying in the desert sun,
And looked the old spread over, we couldn't see anyone..."
--'Mis Raices Estan Aqui, as narrated by John Wayne

It was hot in early September, the kind of heat that will have a coyote chasing a jack rabbit while both move along at a walk. You could see the faintest hope of rain to the east, likely somewhere over the Sierra del Carmen. But that same hope only baked into the rocks and thirsty soil around me, as the mid-afternoon sun blazed from above.

I was on another of my prowls into the lower Big Bend, ostensibly checking on the gravesites near the Tres Negritas. No one really knows who lies there, though fanciful tales and stories abound. I have my own ideas, *pero quién sabes*?

Once done at that sorrowful spot, I decided to follow my nose just to see where it led. Drifting south and then east past remnants of other eras and people mostly forgotten, I began making a large loop beyond the old candelilla wax factory and into the farthest fringes of the McKinney Hills.

In far too soon a time, the hour had come to turn back. I kept to the high ground, wanting to see if I could locate a wagon road that had run down Hannold Draw and across Tornillo Creek. On an old map I had noted some

257

sort of dwelling alongside that road. When that map was drawn, it was the only one so marked for miles around.

Even with the passing of over a century, the ruts for the track could still be discerned. The dwelling itself was also easy enough to find, but the ravages of wind, weather and erosion had collapsed the walls; leaving little more than assorted piles of rocks.

Scouting about one could see this had been a fairly prosperous place, considering where it was and that it dated back to the nineteenth century. The builder had chosen well; close to a known route, close to water, plenty of wood available and during those years what would have been excellent grazing. There were even the last vestiges of long dead shade trees. This falling down, mesquite infested, forgotten rock house had once been someone's life.

After resting in what little shade available I put on my pack and gear again, and set my mind upon the final leg of today's journey. Soon the sun would be setting over the Rosillos, and some semblance of coolness would return to this desert.

My ALICE pack creaked as I shook out the load, my shoulders aching from the weight. Starting up the low hill and away from the ruins, sweat began to pool again under my flat brimmed Stetson and at the small of my back. My feet, having carried me mile after demanding mile, were starting to lodge a protest to more of the same.

Cresting the low rise I stopped and turned, bidding farewell to those despairing piles of rock and rotting wood. Someone else's roots, someone else's life, that I had shared vicariously for only a few precious minutes while resting from my own endeavors.

Turning into the sun, I pulled the brim of my hat down low to shield my eyes and walked over the crest.

And back into my own time and way of life.

259

*"The value of a sentiment is the amount of
sacrifice you are prepared to make for it."
--John Galsworthy*

Along the eastern banks of the Tornillo just west of the bare, roughhewn hills of the Cuesta Carlota, sit the rotting remains of a man's dream from a century and more before. His name was Max Ernst.

If that rings some distant bell in the memory of those who know something of the geography of this area, there is ample reason for that. To this day you hear references to Ernst Tinaja and the Big Tinaja store. On multiple topographical maps you will see words denoting places such as Ernst Valley, Ernst Ridge and Ernst Basin.

Yet Max Ernst's greatest efforts occurred in the immediate acreage illustrated by this photograph. Now known as the abandoned community of La Noria, it once was notated on maps as being Boquillas, Texas.

A side note to this story, if the reader will. Like other locales in the lower Big Bend, there has been more than one Boquillas. Of course, the best known by far is Boquillas, Coahuila, near the entrance for Boquillas Canyon.

Yet there were two other places at different times with that same name on our side of the river. The first is where Rio Grande Village is presently situated. The second, as mentioned above, was also known as La Noria.

That name change can be attributed solely to the energy and desire of Max Ernst. A German immigrant who came to the lower Big Bend in search of a future as well as a challenge; Ernst became a well-established businessman, a county commissioner, a justice of the peace and the local postmaster, among the holding of other offices and duties.

It was as postmaster that Ernst managed to move the name of Boquillas from the Rio Grande Village area. As proprietor of the Big Tinaja Store, it allowed him to consolidate all of his various capacities under one roof. It also allowed him to pursue his dream involving the opportunities and potentials he saw in the community.

260

That was when the population of his dream peaked, roads came and went bringing commerce and people to share in his vision, and to help in the realization of that dream. The new Boquillas, Texas was growing.

Then on September 27th, 1908, that dream was dealt a death blow from a single .44-40 bullet. Max Ernst was murdered from ambush enroute to the old Boquillas while on official post office business. For many years afterwards, the spot where he was shot was called Dead Man's Curve.

No one knows who fired that fatal round. Suspicions and rumors ran rampant throughout the country but no one was ever brought to trial. But whoever did it not only killed a man, he or she also killed an entire community. When Max Ernst was buried, his dream might as well have been placed alongside.

After his unsolved murder, the community became known as La Noria again and the population began to decline. A brief stay in this occurred when the Army began sending troops into the area around 1912, and the locals provided supplies as well as services for the rotating units.

Many of those who have heard of these encampments tend to believe they were only utilized for military operations. That is not exactly true, as they were also used as refugee camps for Mexican nationals fleeing famines, epidemics, religious persecutions and the near genocidal violence of the so-called 'great' revolution.

This helped in keeping up the local population numbers. But when the Army finally packed up and left, and those refugee camps were closed, the corpse of La Noria was planted in a hole just like the body of Max Ernst.

Now all that is left are ruins, eroding rifle pits, near gone trails, rubbish heaps and this decaying cemetery. That and the cactus and mequite, which sing the song of the desert when an arid breeze happens to pass through.

Broken dreams are abundant along the banks of the Tornillo, as well as the occasional murdered one.

"You may not understand doctrine, creed, or rite; but be sure to seek God. No splendid ceremonial nor rigorous etiquette can intercept the seeking soul."
--F. B. Meyer

When I was a kid roaming the Big Bend some fifty years ago, it was claimed by many that all the elk had vanished from the area. Then there were others more knowledgeable who said there were a few still up in the Glass Mountains, hidden away by the rough terrain and a sympathetic land owner who held sway over a good portion of that country.

These days, thanks to both private as well as public wildlife preserves, elk are beginning to be seen far more frequently in the Trans Pecos region. I have heard of them on ranches below Sanderson in fairly large numbers, as well as in the Glass and various other locales across to the Guadalupe Mountains.

I even heard of one cow at Persimmon Gap. Due to empty-headed tourists feeding this animal, she became such a nuisance that she had to be transported to another location. Think about that, folks, before you step forward as an unnatural interloper into the natural definition of 'wildlife.'

However, this particular photograph was taken in Tornillo Basin not more than about two hundred feet from pavement. It was late in the evening and my wife and I were in her Corvette, coming from Persimmon Gap and headed to The Basin for a bi-annual BBNHA meeting.

There were three of these bulls and I took numerous shots of them, selecting this one as representative for them all. This bull was the largest of the trio and you can tell from the background the kind of bare, stark area they were located in. I apologize for the quality, the light was fading fast and giving my little thirty-dollar used Kodak focusing fits.

The shocking thing to me was that at least twenty vehicles must have driven past this very spot just prior to our arrival, and the tracks of the three bulls showed they had actually crossed the pavement. Yet they had gone unnoticed by everyone save for us.

Though I was dressed in street clothes for the evening dinner to come, I still managed to stalk within seventy-five feet of these magnificent animals. Cathy got out of the car and quietly watched my progress. A few other vehicles slowed, saw what was happening, and pulled over to observe.

I would have gotten even closer if not for one of the gathering onlookers' unruly ankle biter, yapping near continuously while the so-called master created even more noise in trying to shush the annoying pet.

A note about good manners and courtesies when coming to the Big Bend as a tourist: unless it is a service canine please leave your dog at home. Nobody wants to hear their ceaseless yattering amid the quietude so many have traveled so far for, and it is for the animal's own safety. Small domestics are only tasty snacks for the many nearby predators.

Ultimately the three bulls moved off completely, drifting down the Tornillo to graze on grass from recent rains. From what I could tell, they were coming from the Rosillos area, perhaps having escaped from a preserve somewhere in that direction. Whatever the reason, to see them like this within the confines of the lower Big Bend was a thrill I have wished for my entire life.

And I thought I should share with others who might understand.

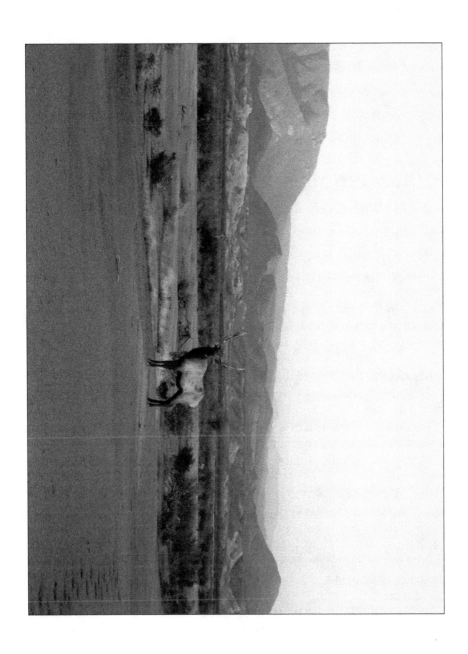

265

"The worst sin---perhaps the only sin---
passion can commit, is to be joyless."
--Dorothy Leigh Sayers

There are a great many places in the lower Big Bend that bring awe and wonderment to those who visit them, no matter the age or life experiences. This area's vast collection of extraordinary rock formations often are the center of such epiphanies, and near countless gatherings of these geological Rubik's cubes are found in every size, shape and shade of color.

One of the better-known examples are the Grapevine Hills, remnants of an ancient laccolith that formed and then eroded away tens of millions of years ago. They are situated to the north side of the Chisos, only a few miles from Panther Junction.

The trailhead is reached by a well-kept dirt road not too far from pavement, suitable for most any sort of motor vehicle. You can see the faintest hints of this natural spectacle from either the north or west park roads, if you know where to look.

Here the biggest attraction is Balanced Rock, and the short trail easing up an arroyo leads right to that very spot. But if you are coming to see only what most do, then you are missing out on so much more.

The photo shown is only one very small part of this visual celebration, and only from one single angle. Beyond the frame are a thousand and more other angles and sights all there for your personal enjoyment, but only if you decide to spend some time to prowl through it a bit.

For the total effect most of us should not go alone. If possible, take a child with you, to reflect upon what is here through their eyes and youthful imaginations.

Watch the look of unfazed wonderment spread across their faces, and remember what such days were like for you at the same age. People talk so often about growing old, some near ceaselessly. Perhaps it is not so much they have grown old as they have allowed themselves to be old.

Going to Grapevine Hills, especially in the golden dawn of morning or last fading light of evening, is a sure cure for such self-imposed maladies.

*"As dust that drives, as straws that blow,
Into the night we go one and all."*
--William Ernest Henley

About four miles north of Panther Junction alongside the road to Persimmon Gap is a grave. It has been there for over a century now, fenced off with a wrought iron barrier that makes it seem even more forlorn and isolated.

It is the grave of Nina Hannold, the wife of Curtis Hannold and she died in September of 1911. Nina was born in Missouri and came to the Big Bend in 1908 with her young family from Logan, Oklahoma. They say it took them two months to get here by covered wagon.

Nina was only 29 years old when buried at this spot, a victim of complications from a third pregnancy. People who come to admire this land's rugged beauty often forget just how tough and unforgiving it can be, especially for those who pioneered it.

More than a few, like this lovely young woman, traveled a long way under harsh circumstances to pioneer this country. They worked from 'can see to can't' throughout each day that followed with little respite, only to die at a far too young age.

The story I heard decades ago was she picked this burial spot herself, it lies on a point of high ground where she used to sit and read to her children. At that time there was a spring situated below the outcropping with large cottonwoods all around, framed by the majestic Chisos Mountains to the south and crowned by endless blue skies.

That spring has been dry a long time now and even the fallen trunks of those cottonwoods have rotted into nothingness. But the mountains and endless blue skies mothering over this lonesome grave are still here, just like they were all those years ago. The somber scene serves as a reminder of one's mortality to those who take the time to stop, walk over and pay their respects.

I think she might have liked that. It gets lonely out here at times, even with all the traffic passing so close by.

269

CHAPTER TEN

CROTON PEAK AREA

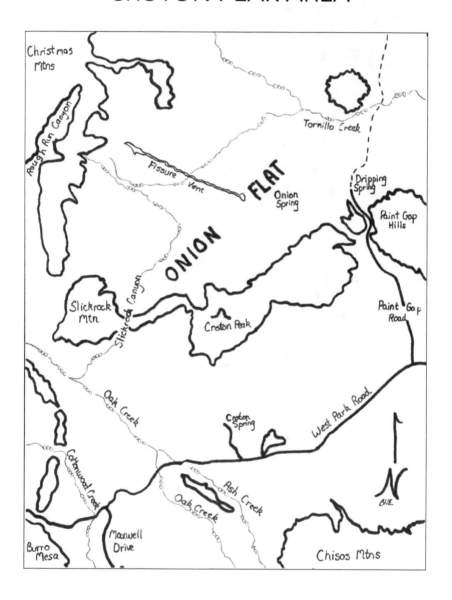

It was late winter some years back, below Croton Peak near the spring that bears the mountain's name. The day was slipping into the dusk of evening, and a sense of peacefulness and belonging settled in like a babe nestled in their mother's arms.

You sit and listen, admiring the signs and scenes of life all around, and watch the sun droop in the west while the shadows lengthen. A chill comes creeping with the faintest waft of a wind off the mountain. Life is most fully appreciated while at the slowest of paces.

Yet over the decades I have observed so many folks in wide-open mode throughout the lower Big Bend, especially in the national park. It is as if they have set their minds on seeing it all in one day. Meanwhile I encamp near places such as this, knowing I will never be able to see all that is worthwhile in one lifetime.

This mad dashing about seems to be epidemical these days, I suppose it is the logical result of our twenty-first century world. A new manner of mortal existence where technological baubles, supposedly created to make life easier, end up mastering us instead. Mankind responds like half-crazed hamsters running frantically on a spinning wheel, trapped in their self-imposed metal cages.

Meanwhile, these human hamsters blast past locations like Croton Spring at flank speed, never aware that such places exist only a few hundred yards away. Like so many other things in their lives, they never attain what they seek as they have no earthly idea of what they are even looking for.

> *"Life is a matter of degrees. Some have life, but it flickers like a dying candle, and is indistinct as the fire in the smoking flax; others are full of life, and are bright and vehement."*
>
> *--Charles Spurgeon*

In the Paint Gap Hills:

When the rains come to the lower Big Bend, a change comes across this mostly parched land that is nothing short of exhilarating, if not near miraculous. If one has ever witnessed the response of a resurrection plant to the merest hint of moisture, one can equate that single event to what happens to this desert as a whole. In effect, it is as if the very soul of these mountains, canyons, arroyos, mesas, creeks and miles and miles of open flats, come to life again.

No more so is this apparent as when the rains come to announce the presence of Spring. Those unfamiliar with this region, locked away in the dreary existence of city life, tend to look upon the season as denoted by a certain date on a calendar pinned to an office cubicle wall. But here there is no specific date, no office cubicle and thank God, no city. Spring comes when it comes and its arrival is as apparent as it is anticipated.

When one shoulders their own brand of solitude during that time and walks into this desert, he or she is in for a sensation of the senses that defies second-hand description or explanation. For it not only delights the eyes with scenes of stark beauty that no camera lens can ever capture, but acts as a natural stimulant without peer for the other four physical senses; as well as that special one that rests within our innermost spirit.

The eyes see the glory of every color, shade, shape and shadow. They dance with joy watching the clouds grow and gather, then turn dark and angry with lashes of lightning streaking down in electrical furies.

The ears hear the sounds of surrounding life of every sort. The bees buzzing about their business, the cooing of the dove nesting, the boom of far off thunder, and the building breeze that delivers the dark clouds bringing forth life-giving rain.

The nose smells the promise of moisture that accompanies that breeze, the aromas of the wild flowers, the scent of the wet creosote, and the occasional musky odor of wildlife huddling in the brush.

You feel the rich, soft, damp earth under your feet, far different in texture than the hard, dried up lifeless dirt of only days ago. The blizzard of large drops of rain that soak you to the skin, the small sting of pea-sized hail that sends you primally searching for cover, and the following warmth of the sun that dries you out yet once again.

Then the taste of cool, clear water running down a rock bed rivulet from the high ground above, satiating your thirst as it does for every other creature who abodes in this place.

And finally, most gloriously, the reawakening of the inner spirit to all things that are truly important in this world and all that accompanies it. That precious time that we can look upon God's Handiwork and give heartfelt praise for just being so blessed, as to stand amidst such indescribable magnificence.

Yes, Spring has indeed finally come.

274

"Imagination... its limits are only those of the mind itself."

--Rod Serling

When one sets out on foot across the many lesser-known reaches of the lower Big Bend, you never really know what you might find. What first appears as a dry, eroded, sparsely adorned flat that would do well to safeguard a single lizard can hold the most fantastic of natural, as well as somewhat unnatural, treasures.

This is the way of our world and the unsuspecting tripwire for even the wisest of human beings: We think and guide upon too much from what we take in at first glance, and never return to ponder more upon what, or who, was in that cursory look.

Though the subject be a painting, a cactus blossom, a bird, a bee or another human being we give their presence short rift; far too busy and preoccupied with other things that we believe to be of greater importance, such as those ethereal goals we set out for.

The old adage of stopping to smell the roses has been neglected to the point of not even being aware of those roses, much less stopping long enough to savor their scent. Potential grace, beauty and wonders galore are there for us wherever we look, but we find nothing because we do not see.

In growing older, I have learned to slow my progress enough to pay more attention as to what might remain hidden at first glance. When younger, I measured 'progress' in miles and if I did not cover at least twenty a day across broken country, that day did not seem complete. Now I usually travel somewhat less in distance, but seem to see so much more while being happily distracted along each journey.

And so it was in finding this place along the lowest parts of the foothills for Croton Peak. Just a few acres of seemingly bland and uninspiring sandstone, but acting on a whim I detoured from my more or less straight line to examine this timeworn landscape a bit more closely. The only word appropriate to describe what was found is 'exquisite.'

This photograph was only one of dozens taken of that locale. Likely a hundred more were waiting for their turn, but the sun was already low on Burro Mesa and I was still a long way from home. Native sandstone mixed with wind, sun and forces from eons of flash floods shaped forms, images and sculptures that boggled the mind and challenged the most agile imagination.

I christened this spot 'Fred Flintstone's Place.' If you sit and study for a moment it actually appears as a smaller, halved section of the penned character's residence from the classic cartoon. It even has the window through solid rock and Fred's bowling ball rests inside, though needing more finishing work to roll down some prehistoric lane.

And all around, wherever you wandered, where other marvelously curious sights formed in much the same way. Beyond here a mere hundred yards away or so were shelters, used by man since time immemorial and blackened by the smoke of ten thousand camp fires.

So if you decide to take a walkabout into this singular land learn to slow down and follow your heart, your spirit and your imagination. The scenes and discoveries waiting for you will make memories for a lifetime, no matter where the path leads from there.

And say hello to Fred, if you happen to see him around.

Yabba Dabba Do, Ya'll.

"We see by life and character, by all that we have made ourselves, by every secret sin that we have cherished, by every battle we have fought and won."
--George H. Morrison

When one sojourns into the lesser accessible reaches of this extraordinary land, you quickly discover there is not a single point on any compass that will not take you to where man once made a life. Whether he was Jumano, Apache, Spaniard, Mexican, Texan or Yankee *norteamericano*, or even from across the seas, the physical remains of his struggle are still here.

Many times, these aging artifacts from different eras can be found in close proximity, usually because of the availability of water, shelter and natural lines of travel. A small microcosm of this continuing refrain is found in this near-solid rock gorge, photographed from the south.

The peculiar cut sits between Slickrock Mountain and Croton Peak, rugged landmarks forming formidable barriers that extend for miles in either direction. It carries the watershed for a good portion of Onion Flat, which in turn becomes Oak Creek, then Rough Run before emptying into the Terlingua near Study Butte.

Large tinajas at the mouth of the canyon abound. Others are hidden in its western walls, fed by cascading torrents of water when the all-too-seldom rainstorm bursts overhead. There are also tiny seeps on both sides. Though the crevice is not very long or impressive in size, it nevertheless has sheltered different clans of man since humankind ventured into this area.

On the bottom end, close by the large tinajas are many metates, used by pre-Columbian Indians to grind their food stuffs. Also present in peaceful co-existence are rotting fence posts and rusting barbed wire from another age entirely.

Well-worn paths are still visible leading in and out. Created first by foot, then hoof, and now utilized by the descendants of wild game hunted by the prior human inhabitants. The biggest predator who currently prowls this ground is the ever-adaptable mountain lion, who has created a wallow on the eastern shoulder to watch what travels below.

Up canyon is a hand dug well some fifteen or so feet deep, covered by decaying wood slats and marked by the remnants of a metal windmill and water tank. Since the canyon is impassable for wheeled conveyances, a near gone wagon road circles to the east about a mile away, threading cautiously along the massive shoulders of Croton Peak. Thus, the influence of yet another time in this very same place.

All still here, all slowly dissolving back into the elements as the desert reclaims her own.

In the end, the scene reminds one that humankind has far more in common with each other than anything that ever sets us apart.

We should take note.

*"Time is the school in which we learn,
Time is the fire in which we burn."*

--Delmore Schwartz

North of Croton Peak and to the northwest of the Paint Gap Hills lies what appears to be a near featureless depression when viewed from afar. It is called Onion Flat, another of those places within the confines of the park that few ever see and even fewer go.

But first impressions can be deceiving and Onion Flat is a prime example of that time-honored truism. The topography, for lack of a better word, is somewhat strange and borders in spots in being otherworldly. If I was asked about a good location for an old Star Trek episode, Onion Flat would immediately come to mind.

Once one journeys into its environs, one learns quickly enough that it is anything but featureless. In fact, it is treacherous enough to have me stop, back up and try a different route from Point A to Point B on more than one occasion. As the quote above implies, you exchange time for knowledge.

In this you come upon some jumbled up terrain just west of Onion Spring, which many years ago was part of Stillwell's Ranch. Forks and branches ultimately leading into Tornillo Creek wander back and forth like some sort of earthy maze, deeply gouged into the soil and with vertical walls that attempt to box you within.

Along the banks can be thick stands of stunted mesquite and catclaw, also acting as barriers. In the end you have one of two choices: swing wide to the south beyond these acres of erosion or find passable entries and exits to negotiate your way through. Being of the sporting type and a bit curious, I chose the second method by bulling my way across until finding a creek bottom that headed where I wanted to go.

281

I had a reason for that and it led me to the biggest obstacle in Onion Flat, the remains of a fissure vent running for miles across the width of the area. On a roughly east to west axis and near straight as an arrow, it cuts almost continuously from the eroded fingers and bottoms all the way to the eastern uplift for Rough Run Canyon.

These fissure vents are found throughout the lower Big Bend, and especially so along the outer slopes of the Chisos and surrounding locales. At a distance they can appear as walls, and in fact were actually used as such by the early pioneers and ranchers to this country.

The old joke for many years has been that post hole digging equipment for the lower Big Bend should include a stick or two of high explosives, as the ground is often that unyielding. That is why you see so few fence lines in the park, the materials were expensive and in some places near impossible to string properly.

So, land owners both big and small utilized natural barriers like these exposed fissures to approximate their property lines. On occasion they were even known to swap sections of land to better suit this natural fencing emplaced eons ago. The Big Bend was one of the last regions in Texas to have open range, and this was one of the main reasons why.

In the photograph you can see the fissure angling toward the Christmas Mountains on the horizon. One other point of possible interest: the high ground for the entire flat sits just to the left, outside the frame. Everything basically beyond that point drains into Slickrock Canyon and on to Rough Run, while most of the drainage within the frame goes northward into the upper parts of the Tornillo.

The Tornillo drainage runs across the middle of the photograph, through a gap in the fissure that you can discern by the green foliage. Several trails and wagon roads used to converge at the gap as it was the only easy way to travel through the flat. Game sign is still prolific today utilizing the same basic route.

And time burns on.

*"As I was walking that ribbon of highway,
I saw above me that endless skyway;
I saw below me that golden valley,
This land was made for you and me."*
*--Woody Guthrie,
'This Land is Your Land'*

I doubt there is hardly anyone of a certain age who has not heard those lyrics before. Woodrow Wilson 'Woody' Guthrie was a prolific songwriter and *This Land is Your Land* was his best-known work.

When most folks think of Guthrie, they think of Oklahoma or Los Angeles or New York City. The more astute might remember the Texas Panhandle, specifically Pampa, where Woody lived as a teenager for a short while. Hardly anyone would associate him with the lower Big Bend, but this is the reason for this commentary.

As the story goes, around 1902 his grandfather had a small place near the Chisos Mountains. Quite by accident, a vein of silver and gold ore was discovered some distance from his grandfather's adobe home. The samples assayed proved to be fairly valuable but for one reason or another the find was never filed. Shortly thereafter the family moved on and the location was lost, save for a somewhat dubious map that became a Guthrie family heirloom.

Fast forward to 1931. It is the time of the Great Depression and the entire family and clan of Guthrie is about two blinks shy of being flat broke. Spurred on by restlessness as well as the slightest hint of greed, Woody and three other family members set out to find this fabled vein that has only become richer with each retelling.

For those who are interested in the details of their odyssey, the epic is found in a novel published some ten years after Guthrie's death in 1967. Entitled *Seeds Of Man,* the book was condensed from an eight hundred page manuscript that Woody wrote in the late 1940s. I have a copy in my private library and trust me, it is far from being among his better efforts.

More so, it was obvious that Guthrie was having difficulty in giving accurate directions to landmarks along the way. He frequently mixed up his norths and souths along with his easts and wests, and was vague in other important matters. Some of this confusion might be attributed to a fifteen-year lapse in memory, but it was so flagrant in some passages one begins to suspect that it was deliberately so.

Now to the photograph. It turns out that Guthrie's grandfather had his adobe home in the large flat shown, south of what some call Slick Rock Canyon and others Slick Rock Gap. You can see Croton Peak to the right and Cottonwood Creek runs the other side of those low red rock outcroppings. This is the same creek, by the way, that flows past the Sam Nail Headquarters.

I have prowled this general area many times and knew of a good deal of the area history attached to it, but had never heard of the Guthrie link until then. As far as the location of the diggings, one might be interested in the byline for Woody's book: 'An Experience Lived and Dreamed.' From what I can discern, there was a lot of dreaming going on when it came to that so-called mine.

However, I did come across a passage where Guthrie actually gave usable directions to his grandfather's homestead. I had to pause and reread it carefully for confirmation because I had been there before. Most everything was gone but it was obvious that someone had lived there.

The homestead was precisely where it was supposed to be.

Now I seriously doubt the silver or gold, but my curiosity does wants to go take another look around someday.

Because whether Guthrie was ever actually there or only knew of this place second hand, the folk poet and songwriter could be very exact when he wanted to, and very inexact when he didn't.

CHAPTER ELEVEN

HOT SPRINGS AREA

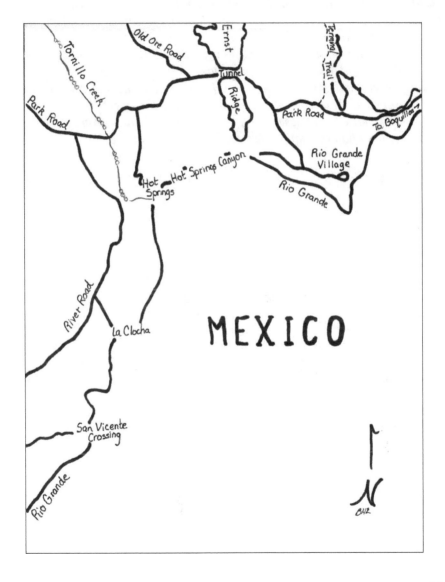

The Hot Springs-San Vicente-Boquillas area is a special place for me, even in the lower Big Bend. There is so much human history in the vicinity, some of which my own family played a small part in. Unfortunately, most of that history is being forgotten; day by day, decade by decade, century by century.

That is a shame because so many of our present societal ills could be healed with the factual knowledge of our shared history. I suppose that as a child I was blessed yet again in this as without television, radio or other distractions, my attention turned to books and the conversations of the adults around me.

More so my parents and grandparents made certain of the subjects I was learning about, including the history of my family as well as the times they lived in. My dad was fond of saying that a man has to know where he came from before he really understands where he is going. He also made me understand that one should never judge someone other than in the times they were living.

When I stand on this desert soil, I know where I came from. It makes me more ready for whatever future the world sees fit to send me.

> "Clay lies still, but blood's a rover,
> Breath's aware that will not keep;
> Up, lad: when the journey's over,
> There'll be time enough to sleep."
> --Alfred Edward Housman

There are more cemeteries, graveyards, *panteóns*, burial sites and long forgotten places of final rest in the Big Bend than what the uninitiated would ever think possible.

Furthermore, the history of such goes back far more in time than even most people who now live here would imagine. In that vein, the area around present-day Presidio comes to mind almost immediately. But so many of these sites are fast giving way to time, erosion, lack of maintenance and unfortunately, vandalism.

Some time ago I began making a conscious effort in documenting some of these spots, as many manuscripts and essays on the subject do not list all that I am aware of.

No two or alike. Each has its own flavor and sense of finality, at least on the mortal plane. So many are anonymous, their life stories lost to perpetuality due to one reason or another. Record keeping was never a strong point in this part of the world and grave registration ranked near the bottom of that particular list.

One of the more interesting and fairly accessible sites is the upper San Vicente cemetery, shown in this photograph. In actuality there is more than one graveyard in this area that bears the San Vicente moniker, as well as others scattered about nearby if you know where to look.

But not too many of these have a pair of concrete tombs to commemorate the dead. Nor do many have an iron fence around other graves to protect them from interlopers, be they man or beast. Also unusual are the steel crosses formed from discarded farming implements.

'Elaborate' is the word that comes to mind considering the era, the populace and the environment.

Yet to the westerly side are simple graves with no markers at all, evidently deliberately separated from the rest. One wonders the reason why. Was it because of an infectious disease such as the Spanish flu and was this some sort of attempt to isolate them, even in death? We will likely never know, but there are other such instances in other cemeteries scattered throughout this harsh land.

Life was hard and dying came easy in the early years of the lower Big Bend, for those who challenged this unforgiving region of extremes. Even the fittest sooner or later would succumb to their own finite mortality.

Yet weak or strong, young or old, by and large not even their names now remain.

291

"Genius does what it must, and talent does what it can."
--Owen Meredith

I have written before of the six-mile overhead tramway that carried tons upon tons of raw ore from the Puerto Rico Mine near Boquillas, Coahuila. In an earlier chapter of this book, I showed photographs of ruins on the tramway's north end where a three-story terminal once stood.

In this frame you are looking north from the first bit of high ground on the Texas side, with the river behind you. You can see the century-old remains of one of the wood support towers as well as the original steel cable laying on the ground.

The support towers and cable run near straight away for another three and a half more miles, with some tough real estate in between. If you look closely center frame, you can see the right of way for both climbing the distant ridge, up and over the horizon.

To the right side in the photo is the canyon where Strawhouse Trail runs alongside the eastern rim, angling toward the Dead Horse Mountains. This range is also known as the *Sierra del Caballo Muerto*.

The Marufo Vega Trail is actually a network of trails, some of which intersect the Strawhouse on top of that ridge. Truth be known, these paths were used for the smuggling of goods and stolen livestock more than anything else.

The lower ground pictured is part of Ernst Valley, named after Max Ernst following his unsolved murder. It comes to a pinch at the canyon mouth, but once the canyon opens up again the valley continues on north for approximately two miles further.

The Strawhouse originated from where Rio Grande Village now sits. It goes all the way up to Telephone Canyon (then known as 'Heath Canyon'), and was utilized by the Army in running land lines for communications during the Villa years.

To accomplish this, an exploratory patrol was sent out via the Strawhouse to determine the best field phone route to Stillwell Crossing. It was decided to make this little jaunt in the middle of summer, and both officers and men had some very colorful names for this country before they were finished.

Now the telephone lines are gone, the tramway rotting away, and those men long dead. Time marches on as memories first fade, gather dust and are later forgotten. Yet the desert remembers, taking careful note of both genius or talent while playing a crucial role in how each succeeds or fails.

El Despoblado, as the Spanish referred to it has always been that way: unimpressed, uncaring and definitely unforgiving.

Yet still watchful.

"Meditation is recalling what we have committed to memory and then turning it over and over in our minds to see the fullest implications and applications of the truth."
--James Montgomery Boice

When you hear the name 'San Vicente' in the Big Bend, you can be talking about several different locations. There is the old San Vicente Crossing on the Rio Grande, which was a favored spot for Comanche raiders plying their bloody trade into and out of Mexico.

In an effort to stop the steady stream of murder and devastation, the Spanish created a series of presidios in the early 1770s. Among them was *Presidio de San Vicente*, *Presidio de San Carlo*s (Lajitas Crossing), and *Presidio de la Junta* (Ojinaga/Presidio).

The garrison near San Vicente Crossing was more successful than others, and the Comanche shifted their favored easternmost spot to Paso del Chisos, below Punta de la Sierra. A small village grew up near the presidio and was christened San Vicente, Coahuila.

Later on two 'San Vicentes' were established on the Texas side, one at the crossing itself and the other located in some low hills to the north. The highest point in those hills is also called San Vicente at times.

My great-great aunt, Mag Smith of Hot Springs fame and blood kin English, came to live in the San Vicente area after being forced out of Hot Springs by the National Park Service. She was there for a couple of years before being forced out again by that same entity.

Aunt Mag then weighed anchor and moved to Boquillas, Mexico for around five years. To say that she stayed at odds with the NPS hierarchy would be putting it mildly.

After she left, the NPS went in with their ill-conceived and executed 'back to nature' program and basically bulldozed the community out of existence. Those homes done in by a dozer blade did not die alone. So did a way of life.

Yet some of these ruins remain in spots where the federal government could not get to them due to terrain, or were unaware of their presence. This photograph illustrates one such place, not too far away from the upper San Vicente cemetery. The bulldozed ruins of others, as lifeless as those bodies in that graveyard, lie scattered about the surrounding flats and hills.

Many a poet over time has expounded upon the question of what is a house without people.

I wonder how they would consider these near-erased ones that no one remembers anymore?

"Cast out into the open field, left in a wilderness where it is not likely that any should pass by, thrown where the cold can smite by night and the heat can blast by day, left where the wild beast goeth about, seeking whom he may devour-such is the estate of human nature: unclothed, unarmed, helpless, exposed to all manner of ravenous destroyers."
--Charles Spurgeon

Like the prop from an old Clint Eastwood spaghetti western, the upper San Vicente cemetery rises out of a nigh lifeless part of the Chihuahuan Desert. As the evening breeze plays with the dust and the greasewood sways in time, one can almost hear an Ennio Morricone tune whistling in one's mind.

But this is no prop and real people have lain here for over a century, mostly casualties of challenging this country on its home court. They had little of the technological advantages we enjoy today and few if any died on the wrong end of a six gun. Their deaths were brought on mostly by illness or accident, while a few had the enviable blessing of passing on due to advanced age.

Even now this land can occasionally reach out and squeeze the very life out of a human being, but back then it was a commonplace event. Death played no favorites. Young and old, man and woman, infant and infirmed, they all came to rest here at a place most have never heard of, much less actually seen. Some were evidently buried with a good deal of pomp and circumstance, but time and the elements have removed all traces of who they were or when they died.

It is a sad and lonely place, a graveyard of forgotten souls neither visited nor likely recalled, dissolving slowly back into the earth from whence they came.

A reminder, if you will, that most every life once had a story sooner or later forgotten.

As likely our own someday.

> *"Mine is a rugged land but good for raising sons---and I myself, I know no sweeter sight on earth than a man's own native country."*
> *--Homer's Odyssey*

This was taken looking downriver from the Langford ruins above Hot Springs. Most people that come here never realize the almost dissolved road drifting by was one the first ways to get here. It continues on past the Langford residence and wanders to and fro through the barren hills, making a wide swing before crossing the Tornillo below La Noria and on to the Hannold Store.

Truth be known there are many such nearby roads, several of which were never noted on any map I know of. Bits and pieces of these tracks can still be found and followed for miles, making for a bewildering web of transportation routes going back to the era of mules and wagons.

When it comes to the Hot Springs area, I have a bit more knowledge than most about these roads and the surrounding terrain. You see, this was one of the several spots in the lower Big Bend where my family established a toehold early on. Many years ago my great-great Aunt Mag Smith managed Hot Springs. That is, before the National Park Service dynamited the bath houses and forced her out.

From then until her death in 1965 she operated other nearby stores and trading posts, including across the river in Boquillas. All the while her feud over what happened at Hot Springs and later San Vicente, as well as two sections of land that once belonged to her, continued on with the federal government.

I suppose the low point came when the NPS claimed she was running guns into Mexico. That accusation shocked our extended family and brought English tempers to a fevered edge. My grandfather and every one of his brothers save for one had been peace officers, a tradition in our family that went back to the Republic of Texas and before.

A few years later our part of the family came back to the Big Bend from the JA Ranch, and Aunt Mag taught my grandfather the candelilla wax business. After all, she was his favorite aunt and he her favorite nephew who had spent many a day with her at Hot Springs. He ended up leasing the Lajitas Trading Post from Rex Ivey on her say so. That's how I grew up with such a close kinship with what was once Lajitas.

Aunt Mag died in 1965, still considered 'persona non grata' by the hierarchy of the National Park Service. They would not even make mention of her name until the mid-1980s.

Her death hit my grandfather hard, doubly so due to the circumstances and our still simmering feud with the federal government. He passed on in 1977, and at eighteen years old I finally understood something of his pain in losing Aunt Mag.

That particular pain is never stronger for me than when I am at Hot Springs.

And to his dying day, my grandfather never forgave the National Park Service for what they did to her.

> *"What is a cynic? A man who knows the price of everything, and the value of nothing."*
>
> **--Oscar Wilde**

You are standing on a low hill just above the northern side of the Rio Grande, looking off in the distance toward Mexico and the Sierra del Carmen. Some three miles away and a hundred years ago, the southern terminal for a six-and-a-half-mile overhead tramway sat at the foot of those mountains, near the Puerto Rico mine outside of Boquillas, Coahuila.

In the frame you can still see the metal cable that ran the entirety of this course lying on the ground. It came to rest there after the tramway was abandoned and has not been moved since.

Just rotting remains of the large wooden towers that supported the cable are present, most have now all collapsed upon themselves due to weathering and age, or an occasional act of vandalism. The rise where this photo was taken had two of those towers situated on it. They were spaced out unevenly throughout the tramway's course, depending on the terrain. Some years back I came across one still standing, I wonder if it does so now.

One only needs the barest knowledge of this country, the engineering and geographical challenges involved, and the era in which this project took place to appreciate the mechanical wizardry and physical effort expended here.

With large buckets suspended from the cable, tons of raw ore were transported by the hour across to the Texas side. Continuing along the tramway, it was deposited at the northern terminal for further transportation to the railway in Marathon.

This was a feat in itself that was first accomplished by freight wagons and Mexican mules. Gradually, they in turn were replaced by trucks from companies such as Packard, Mack and White.

But like most of man's incursions into this desert, sooner or later the land wins out and all those plans and projects are left to wither away. After the end of World War One, the price for ore fell and the tramway stopped running. Rather than have it removed for another purpose, the tramway was simply abandoned in place.

And from that point forward the desert proceeded ever so slowly to reclaim its own. You see, if there is one thing it and its natural inhabitants possess, it is patience.

Out here, patience is one of the essential requirements for survival.

"Every man is put on earth condemned to die. Time and method of execution unknown."

--Rod Serling

In past commentaries I have mentioned the historic crossing along the easternmost branch of the Comanche War Trail, arrowing over the Rio Grande into Mexico from what would become the state of Texas. This crossing was known as 'San Vicente'.

But long before that time and long before it had the name, or even saw the first Spaniard, Comanche or Apache, this crossing was used for thousands of years much like the one at Lajitas and what is now Presidio.

In effect, there were ultimately three locations known as San Vicente. The original was San Vicente, Coahuila, where the original presidio once stood. Planned for by Irish expatriate and later Spanish military governor, Hugh O'Connor, the fortification was built before the American Revolution. It was by far the most successful and ultimately forced the Comanche to use the Paso del Chisos some miles upriver.

As another century or so went by, a sister village on the American side sprung up called San Vicente, Texas. Later another community, further away from the always unpredictable river, came into being. Likewise referred to as San Vicente, it was a mile and a half or so north of the crossing.

So in the end you had San Vicente, Coahuila, San Vicente Crossing and upper San Vicente, and each of these locales had their own cemetery. Each also had its own character, design and history.

In this particular photo, you see the San Vicente graveyard for the Texas side closest to the crossing. Neglected and nearly forgotten, an estimated thirty-eight souls rest in anticipation of the sounding trumpet.

Of that total, only one broken headstone remains as any sort of record as to who was buried here. The inscription is partially unreadable, but in Spanish you can read a date of birth of 1819 and a date of death in 1880.

Think about that for a moment. If this person was born in the immediate area, consider all they experienced in regional history. Ponder upon the number of changes they might have seen and the knowledge they may have acquired.

If a grave could only give voice to that single lifetime.

"In the empire of the desert, water is king and shadow is the queen."
--Mehmet Murat

This is the upper end of Boquillas Canyon, where the Rio Grande cuts through the middle of the Sierra del Carmen and Dead Horse Mountains. It is one of the three major canyons along the river situated on this southern boundary of Big Bend National Park, the other two are the Santa Elena and the Mariscal.

Each have their own adherents and rabid supporters for one reason or another, mostly among the rafting community. There are some who claim that Boquillas is both the deepest as well as the longest, but I suspect some of that may have to do with who is holding the measuring tape.

It is said by others to be where the Chandler surveying expedition came to an unexpected end in the year of 1852. Their mission was to chart the river from El Paso to the mouth of the Pecos, but the Boquillas got the better of them. Their boats were wrecked and many of their supplies lost, and eventually they had to walk across northern Mexico to reach Fort Duncan, near present day Eagle Pass.

Makes one wonder how many of these modern day rafters would be up for a walk in the sun to Eagle Pass, after losing their boat and most of their supplies.

Above the canyon mouth a couple of miles upriver is the village of Boquillas, Coahuila, roughly across from what the National Park Service now calls Rio Grande Village. At one time, this same general area was known as Boquillas, Texas. Around the dawn of the twentieth century, the name of Boquillas was also used for the settlement now noted as La Noria.

Many names are transitory in this country. To my knowledge there have been three Boquillas, three Terlinguas, a couple of San Vicentes and Lajitas crossing went by many other names in Spanish, Mexican, English as well as different Indian tongues.

People come and go, and each time a new group comes they seem to think they are the first ones to see a particular spot in the lower Big Bend, and they rename some of the landmarks yet again.

This peculiar regional tradition continues on to this very day. Folks move in, hang around a few years, and one morning wake up thinking they are now some sort of expert on this country.

Take it from me, all the experts are either dead or smart enough to not ever allow themselves to be considered as such.

CHAPTER TWELVE

PERSIMMON GAP AREA

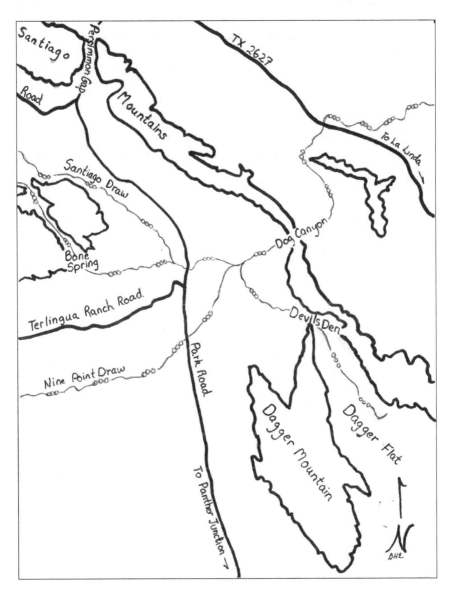

The Persimmon Gap area and the country around contain many places of both historical as well as geological importance, yet they are the very same places that so many speed right through.

More so, most of this area north and west of the Rosillos Mountains contain over 80,000 acres that make up the most recent additions to the park. This mostly consists of the old Buttrill complex, its fading vestiges reflecting a pioneer ranch life that can still be found along any heading you so choose.

Combined with this are little known landmarks and spots that will awe anyone who takes the trouble to seek them out. The hills surrounding Bone Spring alone hide a hundred different places that make the passerby stop and ponder upon.

There is hardly a single section in the lower Big Bend that does not touch the five senses, as well as that special sixth one residing in the sojourner's soul. But the Persimmon Gap area is unique unto itself.

At first glance it promises so little in comparison to where the casual tourist may be going.

But in reality, it possesses so much.

"For a moment of night, we have a glimpse of ourselves and of our world islanded in its steam of stars---pilgrims in mortality, voyaging between horizons across the eternal seas of space and time."
--Henry Beston

The summer sun was setting as I made my way up Dagger Flat, to the spot where it contorts and pinches into suitable form to enter the upper end of Devil's Den. It had been a long, hot day and I savored the coming coolness much like an old man does the cherished memories of a first love.

As the eroded trail from a century ago and more began to ascend, I looked over my shoulder to the mouth of the rocky crevice. Having been over, through and along its shoulders at different times of my life, my appreciation for this natural anomaly was more involved than most. It had also led me to a startling discovery, the presence of a good-sized cave below the crest for the southern rim.

For some reason that has continued to elude me, there is a sizable amount of information about Devil's Den that is either bad or incomplete. Furthermore, some of it could prove even dangerous if anyone took that information without question or verification. Just because a person finds something in print or on the internet does not necessarily mean it is true.

Even the National Park Service seems to have less than a full grasp concerning this unusual area. They take the seeker on a longer, somewhat more difficult route from Dog Canyon trailhead; through brush-choked creek banks, and up the southern shoulder to view the crevice. Because of this and other factors, the casual hiker often comes away with less than a favorable opinion in what it took to make the hike.

311

Truth is there are shorter, easier, more scenic ways to the top of Devil's Den. The biggest problem is how the NPS trail negotiates the cut and on which side. In effect one misses so much that serves as a sensation for the eyes, a salve for the spirit and a ready-made jump start for the imagination.

I mentioned before of being on a trail over a hundred years old, and likely far older than that. This nearly vanished path once ran from at least Dagger Tank to Bone Spring. If you know this country and the folds of the terrain that wiggle away in every direction, you can keep to the track on general terms easily enough.

In doing so you learn to treasure Devil's Den, for this venerable trail goes over the north rim of the chasm rather than the south. As you journey along and up to the crest, the true magic of this improbable place begins to make itself known.

On either side are tinajas and shelters used by man and animal alike, long before any record was kept of their existence. There are also rotting posts and rusting barbed wire fences, including a gap that once stood at the top for the herding of livestock. Once over the crest the section of trail dropping into Dagger Flat is still in passable shape, kept so by generations of wildlife who know the best routes up and over these craggy, roughhewn hills.

And, of course, there is the cave. For those who have stood above and wondered about the hollow sound under your feet, now you know the reason why. Note the smaller 'window' to the left of the cave's entrance. I would be slightly less than surprised if that entire section was a series of cavities underneath the rim.

I stood there on that old trail, staring at the cave and wondering what secrets were concealed there. I also wondered how many other men had stood in this very same spot, wondering the same thing.

Each of us pilgrims in our own mortality, journeying but briefly between those same eternal seas of space and time.

312

> *"It is only with the heart that one can see rightly; what is essential is invisible to the eye."*
> *--Antoine de Saint-Exupéry*

You are standing above the gorge that forms Devil's Den, with miles upon miles of rough, desolate country running off in every direction. It was the middle of a winter that followed hard upon an unusually dry and hot summer, explaining in part the natural starkness of this season appearing even more so.

This perspective might not look like much to the unknowing eye, but what you are seeing is a fairly important stretch of the lower Big Bend. This area forms a natural chokepoint for anything or anybody moving from the Chisos Mountains and surrounding regions to anywhere north. You can see the line of rugged uplifts, stretching away in near solid formation to form a formidable barrier all the way to Santiago Peak, and beyond to Paso del Norte.

Devil's Den, Dog Canyon and Persimmon Gap afford the three main ways to get through this chokepoint from the south. Anything coming from Dagger Flat and most points east passed on the ancient trail that runs along the opposite shoulder of this chasm. To get past the string of rugged uplifts to your front, historically Persimmon Gap and Dog Canyon were the accepted routes through.

Persimmon Gap, seen as that distinct notch in the upper center right, was how the Great Comanche War Trail entered this region. To this day the pass is still used, as it is where you enter the national park from Marathon.

It doesn't take much of a tactician to realize these intricacies in terrain once you are horseback or afoot. It also doesn't take much of one to realize the importance of Bone Spring, which sits near that bisected low string of hills in the upper left edge of the frame.

But with technology and vehicles that can travel hundreds of miles in only a few hours while in air-conditioned comfort, the importance and historical significance of such landmarks are lost to the modern traveler.

Which is why you can't really experience this country until you are out in it, and in turn fully appreciate those who came before.

BE

> *"So, we beat on, boats against the current,*
> *borne back ceaselessly into the past."*
> *--F. Scott Fitzgerald*

Over a hundred and fifty years ago, Dog Canyon was one of the two major routes in and out of the area now known as Big Bend National Park. The other was Persimmon Gap.

The Comanche War Trail passed through the gap, before branching off into different routes leading on to Lajitas, San Vicente, Paso del Chisos and other select crossings along the Rio Grande. Dog Canyon was the favored route for the narrow-gauged Chihuahuan ox carts early on, and is reported to be where Lieutenant Echols entered the lower Big Bend with his Camel Corps command in 1859.

A year later Lieutenant Echols returned with his curious creatures and passed through this general area once more. Echol's diaries provide for some entertaining reading, and deftly describe how fearsome an opponent this country was to those trying to penetrate into its arid bowels.

Later, after a road was established through Persimmon Gap, Dog Canyon faded into obscurity. These days it is a quiet monument to the past usually only explored by the occasional *turista*. A few years back you could plainly see where the ox cart track entered the canyon, but recent rains have made it far more difficult to do so. It probably won't be much longer before those tracks become nothing more than a memory.

This photo was taken at the park boundary line, you can see the fence posts and wire marking the shift from public to private land. A word to the wise: unless you have an invitation from the land owner specifically, stay off his or her property. Trespassing is strongly frowned upon in West Texas and I occasionally see internet 'experts' posting trail routes through this area that actually cross into private land. Please do not do this.

But for the geologically inclined, there is much to be enjoyed here and is the main reason why this frame was selected. In Dog Canyon there are numerous rock formations, inclines, folds and examples of vertical strata. Studying the photo, you can see large slabs of layered rock angling vertically into the sky. Throughout the chasm such natural phenomena can be viewed and speculated upon.

And if you will listen with your imagination, as the evening sun is going down and the canyon walls are slipping into darkness, you might just hear the ghostly creak of an old Chihuahuan ox cart from long ago.

"Before you can make an impression upon another person's heart, you must have an impression made upon your own soul."
--Charles Spurgeon

You are on the south rim of the small but somewhat deep gorge of Devil's Den, looking across the very northern tip of Dagger Flat and on to the Sierra del Carmen. It was winter time in the park, but one of those mild late afternoons that makes you want to start out in a certain direction and walk forever.

Most people, even those who venture to this spot, do not realize that the top side of Devil's Den is actually the very northern tip for Dagger Flat, which runs on for several miles toward the southeast. A heavy rain will send a torrent of water through this crevice that sweeps around and exits through Dog Canyon.

If you are in the Dagger Flat region and want to make for Bone Spring or Persimmon Gap, this is the logical route whether on horseback or by foot. A trail along the chasm's opposing north rim winds down into the flat below. The narrow slit itself is navigable but just barely, and you have to get on your hands and knees at times to crawl past large boulders blocking the way.

This is another place where many folks often zoom by enroute to Panther Junction, in some mad dash to see the park in one or two days. All I can say is good luck with that, because it's kind of like trying to tour the Smithsonian in a nano-second. There is so much to see in these oft skipped over spots like Devil's Den.

On this one shambling foray were parts of the original road that paralleled the present highway to the east, including a partially collapsed concrete bridge that once spanned Bone Spring Draw. There were also the remains of an old candelilla wax camp, dirt tanks dug long ago, vanishing paths no longer in use and of course the crevice itself.

For those who might be interested, my wandering here was only partly due to my natural curiosity. I am currently researching a future historical novel about the Cristeros War in Mexico that occurred in the mid-1920s.

A band of Mexican refugees, fleeing murderous religious persecution, will come through this very spot, headed for Marathon.

And I believe the best way to tell a story is with my boots on the ground.

All one hundred and fifty plus miles of it.

> *"We obviously stand at the brink of a great mystery and our understanding of it can only be minimal."*
>
> **--Colin G. Kruse**

I actually took this shot of Persimmon Gap while enroute to Dagger Flat on a late summer morn, on a day that would include both hundred degree plus heat as well as an occasional downpour of rain. You can already see the humidity building in the desert sky.

Persimmon Gap is the gateway where so many enter what is now Big Bend National Park, and it has served that same purpose from ancient times. Since man first set foot in this region there has only been four basic ways through the rough, imposing physical barrier formed by the Santiago Mountains: Dog Canyon, Javelina Gap, Persimmon Gap and a nameless pass situated along the eastern base of Santiago Peak.

Out of these four it was Persimmon Gap that rose highest in prominence, starting with the use of this natural cut by the Comanche moving to and from Mexico. Though many variations of the trail have been talked about and more than a few arguments started, most everyone will agree the route through Persimmon Gap was one of two major arteries for these raiders and their attending large amounts of booty.

Perhaps that is the best way to describe how the Comanche Trail worked, by imagining the cardiovascular system of the human being. The arteries branched into vessels and then into capillaries, which in turn explain the various river crossings near Lajitas, Ejido de Santa Elena, Paso del Chisos, San Vicente and Boquillas.

There were other, smaller ones also in use. The fact is the Comanche people were at the very pinnacle of their power, overshadowing that of any other tribe or sovereign nation residing or laying claim to this vast expanse.

321

Simply put, they went where they pleased and crossed where it suited their purpose.

As far as the comparison of the human cardiovascular system, one other obvious similarity was present: Human blood flowed in copious amounts wherever those vessels led.

It was their time and their place; it was the land of the Comanche Moon.

It will not come again.

"Now, what is man but soul and soil, breath and body, a puff of wind the one, a pile of dust the other, no solidity in either?"
--John Trapp

Bone Spring is one of those spots in the lower Big Bend that many have heard of, few have gone to and even fewer know much about. That is a shame as there is many a story within the immediate reach of this spring, stretching back through different eras, ethnicities and reasons for being here.

In times before the spring was known as a reliable source of water, though reportedly with visible signs of alkaline content. That did not seem to matter to the pre-Columbian Indian who first came to this region, as metates can be found in the vicinity that a man can stick much of an arm into.

Furthermore, many old trails as well as some of the first primitive roads passed through here, routes built upon or traveling along those same footpaths formed in prehistoric times. They angled in from Dog Canyon, Devil's Den and other points on the compass including through Bone Spring Canyon, running due north in the direction of Persimmon Gap.

In between the coming of the Comanche and the first pioneer ranchers, the spring was called the 'Guaronza' as well as other variations of this Mexican colloquial term for a Huisache tree. The name was changed to Bone Spring by the first Anglos, who noted the many bones of dead animals who apparently had been trapped in bogs moistened by the seep.

Ownership of the spring changed several times during this period, but one man's presence loomed large over them all. He was Monroe Payne, the son of a Black Seminole Indian.

The Payne name has been intertwined with the history of the lower Big Bend for some time now. Early on they were Army scouts and able fighters, with Monroe's own father earning the Medal of Honor. Later the family became known as cowboys, and were known throughout this country as some of the best cowboys and wranglers to ever sit a horse.

In that vein Monroe was hired as a ranch hand for the Buttrills, settling in at Bone Spring. The rock house in the photograph was where he lived for many years with his wife and seven children. In the background you can see Dog Canyon and Devil's Den, giving one a better idea of the importance of this water source for the different people of different eras who passed through.

Now the spring is almost gone, sucked dry by the invading mesquite that preys upon these spots when left uncared for. The nearby windmill and water tank are equally disused, having not done their assigned duty in decades. The rock house where the Payne family dwelt is nothing but decaying ruins, its sturdy foundation and walls stubbornly holding on against the implacable desert.

Only the metates remain intact, yet another irony of this land where the most ancient human denizens left the best-preserved marks of all.

CHAPTER THIRTEEN

ROSILLAS MOUNTAIN AREA

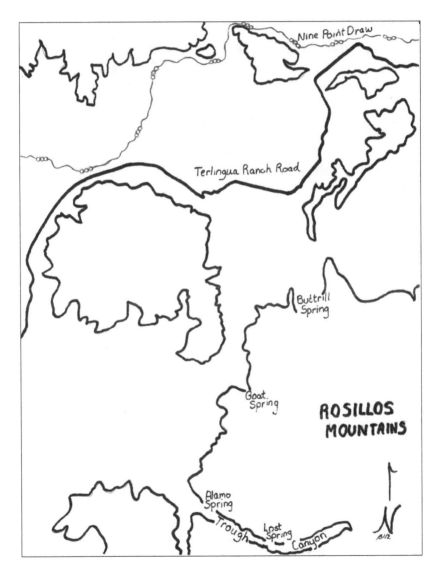

Much like the neighboring sections that make up the Bone Spring area this acreage, once part of the Buttrill Ranch complex, is the latest addition to Big Bend National Park.

Donated by newspaper magnates and well-known philanthropists Houston and Ed Harte, this largely undeveloped part of the park still contains many intact pieces of a working ranch. Unlike the other ranches taken over by the federal government to formulate the park, these sites have been left untouched from the blade of a bulldozer or the wanton destruction of high explosives.

This in itself makes the area a treasure trove, to explore and better understand how the first ranching pioneers lived and went about their daily business. It serves a two-fold purpose in that manner, exposing newcomers to the first slightest taste of that life while resurrecting the misplaced memories of those native to such an environment.

Finally, there is the land itself. The Big Bend is a tangled, three-dimensional natural maze of conflicting landscapes, geological strata and vistas that bend and stretch the imagination of the individual.

Here you can experience in full force that effect and wonder at the intricate causes of it all.

328

"Kingdoms are but the lengthened shadows of kings."
--Charles L. Feinberg

Once upon a time and really not that long ago, the lower Big Bend teemed with a Texas institution you don't see much anymore: the working ranch.

Now I am not talking about a forty acre 'ranchita,' or an exotic game preserve, a nature conservancy, or a glorified tax write-off for the rich and want-to-be famous, and I am not saying that any of those are necessarily a bad thing.

But my memories, my heart, goes back to those places where generations of hardy men and women lived on working ranches both big and small, and who labored near ceaselessly to bring forth a living from horses, mules, burros, cattle, goats, sheep, chickens, and the grains and grasses to feed those animals.

Each had their own vegetable garden, their own pets (be it dog, cat, lizard, crow or perhaps even a javelina) and each had their own individual histories and traditions. There were also the shared regional courtesies such as no spurs inside the house, taking your hat off when indoors, never opening a gate or gap without closing it and no one; no matter what name, nationality, color, creed or political affiliation ever went away hungry.

Among these better-known ranches of yore was the Buttrill Ranch complex north of the Rosillos Mountains. The Buttrills or 'Buttrells,' as you sometimes see in older documents and maps, were a pioneer family who came to this area in the mid-1880s. Their name and their original ranch was also inextricably linked with yet another pioneer family, the Paynes. The Paynes were descendants of Black Seminole Army scouts and some of the best cowboys found in this region.

In the decades that followed the Buttrill was divided up, sold and resold, and later known at times as the 'North Rosillos Mountain Ranch,' the 'Panther Ranch,' and ultimately the 'Harte Ranch,' before being donated in the late

1980s to the National Park Service as the last sizable addition to Big Bend National Park.

However, for me it will always be The Buttrill, for they were here first and worked the hardest in attempting to bend the will of this stubborn, circumspect land.

They were the true believers.

Now their headquarters, their foreman homes, their line shacks, their barns, outbuildings, corrals, loading chutes, dirt tanks and water troughs sit decaying and empty; as that very same stubborn, circumspect land slowly reclaims its own.

Their lonely shadows grow long in the late evening of the desert, sad remnants of a hard-won kingdom now defunct and of a time now since passed.

"Past the first hill on the desert
Is another hill I can't see
And the hill that keeps hiding
Is the hill that keeps calling to me..."
--Marty Robbins, 'The Bend in the River'

It was a hot late afternoon as I stood on a hill above Buttrill Spring, surveying what lay before me for as far as the eye could see. Sweat was forming inside my hat band and trickling down my back, and my breathing was still coming to me hard from that last climb. Since early morning I had been making a large loop along the northern and western slopes of the Rosillos Mountains; working my way back and forth and up and down, following my nose just to see where it might lead me.

From above and behind I had drifted down from Goat Spring, heading back to my truck that was parked still some three miles or so away. My calves ached and my feet protested just at the thought of the idea.

Anyone who has ever been on this side of the Rosillos can attest to the acres upon acres of round red rocks perched haphazardly in every direction. Walking across this area is like trying to balance your way through a turbulent sea of bowling balls, each in turn ready to roll from under your weight with one misplaced step.

Thinking back to the era when this was part of the Buttrill Ranch complex, one wonders how you could work some of this country on horseback. It is difficult in spots for someone with a pack on his back, but a disaster looking for a place to happen when it comes to a horse carrying a man.

Spying over the landmark spring to the Santiago Mountains and beyond, a feeling of awe and being mighty small in the bigger picture of things swept over me. If a human being needs to stay in touch with their humility, all they have to do is spend some time alone in this land. It will humble you in ways like only an irrefutable measure of true insignificance can.

331

While an evening breeze teased me with the slightest hint of a coming coolness, and my eyes took in what was below and around, the lines from an old Marty Robbins ballad came to me. These days fewer and fewer have ever heard of Robbins, but he was a very talented man in many ways, and one of the good guys in a simpler world that has since moved on. He also had a genuine love for the desert and the American Southwest in general.

Mr. Robbins would have surely found some inspiration in this grand scene that unfolded itself to the far horizons, some lyrics to convey something of the stark beauty that was here. Of all his many gifts, that one is his most memorable.

As for me I just smiled and sighed at being able to see it for myself, aching feet and all. It's a big country and I'll never see it to completion but I'm sure going to try.

And I moved on, aiming for that next hill.

"The dawn of knowledge is usually the false dawn"
--Bernard De Voto

I was working my way south along the west side of the Rosillos Mountains, headed for Trough Canyon when this photograph was taken. Behind me was the pass leading up to this higher country and to the front was another pass that eased off into Tornillo Basin and Onion Flat.

The purpose for this particular prowl was to scout out the country for a future historical novel, where a fast-moving cavalry detail utilizes both passes as a short cut to Persimmon Gap. It looked really good on paper, but I knew that I needed to put a pack on my back to make certain.

Thing is, a fellow usually has to put boots on the ground to see if such a route is feasible. You can look through topographical maps both old and new, stare at Google Earth until your eyeballs fall out, and still not have a clue as to what is actually there until you go see for yourself. If the lower Big Bend is anything else, it is both surprising as well as tricky.

As one can plainly tell here, any mounted man taking this route would have to ply his way along rather carefully. Better yet, if the horse was mountain born and bred, let the animal pick the best route as he usually knows more than the rider. Wrong horse, wrong man, or both trying to push too fast would result in a crippled mount and a rider afoot.

This country immediately west of the Rosillos proper has fields upon fields of tens of thousands of such rocks, with all the stability and grip of a bunch of greased cannon balls. The pass in front of me was feasible enough and the one to the rear near Alamo Spring was negotiable, but this stretch in between was a bone breaker and horse killer of the first order.

After sizing up the surrounding terrain, I sat down and started panning the lower elevations with binoculars. Seeing some better ground below, I reshouldered my gear and changed course. It wasn't the first time that I had to

334

do this, and certainly wouldn't be the last. To borrow the phrase with a bit of the pun, "it goes with the territory."

Ultimately my imaginary cavalry column would have to swing wide to the west between the two passes, giving up straight-line distance for safety and speed. Like so much of what is found in this region, the shortest way is often not the surest nor the fastest. To not understand this basic tenement of this land is a sure way to grief, or to break your neck or someone else's.

That, in a real fashion, is the true essence of the lower Big Bend. She is very much a beautiful woman, but about as treacherous and deceitful as any beauty turned bad can be.

Yet I keep coming back, even after so many forays over the decades and after being made to feel a bit foolish on occasion. It seems the more you learn, the less you know. When some well-meaning person refers to me as an 'expert' concerning this country, I literally cringe inside.

The dawn of knowledge is indeed often enough a false dawn.

Reckon that goes with the territory, too.

336

CHAPTER FOURTEEN

CASTOLON AREA

Not too long ago La Harmonia Store burned down at Castolon, taking with it the last living memory of a type of regional business once known as 'the trading post.'

It died the victim of an errant fire and large amounts of combustible undergrowth that had been allowed to encroach too closely. However much like the mythical Phoenix, there are already plans afoot to rebuild the store to what it was.

Arguably the last trading post still standing is the one at Lajitas, but it is now a golf pro shop and has been altered dramatically from the time it was first built. La Harmonia remained somewhat true to its spirit and name, and has stood there much the same as when it was converted from an Army barracks around 1920; the third of three stores in Castolon at different times. Ironically enough, it was nearly lost to fire back in April of 1935.

During its decades of private operation, La Harmonia was the center of community life not only for Castolon but nearby farming communities stretching up and down and on both sides of the river. It was where you came to buy, sell, trade, barter, borrow, get your mail, socialize, seed your oats or just enjoy the cooling shade.

One by one, those communities were abandoned and then reclaimed by the Chihuahuan Desert. The store and the few surviving residences kept by the National Park Service were all that was left of what was a teeming, vital part of the lower Big Bend.

I hope the many good folks involved in trying to rebuild La Harmonia get the job done. It needs to happen.

"Far better it is to dare mighty things, to win glorious triumphs, even though checkered by failure, than to take rank with those poor spirits who neither enjoy nor suffer too much, because they live in the gray twilight that knows not victory nor defeat."
--Theodore Roosevelt

In the lowest parts of the Big Bend of Texas, along the Rio Grande between Castolon and the near forgotten farming settlement of La Coyota, Blue Creek enters the river. Many years past there was a crossing situated here, and to this day both wild as well as domestic animals wander to and fro across a manmade border they have no knowledge nor concern for.

Some distance above this large, usually dry waterway, a nameless fork leaves Blue Creek heading almost due north. It in turn has numerous branches of its own that come into the broad bottom from both east and west, and all points on the compass in between.

You can look on any map, whether modern or from the time of the first pioneers and find absolutely nothing other than topographical lines going hither and yon, divided by the single blue strokes denoting these different creeks. Most would not even consider going this direction, for as the old police adage goes: 'Move along folks, nothing to see here.'

But there are things to be seen. Though not a single notation exists on those maps, there are spots that make one just stand for a moment and ponder. Near vanished roads, crumbling ruins, wells, rock corrals, Indian camps, springs, seeps, tinajas and trails hundreds of years old are hidden here in the desert; almost completely secured in their isolation from the casual interloper.

On this day I scouted from the river all the way up near The Chimneys, prowling where my senses led as I zig-zagged my way along. That is how this photo came about, in my wandering I stumbled across the remains of a windmill, some rock pens and what might be a solitary grave.

Off to the side was the long dormant, rusting hulk of a Continental flat head four that once powered a Star automobile. Since they haven't made Stars in nearly a century, you get the vaguest impression as to how long these timeworn relics have been sitting here.

Many come to this country thinking they have found something undiscovered, where no man has ever trod or labored before. In my own lifetime I have heard such talk countless times as the population of the lower Big Bend ebbed and flowed.

But this is no new 'undiscovered country.' In fact, it is far from it. It is a very old land and no matter where you may venture, you are walking among and upon someone else's life.

One needs to always remember that and to remember them.

"It may be said with a degree of assurance that not everything that meets the eye is as it appears."

--Rod Serling

When you are on higher ground in the lower Big Bend, most likely you can see for a considerable distance in at least one direction. More so, you will be impressed with not only the view but the seemingly vast emptiness that at times appears prepared to swallow you whole.

That much is obvious on the first cursory glance. But what is not so obvious is that seemingly vast emptiness is, in reality, anything but.

Consider this photograph: If you look closely in mid frame, one will see the contrasting reflections of The Chimneys, a line of low-lying rock formations that have provided man a home for thousands of years.

To the immediate left is Kit Mountain, where seeps and tinajas can be found round about. Amid those are a few springs, including the one that supplied the ancient residents of The Chimneys. They had shelter in the rocks, water from the springs and the availability of abundant game drawn to both.

On the horizon lies Anguila Mesa, which in turn is part of the Sierra Ponce. The southern boundaries of the mesa are abruptly defined by Santa Elena Canyon. No telling how long man has situated himself in the varying shadows of that chasm.

There are numerous other such spots scattered throughout this desert and in the unlikeliest of places. Where one would swear the nearest water would have to be the river itself, it beckons to the more attuned only mere yards away.

As time passed man became aware of these hidden locales where he in turn lived, struggled and sometimes died within their confines.

Little of this was documented but it did happen. The enduring marks left by those who came before, be it pictograph or piled rock or charred overhang or a rusty piece of wire is still found out here, giving indisputable testimony to both their labor and lives.

Perhaps that fact is something for the reader to think upon, next time one stares off into that seemingly vast emptiness.

It is not empty. Human endurance for the ages, even triumph, is all around you.

"May I deal with honor,
May I act with integrity,
May I achieve humility"
--Robert K. (Soupy) Campbell, CDR., USN

You are standing at the cemetery for the long-abandoned farming village noted as 'Coyote' on USGS topographical maps, but the real name was La Coyota. What still remains of it sits about two miles upriver from Castolon, just east of the mouth for Alamo Creek.

No one seems to know exactly when La Coyota was first established, or when the last occupant finally moved away or died. Suffice to say that like most of the other nearby agrarian communities it came into being sometime in the 1890s, reached a zenith in the 1910s-1920s and then faded off into nothingness by the late-1930s.

At no time having more than a dozen families or so, there is not much left that hasn't been nearly obliterated by time, weather or a National Park Service bulldozer.

But there is the cemetery, occasionally still looked after by the descendants of those who once toiled on this land. After the verdant farm fields returned to their natural form, this burial site became a landmark used for other purposes.

When I was a small child, it and the mouth of Alamo Creek served as a conduit for candelilla wax loads coming across the river. At that time Ross Maxwell Scenic Drive did not even exist; instead there was only a patchwork of mostly unmaintained, decaying dirt roads going back to the dawn of the Twentieth Century.

I think my grandfather knew every one of them, as well as the attending back trails and creek beds that he navigated in his old GMC. He could do so just as well in the dark with no headlights as he could by a mid-day sun.

It was at night when we made our runs, picking up loads of wax in the wee hours at spots like Terlingua Abaja, the Dryden Place, Sublett Store, or the

345

dozens of ruins strung like a string of adobe and native rock pearls along the northern side of the Rio Grande. And, of course, at the mouth of Alamo Creek below La Coyota Cemetery.

Now let me tell you something: there's few things spookier in this world than sitting in silence below the moonlit shadows of a decaying graveyard, watching other shadows of men and burros crossing that river like so many will-o'-the-wisps. Furthermore, that sort of experience is especially memorable when you aren't much beyond wearing diapers.

With that in mind, there may be some who question why any man would take a four-year-old boy on such a nocturnal adventure, even when that four-year-old was begging to go. But all the while he was teaching me, showing me, educating me in ways that few others can ever appreciate or even imagine.

When someone makes the comment that I know a bit about the lower Big Bend, he is the man who deserves the most credit for that. When something happened in my life where I had to make do or die, he had already led me up that trail by example all those many years ago.

And though he has been gone now for over forty years, he still lives and breathes in my heart. For he was the one who guided me most in becoming who I am.

Or at least, the better parts.

347

"We dance round in a ring and suppose,
But the Secret sits in the middle and knows."
--Robert Frost

You are looking up a small, curious crevice known as Tuff Canyon. 'Tuff' is a type of rock made of ancient volcanic ash following an eruption, and the result is quite visible in the walls of this steep arroyo. It sits alongside Maxwell Drive on the way to Santa Elena Canyon, about two miles northeast of Castolon as the crow flies. When you follow the road, the distance is more like three as it has to wind around Cerro Castellan.

The dry run forming the bottom has quite a story itself. You see, it is the same one that has its watershed in the Blue Creek Canyon of the Chisos Mountains. The creek actually begins along the southern lower reaches of Emory Peak, the highest point for the range.

From that locale it winds and wanders out of Blue Creek Canyon, past the old Homer Wilson foreman's place, and continues on for nearly twenty miles before depositing itself into the Rio Grande just west of Cottonwood Campground. To walk this dry run out is to see a good slice of the park, as well as an interesting one.

Providentially, the creek parallels Maxwell Drive in several places along the way. Those last three miles to Castolon contain so many unusual rock formations and sights that you could spend the entire day in the near vicinity, and not even come close to seeing it all.

That is one of the enduring fascinations of the lower Big Bend; unusual things in unusual places scattered about indiscriminately, often with little to no reason or rhyme to it. A dreamer's paradise as well as a geologist's nightmare, you might say.

Since it parallels Ross Maxwell Drive along several sections, the run is easily accessible for short day hikes. In fact, the roadway actually crosses Blue Creek in the pass between Kit and Goat Mountains.

You can park your vehicle on the shoulder, arm yourself with a topographical map, canteens and victuals, and spend a pleasant couple of hours actually seeing and experiencing parts of this wondrous land in blissful solitude.

Meanwhile many carloads of others will merely drive on by, eyes glued to the pavement in a mad rush to see the sights of a lifetime in a single day.

*"So as through a glass, and darkly
The age long strife I see
Where I fought in many guises,
Many names, but always me..."*
*--George S. Patton, Jr,
'Through A Glass, Darkly'*

When traveling the West River Road off Maxwell Drive in the national park, few realize that it's not the original 'river road.' Yes, the route used now has been there for a long time, going back to the beginning of the twentieth century. But the original road goes back even further and was far more traveled during its heyday.

This first track ran mostly parallel with the river from Castolon to Buenos Aires, which was once a farming settlement and now serves as a primitive camp ground. The route was only a section of the total sum stretching from Lajitas to Johnson Ranch. Initially utilized for regional commerce, US cavalry units stationed in Castolon routinely reconnoitered to these two opposing locales.

It also made for part of the Army supply road that ran to Fort D. A. Russell, initially known as Camp Marfa. The fort was headquarters for detachments throughout the Big Bend region. After an airfield was constructed at Johnson Ranch, vehicles reached the landing strip by this route.

The airfield itself proved to be a main stopover between San Antonio and El Paso for Army aircraft, providing aerial reconnaissance along the river. This led to an ongoing rivalry between the cavalry and the air arm, much like the same that was occurring between cavalry and armor.

That dispute was finally settled by gifted military strategists such as George C. Marshall, Dwight D. Eisenhour and George S. Patton. Each intuitively understood the maelstrom of destruction the Nazi Blitzkrieg was

351

bringing, and though possessing the very heart and soul of a cavalryman Patton understood armor best of all.

Suffice to say, the cavalry lost out.

Yet times were also changing along the river. Johnson Airfield was shut down and the Army packed up to fight a modern war in far flung places around the globe, led by those very same men and others like them.

Meanwhile, this part of the road slipped back into near anonymity. Ultimately the National Park Service found out what the Army already knew: it was constantly being washed out by rainstorms and river floods. So this particular section was abandoned in favor of the road presently in use. It was then forgotten other than by long-time residents, smugglers of all sorts and an occasional near lost Border Patrol agent.

Not too long ago I hiked the abandoned portion. Zig-zagging along my way were ruins, stunning rock formations and vistas to fill one's spirit with pure pleasure. There were thickets, too, the kind to make a man think he was back at jungle warfare school in Okinawa.

This photograph was taken where the road was forced to higher ground, the river pressing hard against a bluff below. Actually, I should say 'roads,' as the Army tried more than one variation during its tenure. You can see what is left of this particular track angling over a low rise by the rock overhang, which in turn frames the mouth of Santa Elena Canyon some eleven miles away.

My thoughts went to how many patrols rested here, making use of that overhang as a brief respite from the blistering sun. How many men complaining about the heat and dust, or why they were in such a remote, godforsaken land. How many times waiting for the call or sign to move on.

It is the way of the fighting man since time immemorial.

The verse above ran through my mind as I stared at that road and that rock. The lines come from a poem Patton wrote after leading the first ever American tank brigade into combat during The Great War.

That was what they used to call World War One before mankind had the misfortune of learning to number them. Patton was just a young cavalry lieutenant when this road was patrolled, men who had known him sat under that rock at one time.

Maybe he had himself.

Quién sabes?

It was time for me to move on in my own time and place, while still paying proper homage to the past.

353

CHAPTER FIFTEEN

EL SOLITARIO AREA

Of all the areas that intrigued me during my raising in the Big Bend, El Solitario was near the top of the list. I was brought up on stories of these mountains; strange lights in the sky, compass needles that swung from side to side, buried treasure and haunts and ghosts of every guise and description.

Then there is the eerily unnatural terrain itself, like the incredibly large stone fingers along the western slopes that folks in the Rockies call 'flat irons.' No one had to jump start my imagination on that one; early on I would look across Fresno Canyon and speculate they were the claws of some gigantic monster, trying to free himself from his stone clad tomb.

As I grew older and learned more, I found that for each of those fantastic stories there was at least the smallest kernel of truth. I also learned to appreciate the unsolved Rubik's Cube that passes for geology in this range. Though it is now sixty years later and counting, I can still imagine that monster trying to dig himself out from all those billions of tons of rock.

And sometimes in the wee hours I can hear his groaning drifting down the canyons, carried along by a night breeze...

"The whole difference between construction and creation is exactly this: that a thing constructed can only be loved after it is constructed; but a thing created is loved before it exists."

--G. K. Chesterton

El Solitario is a caved in laccolith; meaning that hundreds of millions of years ago during a period of intense volcanic activity, it was a gigantic bubble of lava and rock. After it cooled and portions of the laccolith began to erode, some of the softer parts gave way and the dome collapsed within itself.

Adding to the general geological confusion is this same bubble blew up underneath the far more ancient Ouachita mountain range, the remnants of which are found from the Rio Grande across into Oklahoma and Arkansas. This made for what *El Solitario* is today, a bewildering maze of rock formations that has left many a geologist completely stupefied and drooling out the side of his mouth.

What remains of the laccolith forms a basin with ridges of peaks and uplifts encircling it about. From a thousand miles in space, this natural phenomenon can be spotted with the naked eye. Due to its bullseye appearance, one might mistakenly believe it was ground zero for a large meteorite impact.

In this photograph one can see the flatirons of *El Solitario* and the large cavity that sits in the midst of them. I have always been fascinated by that odd landmark, which in turn is made up of countless other anomalies that transform these mountains into the enormous puzzle they are. Looming over it all is Fresno Peak, the highest point in the range.

There is no telling how many thesis papers, manuscripts and books have been printed on this one area over the decades, and then unceremoniously dropped into the well-known circular file because they have been proven wrong yet once again.

That is the fitting lesson to be learned about this country, you spend your entire life trying to learn its secrets only to be made painfully aware of your pitiful level of ignorance.

Sort of keeps a man humble and cognizant that there is an All-Knowing God on high.

*"The longest journey
Is the journey inwards
Of him who has chosen his destiny."
--Dag Hammarskjold*

There are three major drainages for the basin of *El Solitario*. As you are facing south, they are referred to as the Left Hand Shutup, the Right Hand Shutup, and the Lower Shutup.

The Right Hand and Lower Shutups drain into Fresno Canyon while the Left Hand ultimately empties into Terlingua Creek. Of the three, the Left Hand is by far the easiest to navigate and was coincidentally where the western property line extended from our ranch headquarters along the Terlingua.

My dad and my grandfather enjoyed prowling this country on horseback, trying to learn more of it and the stories of its known history. The yearning to see what lies over the next rise or around the next bend has always been strong in my family. I suppose that is what drove my ancestors to push out with Boone through the Cumberland Gap, then across Arkansas Territory and south of the Red River while Texas was still under Spanish rule.

Be that as it may, as a child both of these men enthralled me with many a story of what lay 'Out There.' One of the more intriguing was of a rock dam on the Left Hand Shutup. Dad would on occasion visit the site astride his favorite horse Pedernal while scouting the surrounding countryside.

At that time good water was available and a palm tree provided shade, making for a true oasis of green in the middle of a hard, parched land. Dad told me that someday he would take me there. That someday never came.

Some forty years later I base camped at Tres Papalotes, finally making it to that very same spot. The palm tree was long gone and there was no water, the dam had filled up with creek gravel and silt. It won't be too much longer before the dam itself is gone, as time and erosion are wasting it away.

I sat on the adjoining rise for a long while and thought about things of the heart and people of my past. Both Dad and Pedernal have now been dead for decades. But I hope they still ride together in another 'Out There,' into that undiscovered country where no mortal eye or presence is allowed.

Then I put away my thoughts, saddled up and pushed on to what lay around the next bend.

It's a family tradition, you know.

"In design, in size, in number, in excellence, all the works of the Lord are great. Even the little things of God are great."
--Charles Spurgeon

Working your way through the Solitario, you never know what wonderfully strange, almost otherworldly sights you might stumble across next. What has occurred in this eroding laccolith presents mute testimony to a cataclysmic power impossible for the human mind to fully comprehend.

Throughout much of the range, vegetation is sparse. Any green living thing acts as almost an afterthought in setting off the stark, desolate, craggy terrain surrounding it. Many of these plants are almost as hardy as the rock formations they grow among; ocotillo, cat claw, yucca, mesquite, an endless variety of cacti, and seas of lechuguilla that stretch out in every direction.

Even the small, apparently fragile resurrection plant has its own miracle of existence. Lying dormant and seemingly dead for months on end until a rare giving of moisture, and within hours it will turn into a verdant color worthy of any jungle.

But when this land is dry, which is the vast majority of time, most of the splendor found in color comes from the rocks themselves. I have often referred to this range as God's Own Rock Collection and a casual walkabout within its environs will quickly explain why.

Conflicting, bizarre, twisted, out-of-place formations greet the eye wherever it sets, and time and again the mind finds itself asking what forces could have possibly caused this or that to happen.

If there ever was a place that could be termed a riddle wrapped within an enigma and then shrouded in mystery, *El Solitario* would be a likely candidate. There is an old regional adage that goes, "When God created the world, He took all that He had left over and put it in the Big Bend."

El Solitario is where He put His Rock Collection.

It is, for lack of a better term, beyond magnificent.

"He enjoyed long stretches of pure delight such as only a seaman may know, and moments of high, proud exultation that only a discoverer can experience."
--Samuel Eliot Morison

In the past I have referred to this area as God's Own Rock Collection, and this frame pretty much expresses why. It is only one of so many strange, weird and wonderful sights you come across on foot in this country, and why I have always been drawn back to it.

On this day we had started near Post Mountain where the west branch of the Military Road tops out of Fresno Canyon, down the canyon itself and then turning into the Righthand Shutup. We continued until near Burnt Camp before reversing direction back to where we came from. It was quite a little walkabout, and one of the more memorable ones in a host of such memories.

There are three of these shutups, each serving as a giant drainage system for the Solitario basin as well as its surrounding uplifts. Each has its own character, challenges and moments of awe where you stand there slack jawed and wonder to yourself; *'How did this happen?'*

The Righthand Shutup is not the easiest way into the range and calls for occasional climbing, including a couple of drop offs some fifteen to twenty feet high. Of course, one should remember the term 'easy' should be used but sparingly in the lower Big Bend. The terrain, the temperature extremes, the lack of water and the remoteness itself will conspire against you on any given day.

Yet any of those given days can also bring sights that few others will ever see. For with the many defiances of the desert come the discoveries of abrupt anomalies that strain one's ability to adequately describe.

One of these sits at the lower end for the Righthand Shutup. As you turn into the crevice and the walls close in, off to the side stands a pillar of gray volcanic rock nearly twenty feet high, like a stone sentinel on guard at the entrance. It in turn is situated among impossibly diverse arrays of other rock formations and types, each lending to this surreal scene.

You can tell from the photo how odd and incongruent it is to the surroundings, and how improbable the mere presence. Yet there it is, looming over you as you walk into the confines, almost as if it has knowing eyes that follow you to gauge your character and purpose.

After all, what better to watch over God's Own Rock Collection than a solid stone sentry to guard the treasures found within?

365

"Life is trying things to see if they work."
--Ray Bradbury

It is the earliest days of Spring in the Lower Shutup of the Solitario Mountains, or '*El Solitario*' as often marked on older maps. You are facing roughly south, just above where the canyon walls narrow to a vee barely wide enough for a man to pass through. To your right and near the top of the rim are a series of caves.

Below this point is a drop off that falls away to where the floor of the crevice continues on to the Fresno. They link together just above the ruins for the original Buena Suerte.

You can't get down to the lower floor safely without a good rope, and you have to work your way through a crazy, jumbled up mess of rock and boulder to do so.

But you can climb out of the shutup on the western side behind the caves and negotiate your way around. That is the way to go if of a mind to reach the lower desert, and the Lajitas as well as Fresno areas.

Many folks come and drive around the inner perimeter of the Solitario basin in a four-wheel drive vehicle, or perhaps on a motorcycle or a mountain bike. They run pell-mell along the confines of the primitive roadways, often enough just to see how fast they can go.

Then they come out and tell others they have been to the Solitario and there really isn't much there to see.

But they haven't really been there, not by a long shot.

> *"Of all the mathematical disciplines this is the hardest: to number our days. We count everything else, but we do not seem able to use our days rightly and with wisdom."*
> **--James Montgomery Boice**

It might not look like much to many, just a dry creek running through the even drier reaches of the eastern side of The Solitario.

But there is history here to be remembered. Several years ago I scouted this country to find some sign of the Telephone Trail, likely the first wheeled route that went through these rugged, desolate mountains.

Please note this path had nothing to do with Telephone Canyon or the trail to it in Big Bend National Park. Rather, this was the service route for a telephone line that ran from the Mariposa Mines at the foot of California Hill up to Marfa, Texas. This was during the dawn of the twentieth century and the wire was one of the first of its kind in this country.

Most people who live in the lower Big Bend these days have never heard of this particular trail, yet in its time millions of dollars were made or lost over the telephone lines it helped maintain. Knowledge is power, and near instant knowledge along a distance that took a mule team four days to cover made that power vastly more so.

Along this creek bed I discovered a few remaining traces belonging to the line, most everything else has been removed or deteriorated away into nothingness.

Someday I will go back for a more thorough exploration to determine if anything else can be found. However, that time needs to be soon or there will be nothing left.

Just those dry creek beds, running hither and yon across the face of an even drier land.

*"We shall not cease from exploration,
And the end of all our exploring;
Will be to arrive where we started,
And know the place for the very first time."*
--T. S. Eliot

You are standing atop Fresno Peak on the southwestern side of *El Solitario*, facing roughly west. The mountain stands some 5,060 some odd feet tall, and is the highest point of this collapsed laccolith. Aptly named it towers over Fresno Canyon, which you can see snaking back and forth some 2,000 feet below.

Beyond is The Llano escarpment, forming the western wall for this rugged chasm. To your left that highest bit of ground in the escarpment is Rincon Mountain. Behind it, on the horizon, are the blueish ranges of Chihuahua. My dad always said the really big mountains were in Mexico, and as usual he was right.

Behind you is Needle Peak and off to your north sits Burnt Camp, Los Portales and the Righthand Shutup. Due South is Chimney Rock. Any direction you want to go from here is across rough, unforgiving country dotted mostly with sage, greasewood and lechuguilla.

This terrain is also strewn with rocks and boulders of every size, shape and description; heaped and stacked upon each other in haphazard fashion. There is not an easy mile to be had, even in a land where anything termed easy is usually anything but.

It is a solitary, lonesome place, though not near as lonesome as it used to be. So many more people are here now than I can ever recall, with so much more technology that allows them to do so.

But the desert remains, still mostly unbent by man's will and machinations.

I hope this will always be so.

372

"The line dividing humanity is not racial, political or even religious, but spiritual. That line runs through every human heart."
--Bruce Waltke

If one were but a single drop of rain that fell into the large laccolith known as *El Solitario*, and if you were joined by enough of your fellows, there would be a good chance of being funneled through this narrow gap enroute to Fresno Canyon.

Though rain is a seldom seen commodity in this basin it has been known to come in raging torrents, while flashes of lightning strike the nearby peaks and high ground amid thunder that booms like God's own artillery.

It is an awesome rendering of nature's orchestra of sound and sight, combined with strains of smell, taste and touch to highlight certain notes in the performance.

Then another rumbling starts, somewhat like the thunder but different in tone and style. More uneven, more earthy and even to the uninitiated far more ominous.

That single drop of rain, now in the company of an untold number of others, has combined to form a mighty army rushing headlong to attack all that lays before them.

They go over, slice through and ultimately sweep away any and all obstacles within their reach, including solid rock. Over the eons this army has shaped and fashioned all manner of unnatural sculptures that defy description. Some of their effort can be seen here, the remaining rock left stark and purposeful.

Yet at this very same spot that same army left life-giving elements that bring the sprinklings of seasonal verdancy alongside seasonal destruction.

And the desert stoically accepts both as it prepares to blossom anew.

374

"There are two things to aim for in life: first, to get what you want; and, after that, to enjoy it. Only the wisest of mankind achieve the second."
--Logan Pearsall Smith

You are high above in the southern part of the basin for *El Solitario*, near the old gold mine that sits on the eastern side of the main dry wash feeding the Lower Shutup. The lens of the camera is pointing roughly west, with Needle Peak in the foreground while Fresno Peak stands behind on the horizon.

This mine sits almost astraddle of the Presidio-Brewster county line amid the farthest lower reaches of Eagle Mountain. Not marked on any of the 1:24,000 topographical maps, it was nevertheless an operation fairly well developed. The dirt road you see in the distance was for diggings scattered around Needle Peak, as well as the ranching efforts that took place here.

There are also a series of old wagon roads that climb out to the southeast, before you are completely boxed in by the Lower Shutup. One heads toward Black Mesa and California Hill, one toward the Escondido, and a third strikes out for Chimney Rock and Fresno Mine.

When I was a kid, many used to say there was no gold in the lower Big Bend. Well, there was. Like most anything else that has to do with rock or minerals, this country has some of the substance hid out someplace.

The problem usually lies in there not enough to make the extraction profitable. Another one of those little Catch 22s about this land that happens time and again, generation after generation.

And for those who have seen Elephant Tusk in Big Bend National Park? Yes, Needle Peak is very similar to it in shape, though quite a bit smaller.

Not to mention drier, too. They used to pump water all the way from the well at Burnt Camp to the diggings just south of Needle Peak. The pipes are still there.

Like most everything else in this perpetually parched place, it almost always comes down to water.

> "To most of us nothing is so invisible as an unpleasant truth. Though it is held before our eyes, pushed under our noses, rammed down our throats — we know it not."
>
> --Eric Hoffer

It was several years ago now, though in my mind only yesterday. Seems that time has a peculiar habit of slipping by unnoticed, even when we thought we were paying attention.

My sons were still at Annapolis and each spring break they would bring their midshipman friends to roam hither and yon throughout the lower Big Bend. Though I was never easy on this latest iteration of American fighting man, we always seemed to have more wanting to come than room to board.

In fact, our little expeditions picked up the unofficial moniker of 'Mr. English's Afghanistan Training' inside certain rooms and offices at Bancroft Hall.

This particular photograph was taken in the Right Hand Shutup for *El Solitario*, while moving into the basin from Fresno Canyon. As you can tell it was just before the first sprinkles of spring, the country was suffering from one of those spells that sucks the moisture out of man, beast and all things green.

My younger son, Ethan L'Amour, was pulling point this day and scaling up behind him was Joe Gehrz. Ethan is presently skippering his own patrol boat in the Persian Gulf while Joe is a Navy flight surgeon.

Like I said, time does have a way of sneaking past.

One special note concerning the photo, there is no color enhancement occurring in the frame. Anyone familiar with this land would say it is about as close as a camera can reproduce.

The country itself is that contrasting, and my used little thirty-buck Kodak works about as well as anything else in recording such moments that I want to remember.

Because as time gleefully plays its guileful tricks upon we mere mortals, it makes me aware of yet another one of those unpleasant truths.

Even as that same time continues to slip away.

CHAPTER SIXTEEN

DEAD HORSE MOUNTAINS AREA

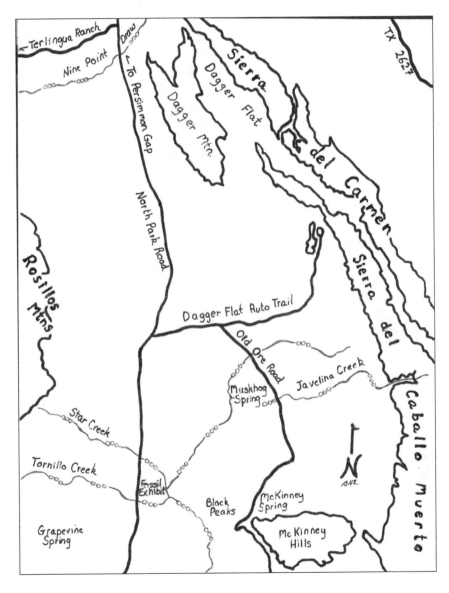

No one seems to be really sure where the Dead Horse Mountains begin and where they end. They come out of the Boquillas area on our side of the river, closely intertwined with the northernmost section of the Sierra del Carmen, which runs for miles upon miles into Coahuila.

Not even cartographers seem to have a firm grasp on this, as one set of maps show a section of the range as the Dead Horse while another lists them as the Sierra del Carmen. To add to the turmoil, many times they note the Dead Horse Mountains as the 'Sierra del Caballo Muerto.' Most folks stick to calling them the Dead Horse, as it is shorter and simpler for them to pronounce.

There are several different stories as to how these isolated, inhospitable mountains were first christened. Some say Texas Rangers killed a remuda of Indian ponies there. Others claim the rangers shot their own horses to avoid them being taken by Indians. Finally, a few will say it refers to some surveyor's mount that fell to its demise inside one of the many canyons.

As usual a perpetual state of confusion about places and names reigns supreme in the lower Big Bend; attended to and enlarged by conflicting facts, legends, myths and even an outright lie or two.

Which is likely as it should be, as this land would not have the same flavor without all the speculation piled upon lore and mystery.

"The Promised Land always lies on the other side of a wilderness."
--Havelock Ellis

It was nearing the end of a long, hot day on my thirteenth mile with two more to go. I had been swinging a jagged, uneven loop across the western slopes of the Dead Horse Mountains. During my prowl I wandered up both main forks for Javelina Creek, their canyons cutting across the face of the range with deep incisions.

Not many folks spend much time here on foot. There are no trails to speak of or roads that provide easy access to this area, and there has never been much human activity compared to other regions of the park. During my scout I had only found a shard of broken glass, a bent rod of rusty iron, and part of a decrepit barbed wire fence so old and useless you could actually walk underneath it.

You get to most spots in the Dead Horse by breaking your own trail and a quad map comes in handy, along with some experience as well as common sense. You might even say the common sense is essential, as some others have discovered to their discomfiture. This country is where the game ball marked 'Darwinism' is always in play.

It is rough, dry, thirsty land that from a distance seems hardly able to keep anything alive; be it insect, animal or plant. Usually it swelters in shades of dry earth tones, with a dash of reddish accents in the canyons for a bit of contrast. The long-standing joke about the lower Big Bend receiving only two inches of rain during Noah's Flood takes on new meaning, as the Dead Horse likely only got about a tenth and it was mostly blowing sideways.

But this summer, this late July, God had been more than gracious. Though most all of the more easily reached tinajas were dry, the land itself was greener and more verdant than I have ever seen before or imagined possible.

Stands of prickly pear appeared as if decked out for Christmas, with multitudes of red tunas contrasting boldly against the green pads. There was

381

grass, good grass and the ocotillos were covered with the leaves they are so seldom seen sprouting. All this in turn set off by spreads of wild yellow flowers that are usually burned off by mid-May.

In some parts for as far as you could see were yucca, sotol and lechuguilla stalks reaching upward into the crystal blue sky, like lances of massed warriors waiting to do battle. Texas persimmon and Mexican buckeye, along with honey mesquite and other varieties of shrubs and trees, filled the canyons and arroyos. All sorts of birds and insects made their presence known, including legions of bees buzzing about their business.

There were hawks, far more than usual and one golden eagle that I stirred up along the south fork for Javelina Creek. Their natural prey, the cottontail, were out and about in force, along with their long-eared cousins the jackrabbit. Muley deer, big, fat and sassy, bounded away in every direction. Life had come to the Dead Horse Mountains, in a style and variety seldom seen by human eyes.

And I was alone in the audience to this rare, marvelous show; a once in a lifetime walk through a kind of Garden of Eden, or as close as this desert land can get.

I felt honored, even humbled, to be there.

383

"The tragedy of life so often is, not that we have no high impulses, but that we fail to turn them into action."

--William Barclay

Sometimes I get the feeling about something, a nagging impulse about certain spots in this desert as if I can sense where something might be. On occasion I have half-jokingly referred to the sensation as being some 'little guy in the back of my head.' He has been there throughout my life and nowhere more vocal or persistent than in this country.

Because of him I am on occasion led into the most unusual, secreted places not found on any map, written of in any book or spoken about by anyone I have known. This walkabout proved to be one of those times, as well as one of those places.

Recently I have been prowling the western slopes of the Dead Horse Mountains. The overlying purpose for these trips was 'boots on the ground' research for a historical novel I have in mind. But just as likely it was a case of filling the need of going where few others do, especially around mid-August.

I was searching for a watering hole for horses and mules to fit the plot, and found the assorted tiny seeps and small tinajas bone dry. There was a strong suspicion of water up a fork for Javelina Creek, but that section would be hard going on foot and nigh impossible for mounted stock.

A few weeks later I saddled up and pointed my nose north, heading for Dagger Flat. Frankly, the path chosen did not look promising other than some dirt tanks along the way. All had been empty for a long while, sucked dry by infesting copses of stunted mesquite.

However, that 'little guy' was encouraging me onward, pushing me up a route that was not the easiest in either features or contour lines. Working my normal zig-zag pattern as I ventured along, I wondered if one or both of us had lost our minds.

That unsettling surmisal lasted until the draw narrowed into what first appeared as a natural box on three sides. It was only when mere yards away you realized the bottom took a ninety-degree jag, losing elevation rapidly. Though it had not rained enough to flow in months, there were copious amounts of water in ponds and tinajas both above and below.

The signs and sounds of wildlife increased in the small valley beyond. I continued along, spooking up several muleys who bounded away, slicked off and broad with plenty of green grass and attending vigor.

"You ain't seen nothing yet," whispered the little guy to me. Even in the growing heat with sweat trickling down my back, I picked up the pace.

Two miles later the gulch narrowed dramatically again, this time into a small canyon. Sheets of rock on either side, sheets of rock along the bottom and dozens of small tinajas dotted the way. Some were dry but many others contained sizeable amounts of the liquid desert gold.

Picked over skeletons of animals of all sizes lay scattered about. The reason was clear: just below the rim rock were several shelters and caves, so well used by assorted predators the ground in front was beaten down. Above the rim rock, carrion birds perched patiently or took to wing for a better view of a possible meal. Like most everything else in this complicated land, these small tinajas served double duty for the taking of life as well as the giving of it.

The canyon funneled me to where the creek took another sudden zag and dropped completely away among large boulders. I eased to the edge and looked down a forty foot pour off, with a near full tinaja just below me. It interrupted the drop ever so briefly before it spilled away again to another pond of water further below.

The attached photograph was taken from the top of one of the canyon walls, you can see the second pond near center frame.

And the little guy smiled.

"We look back upon our life only as on a thing of broken pieces, because our misses and failures are always the first to strike us, and outweigh in our imagination what we have done and attained."

--Goethe

The truth in Goethe's words came to mind as I stood on a hot June day in a nameless place, studying the residue of someone's broken dreams decaying before me. Not more than about two hundred yards away ran the skeleton of the long-abandoned Ore Terminal Road, still visible from the knoll above.

The Ore Terminal Road began at the northern terminus of the overhead tramway for the Puerto Rico Mine, situated south of the river near Boquillas. Once the raw material reached the terminus, it was loaded onto wagons and trucks. From there, the material was transported to the railway in Marathon for shipment to processing plants back east.

This road was specifically constructed for the task, and was a real improvement over the still functioning Old Ore Road opposite the McKinney Hills. A quirk in fate left this route to dissolve back into the desert after the National Park Service took over. There is not even a marked trail through here anymore.

Which, by yet another quirk of a more personal nature, is why I come to this area. Crowded close against the lower reaches of the Dead Horse Mountains, it is not a spot where one usually passes through enroute to someplace else.

Your destination has to be these desolate hills and quiet valleys. I had started on foot just below the junction of the Old Ore and Dagger Flat roads, and night fall would find me still an hour and a half out navigating under a half moon. There are few things more peaceful for me than prowling through the desert at night, dead reckoning by what God provided above.

And what of the link between the photograph and the quote? The common tie remains in the Goethe adage and those quirks of fate mentioned before.

These rotting remains were once a mine shack, built many decades ago to work cinnabar diggings embedded in the near vertical walls of an overshadowing uplift. The shafts are still there, along with chunks of low-grade ore and mounds of slag. There is no road and no trail to the tunnels, my best guess is some sort of trolley system was used to gain access to the site.

It was, for all intents and purposes, a shoe string budgeted sort of operation. From what I can determine not much is known about the mine, and its bare existence depended on the Ore Terminal Road running close by.

When the road went away, so went this mine and from the looks of things it never even began to repay for the paltry investment.

But whoever built this had a dream, an entrepreneur's plan to better their station in life. When they departed it was likely with not much more than calluses and aching muscles, as well as some hard-earned money lost literally down a hole.

I hope there were other, more successful efforts in their lives and that is just as likely too. Sooner or later, this kind of hard work and determination has to pay off someplace.

And that is how the quote and these quirks come together.

389

*"There was no desert in his heart, though
there was a desert around him."*
--Charles Spurgeon

If one wants off the beaten track taken by so many, the Dagger Flat area is a good place to shoot for. Snuggly nestled between the northernmost reaches of the Deadhorse Mountains and the Sierra del Carmen, the encircled landmark is some six and a half miles long and shaped roughly akin to a boomerang.

Dagger Flat is one of those places in the national park where few venture to, and often enough for good reason. Even the name seems inhospitable and uninviting, and I have seen that country so barren and dry that you would think a single, half-starved lizard would be hard put to survive.

It is also somewhat difficult to get to. The closest vehicular avenue is at the end of Dagger Flat Road, which actually ends a mile and more away from the nearest part of the flat itself. That is measured in air miles, by the way. Walk out even the shortest route and most folks would swear it was three.

My goal for this trip was what I call Hidden Canyon, though I know of no given name for it in neither map nor memory. The name came about after sitting less than a hundred and fifty yards away one day, and never discerning a single clue that it was there.

The wash feeding it is plainly visible due to the accompanying greenery, but the terrain features and gradual slope fool you. The arroyo appears to merely brush against the retaining higher ground before continuing on to the mountains in the southeast.

In reality, that seeming continuation is actually another draw running in from those mountains, and the two collide almost head-on at the opening for Hidden Canyon.

This one gorge carries not only the watershed for half of Dagger Flat and the surrounding uplifts, but also for those southeastern mountains. Furthermore, numerous creeks cut through solid rock at almost every point on the compass to get there.

In the frame you can see the fringes of storm clouds to the front, while a solid, sullen gray mass was locking in behind me. You don't want to be here when the rains come, yet here I was.

I knew the canyon corkscrewed for another mile and a half before emptying into open country again.

I also knew there were some good-sized pour offs along the way. The retaining walls on each side grew both higher and steeper as you went along, making it difficult or even impossible to climb out.

Finally, I knew I was still about seven and a half miles from where I had parked beside Nine Point Draw Bridge, and the day was already slipping past the mid-afternoon hours.

Only a fool pushes his luck that hard in this desert, especially when by himself and in such a remote spot. So I took this photograph and backtracked my way out of there, trekking toward Devil's Den. Another mile or so and I would be in a different watershed, away and safe from what was likely to occur here.

Rain splattered off the flat brim of my Stetson while thunder boomed and rolled behind me. The quiet, insistent song of the desert sirens that had brought me to Hidden Canyon now turned into a roaring rage, like so many furious felines whose prey has slipped away.

Those same dark, ominous looking clouds settled upon the mountains and hills, letting loose with their payloads in a pent-up fury.

But I will be back. Another day, perhaps another route, but to the same canyon.

Whether whispering sweetly or wailing in frustration, those sirens still call out to me.

CHAPTER SEVENTEEN

ON THE ROAD

I don't think many folks these days understand what an undertaking it was to build paved roadways through the Big Bend region, or just how important these were to people on both sides of the river.

Prima facie evidence for this was the highway constructed between Presidio and Lajitas. Officially designated as Texas FM 170, it was known locally as 'The River Road' or 'El Camino del Rio' from about the day it was first finished, which did not occur until 1961.

Up to that time travel from Presidio to Lajitas was slow, onerous and full of detours and round-about ways for most of its length. At times, the road actually crossed over into Mexico for about a mile and a half. But now one could drive the distance in just over an hour in air-conditioned comfort, which was in itself an almost sinful luxury during that era.

With the completion of The River Road and TX 118 some ten years before, the lower Big Bend was finally fairly accessible to the rest of Texas and ultimately the rest of the world.

More so than any other change since man first set foot in this country; these two roadways made the biggest difference for those living here, and again on both sides of the river.

Civilization was coming and nothing was ever the same again.

"I felt my lungs inflate with the onrush of scenery—air, mountains, trees, people. I thought, 'This is what it is to be happy.'"
--Sylvia Plath

In the many childhood memories occupying my mind are this road and this hill. The road is Texas FM170, also known in my part of the world as *The River Road*, or *El Camino del Rio*. The uplift has been called 'Big Hill' since even before this particular blacktop came into existence.

You've maybe seen or heard of the old Robert Mitchum movie *Thunder Road*, or maybe even listened to Mitchum sing the accompanying hit song. Well this was Thunder Road for me, a narrow two lane highway snaking itself along the Rio Grande through mountains, canyons, dry creek beds and curves of every sweep from Presidio to Lajitas.

I was nine years old and my Dad had a brand new 1967 Mustang GTA 390. To his dying day, that Ford was his favorite car ever. It was basically the same model of Mustang that Steve McQueen drove in the movie *Bullitt*, save that Dad's was white with a red interior and had the C6. The automatic transmission was a nod to my Mom to keep her from having to row through the four-speed manual.

She still hated that car, though.

But dad didn't and neither did us kids. He knew only one way to drive it too, and that was wide open. When Dad strapped on his Mustang, Steve McQueen himself had nothing on him. My father was an outstanding driver with a feel for an automobile that few others could duplicate, and his favorite workout for that little white pony car was on River Road.

I look at this photo and I can still hear that big block FE Ford V8 straining, screaming up this hill while those bias ply wide ovals squalled for mercy at each flick of the steering wheel. Dad had his Ray Ban aviators on, grinning.

Hitting each apex just right, setting himself up for the crest where the road seemed to disappear for a moment and the horizon went away.

Then he'd hammer on that Holley four barrel and manually grab a lower gear using the Mustang's console shift, shooting down the other side.

There were no trees like in the quote, nor any other people. Just him and me, having another go at our own personal Thunder Road, Robert Mitchum singing in my head.

And I was happy…

"Highway run,
Into the midnight sun,
Wheels go round and round,
You're on my mind..."
--Journey 'Faithfully'

In all the many journeys I have taken in my life, and of all the innumerable roads that made up those journeys, there are only two that occupy the highest tier of both memories and sentiment---the River Road between Lajitas and Presidio, and the Davis Mountains Loop.

Living on a ranch or at the trading post in Lajitas did not leave much time for any sort of vacation, the days as well as some of the nights were often long and the attending tasks unending.

Getting away for even a few days was almost unheard of, save for a death in the family or an occasional holiday such as Thanksgiving or Christmas. Yet there were day trips and often enough those took in one of the prettiest places on earth, The Davis Mountains Loop.

Now you might think that a bit of hyperbole. But when it is 118 degrees at Lajitas or a 115 along Terlingua Creek with not so much as a swamp cooler, and it is so dry the devil himself can't spit, the verdant coolness of the Davis Mountains was like a veritable heaven on earth.

We would pack up a lunch basket and leave around daybreak, heading north through Alpine. All day we would wander about taking in the fort, the state park, the Rockpile, or just enjoying a cool, shady spot at one of the many picnic areas along the way.

Sometimes we would stop by the Prude Ranch and my grandfather would visit with John Prude about livestock, range conditions or the like. Then dusk would find us headed back to all those neglected chores and the additional long hours needed to finish them.

But it was so worth it.

Years later I would make my own solo trips when I could squeeze in a day off between two jobs and trying to finish high school. It was a chance to get away from hard times and more of those long hours, at least for a little while.

Afterwards, while in the Marine Corps and on leave, I would feel that pressing need to get away from everyone and everything else, if only for a day or so. This road was where I often chose to go.

The years passed, then decades. In the interim I married and we started a family. Cathy and I spent our honeymoon here and later some very special times with our two growing sons.

Then more years slipped by and I was a senior trooper in the Texas Highway Patrol nearing retirement, part of a detachment working special duty for border security. While most everyone else was on interstate, I ended up here as I was about the only one who really knew the road and surrounding area. It was the one single benefit of being away from my family.

Now I look back and wonder where all the time has gone.

So much has changed, so much that will never be the same again as people and civilization continue to fill every nook and cranny of what was once a vast, empty land.

But that narrow, winding road, shaded picnic areas, and those verdant mountains where the cool breezes blow still remain.

I need to go again.

"Books are good enough in their own way, but they are a mighty bloodless substitute for life."
--Robert Louis Stevenson

When one drives the River Road between Presidio and Lajitas, there are sights that make one want to stop their vehicle and go exploring, if only for a few minutes. This narrow, two lane highway twists and turns alongside the Rio Grande, leading you through a bewildering variety of views and landscapes.

Some of the more stunning are found among the many canyons feeding into the river, both from the north as well as the south. On the Texas side alone, there are dozens that have carved themselves into the face of this rugged land and that hide all sorts of secrets. Those would include the most precious desert resource of all: good water.

Thus, one should not be surprised by the accompanying signs of human habitation; ruins and rotting leftovers of someone's struggle to make a life. So many now come into this country with every kind of modern technological device and bauble imaginable. It is this technology, and it alone, that has allowed man to bend the will of the desert into what we see these days.

But put yourself here a hundred and fifty years ago, or a hundred, or even sixty and see how well you fare then. Remember, the River Road between Lajitas and Presidio was not even fully opened until John F. Kennedy became president.

It was in this stretch where building that highway became such a challenge. Redford, once called Polvo, is situated behind you. The dirt road from Presidio to Redford was fairly well traveled in the decades before the completion of FM 170, regional commerce and the US Army saw to that.

But once the road reached the canyon country, near a tiny settlement called Domingo, that all changed abruptly. The land became surreally rough, and the passages narrow and few. The mishmash of wagon tracks and trails all came together in a combined effort to squeak their way through. When the rains came, this infrequent traffic flow ground to a halt.

Think of the isolation. That in itself was enough to drive off all but the hardiest and most self-sufficient. Then there was the oppressive heat, the endless hard work, the sicknesses, the border troubles running both directions and most importantly, the unforgiving nature of the land.

The desert does not give in easily. 'Struggle' was not a noun or a verb found in a book out here, it was what one did daily just to survive.

"There is a peculiar freshness and charm about early morning praises; the day is loveliest when it first opens its eyelids, and God himself seems then to make distribution of the day's manna, which tastes most sweetly if gathered ere the sun is hot."
--Charles Spurgeon

There is a small roadside park about ten miles south of Marathon enroute to Persimmon Gap, nestled alongside the highway as it makes its way past the crumbling ridges of the ancient Ouachitas. During the years that we were living in Ozona, this was my way station for an early lunch when headed into the national park.

This shot was taken fairly early in the morning at the start of one of those jaunts, you are looking in a southerly direction toward Santiago Peak. The range to the left of the uplift is referred to as the Santiago Mountains.

These desolate, craggy obstacles run in a line roughly southeast to northwest, from the area where they meet the Sierra Del Carmen to the point where the Santiago Mountains blend into the Del Norte range.

There are few passages through them, which makes the one that forms Persimmon Gap so important. Persimmon Gap was where one of the main branches of the Comanche War Trail crossed into the lower Big Bend. Likely enough, it was used a long time before the Comanche ever came to this country.

This roadside park is another spot that most folks drive by without giving a second thought to, often at a high lope while trying to see everything in the Big Bend in a couple of days.

401

But if you have the time you can pull off and just sit a spell at one of the shaded picnic tables, taking in all that is around you while letting the strains and rigors of modern living ooze out your pores.

Because here is life in abundance. Both incredibly old yet at the same moment newborn, surrounding you with its presence in sound and smell and sight. Take what is needed to feast your spirit upon it.

You may not pass this way again.

"Faith cannot find a home on this side of the stars. It has caught a glimpse of the Infinite, and it can never be content with anything else."

--F. B. Meyer

There is a magic moment at the end of some days in this country, a duration in time of only a few minutes as the sun slips over the horizon and everything in the desert is bathed in a golden sheen of a dying day.

At no time does it appear starker, yet in the same moment a feeling of peace and of belonging fills the soul with utter contentment and grace. This was one of those days and one of those moments.

We had been up the eastern side of the Rancherias Trail in the state park and were pacing ourselves against the setting sun in returning to our vehicle. It was January, and the warmth of the day was quickly receding as a chill began to spread in tandem with the lengthening shadows. All around, if one was paying attention, this singular land and its inhabitants were making the change from day to night.

For those brief few movements of the hand sweep of a timepiece and just as we reached the parking area, everything for as far as the eye could see lit up in variations of a golden hue. The desert glowed as a mother does upon first holding her newborn.

Then the sun dropped below the far mountains, the gleaming aura faded, and a full moon peeked over a saddle to the east. Another day was done.

They say there is no gold in this desert; at least not enough to gain anything of any real worth from.

They'd be wrong.

"Learning never exhausts the mind."
--Leonardo da Vinci

About five miles southwest of Marathon sits old Camp Peña Colorado. Known to many of the region's generational locals as 'The Post,' this spot is part of my earliest memories as a small child. Anyplace in the Big Bend with such a large amount of water sticks in the mind of anyone native to this arid land.

Camp Peña Colorado is one of those storied places of the Big Bend with an active past going back thousands of years, dating to when man first came to this country. It was located on one of the main branches of the Comanche War Trail running from Comanche Springs to Persimmon Gap, before dividing again for multiple crossings along the Rio Grande.

Once the Comanche was finished, the major hostile clans consisted of the Mescalero Apache under such able leaders as Victorio and Alsate. The camp was established by the Army in 1879 at the base of Peña Colorado Bluff, also known also as Rainbow Cliffs, and served as a stepping off point to blunt the near continual raiding.

During the first six years it was manned by buffalo soldiers of the 24th and 25th Infantry Regiments, along with elements of the similarly formed Tenth Cavalry. Soon a road was established to link Fort Clark to Fort Davis and the railroad came in 1882, establishing the nearby town of Marathon as a water stop. Traveling to most any locale in the lower parts of the Big Bend usually meant going through here. Wagon roads from the south serviced an area from Lajitas across to Boquillas and beyond.

After the vanquishing of the Apache, detachments remained stationed here as military escorts when needed, as well as to assist what little civilian law enforcement existed. Illegal activities have always been a big problem in such a desolate, unpopulated expanse so close to an international border.

The Army closed the post in 1893, leaving little more behind than a few buildings and a cemetery. Sometime later, those buried were exhumed and their remains moved to San Antonio for reinternment. Rumor has it that one of those graves, for some reason, was left undisturbed.

The Post became part of the Combs Cattle Company, serving as a favored spot to conduct seasonal round ups as well as an occasional campground for patrolling Texas Rangers. In 1935 David St. Clair Combs, pioneer and founder for the cattle company, donated the land to Brewster County as a public park.

So began a new mission for the venerable post; one of socials, dances, weddings and family get togethers. It also remains a burial place, on private property close by is the supposed grave of that solitary soldier as well as the final resting spot for Monroe and Jesusita Payne.

Buried nearby is their nephew Blas Payne, cowboy extraordinaire and long-time employee of the Combs Ranch. Their ancestors were Black Seminole Indians, who came to the Big Bend as army scouts and pioneers in their own right. The Payne family story is an essential element to the far larger mosaic of the Big Bend itself.

And now, after the passing of nameless Paleo-Indian hunter gatherers, as well as the Comanche, the Apache, the Mexican freighters, the Buffalo Soldiers, the pioneer ranchers and lawmen; now it is only a quiet park to enjoy the shade, listen to the sound of water, and take a moment to recall.

For here, in a place few know of and even fewer make the effort to see, is a good chunk of the history to this captivating land in near consolidated form.

CHAPTER EIGHTEEN

FAMILY ROOTS

My family first came to Texas in the early 1810s, pushing across the Red from Arkansas Territory and settling around what is now Bonham. Soon afterwards, others fanned out south and west into various parts of the Lone Star State.

In the eight generations to follow, the men of my clan were basically involved in three different occupations: being a peace officer, a soldier or a cowboy. Of those three, they were cowboys most of all and remained pioneers at heart.

That spirit led them into the Nacogdoches area in the late 1820s, the Nueces River country by the 1850s and into the Big Bend region not too much later. In between there was more than one foray south of the Rio Grande, sometimes for years at a stretch.

Yet the Big Bend called to them most of all, that siren song of desert and mountains unlike any other. They learned to appreciate the spectacular beauty of this rugged land,, as well as the challenges and accompanying dangers that were all part of it.

They saw the hungry, sickly children from across the river, healthy men who fell out of the saddle from heat exhaustion, wild and domestic animals alike that died from lack of water and the bloated bodies of human beings who were usually only looking for a better life.

And in the gravest extreme they palmed a pistol or shouldered a rifle to defend their own against all comers, animal and man alike.

Now looking back on them and their kind, I don't think they would have had it any other way...

"Heroism, the Caucasian mountaineers say, is endurance for one moment more."
--George Kennan

The history of my family in the Big Bend goes back to the early 1880s, even before if one counts just passing through. Of all those who made this region home and that had English blood coursing through their veins, one of my great-great aunts was surely the most well-known and talked about. To us she was just 'Aunt Mag,' but to most everyone else she was known as Maggie Smith.

Margaret English Smith was not only the best known of our clan, she also lived in this country the longest, totaling some fifty-five years or so. A little sister to my great-grandfather Edward Benton 'Ben' English, she first came here as a child from Carrizo Springs. Her father, John Placeed English, had a ranch southeast of Sierra Blanca.

This was during the years of the Great Mexican Revolution, and some folks were understandably concerned about my great-great-grandfather using his young daughters as cowhands in such an isolated spot along the Rio Grande. One of those was a certain young Army cavalry officer by the name of George S. Patton, Jr. He makes note of those misgivings in his memoirs, but then added the girls proved to be as good with a horse or a rifle as many of his troopers.

Aunt Mag soon married her first husband and they moved to Bullis Gap, some five miles from that same river in the extreme southeastern corner of Brewster County. After he died of influenza, she ultimately remarried and opened a store near the Rosillos Ranch turnoff in what is now Big Bend National Park.

Around 1942, Aunt Mag and her second husband Baylor were approached by state officials to run Langford Hot Springs, which had recently been purchased for the planned national park. They accepted and made their headquarters at the old trading post you see in the photo. Thus began the most widely known and recorded chapter in Aunt Mag's life, a litany of border stories that have reached the point of legend in their telling and retelling.

In 1944, Byron died in a hotel fire in Alpine. Now alone with several children in this remote, solitary land, Aunt Mag was left to find her own way. Many people of lesser spirit, both men and women, would have folded their tents and moved on. Not Aunt Mag, the word 'quit' was not in her vocabulary.

She not only survived these challenges, she prospered in them in the ways that really matter. It has been said the truest mark of philanthropy is in doing for others who cannot return in kind. If that is so then Aunt Mag was as loyal to that calling as anyone, though she would have vehemently denied any such sentimentality.

To the scores upon scores of fellow human beings she gave sound advice to, carried on credit, nursed when sick, acted as midwife for births, paid for burials and provided a source of income for; she would likely remark that it was only 'the cost of doing business.' However, I strongly suspect her idea of business consisted as much of the heart as it did numbers on a ledger.

That many of these were Mexicans on both sides of the river mattered little to her; they were simply folks in need of help. She spoke their language fluently, adhered and respected their customs and traditions, and extended her friendship to each and all. One of the many reasons her stories have lived on long after her passing is because these families continued to live along that river. She was loyal to them in deed, and they in turn were so in memory.

But with the encroaching officialdom of federal bureaucracy, an undeclared war of wills ensued. This is not an unusual event in my family's history, as most of my kin considered feuding with the Mexican as well as American governments a favorite pastime. The battles roiled back and forth over the years, mostly due to her own perspective of what was allowed in the Hot Springs area, including the smuggling of candelilla wax.

Some might say that Aunt Mag was a force of nature, and she fought a good fight as only a true force of nature can. Ultimately, she was forced from Hot Springs and moved to San Vicente until being forced out again by the National Park Service. With that she moved her operations across the river to Boquillas, until the Mexican government did the same.

She had a place just outside of Alpine and lived there until offered the opportunity to run the trading post at Study Butte. But even a force of nature has a limited time on this earth, and Aunt Mag passed away in April of 1965. The ones who grieved the most were those she had helped the most, who had nothing to pay her back other than with their tears.

During those years and the ones following her death, the National Park Service considered Maggie Smith 'persona non grata,' even going as far as accusing her of being a gun smuggler. Such a claim was so ludicrous on so many levels as to be laughable, if it did not hurt her and my family so much.

Every reference and even mention of her name was struck from park literature, no one at the NPS would hardly utter her name. If they could not destroy her while alive, they would attempt to do so while defenseless in her grave.

Nevertheless, the stories and memories lingered, kept by those who most treasured such a rare breed. Beginning in the 1980s, a softening in the park's approach occurred in regards to Aunt Mag. Now it is almost a full-blown love fest with prominently displayed photographs, signs and other potpourri celebrating her life and many contributions to her fellow man.

Yes, they presently reverence Aunt Mag and that is a good thing. But it would have been sort of nice to let her know while she was still alive.

"For unto us a child is born, unto us a son is given: and the government shall be upon his shoulder: and his name shall be called Wonderful, Counseller, The mighty God, The everlasting Father, The Prince of Peace...
---Isaiah 9:6

CHRISTMAS IN LAJITAS, 1961

There are many Christmases that stand out in my memories, some for good reasons and others not so much.

Like being on the fringe of the 38th Parallel in South Korea, sitting in an unheated tent trying to eat 'Christmas dinner.' It was so cold that by the time I found a spot to sit down, my formerly hot chow had already started to freeze.

Or high in the Sierra Nevada somewhere along the California-Nevada line, a solitary campsite in the snow with only a fire to keep me company. Every now and then the warming blaze would pop, sending glowing embers into the frigid air as if they were joining with the vast marquee of stars above.

In a dark room and a dark place in 1983, staring at a wall right after the Marine Barracks bombing in Beirut. So many friends lost, so much hate inside. It felt so cold then, it was like the room was freezing even with the gas heater up full blast. That was when I realized it wasn't the room, but me.

All those years while in the Texas Highway Patrol, usually working either Christmas Eve or Christmas Day, or maybe both. The bad wrecks, the drunks, the domestic disturbances, the frustrated motorists, and hopefully a moment of quiet near the top of Lancaster Hill, on old US 290.

That was almost a tradition for me, sometimes the moon was so bright that you could see a day's walk in front of you. An interlude of reflection for the real reason for the season to get your head thinking straight again, and then back to work.

Then there are the Christmases when growing up in the Big Bend, this photograph illustrates the first one I can really remember. It was taken inside the living quarters of the Lajitas Trading Post and everyone seems to be enjoying themselves. Dad has gotten a new jacket and jeans. Mom looks like she has received a pair of slacks, standing front and center while talking in mid-photo.

My grandfather is playing with little brother Lyndon while grandmother is getting ready to cook something. She always was a really good cook, among many other things. Meanwhile I'm showing off the best part of me, the back of my head as Tia Maggie captures it all with her camera.

Dad has been gone a long time now and grandmother passed away some years ago. My grandfather has been dead for decades, the victim of a massive heart attack at too young an age. We lost Tia Maggie just this year.

Mom is still around, though, and is still front and center as the life of the party.

I sit here in my study surrounded by the mementoes of my life that followed this photo, and the memories. Yes, there were good Christmases and bad ones, but thank you so much Lord for all of them and for what Christmas really means.

"Actually, all education is self-education. A teacher is only a guide, to point out the way, and no school, no matter how excellent, can give you education. What you receive is like the outlines in a child's coloring book. You must fill in the colors yourself."

--Louis L'Amour

On occasion people ask me, "How long ago was it you lived in the Big Bend?" Well, far enough back to be in this photo. The location is Terlingua School and it was Christmastime, judging by the presents being waved about and the black boots of a Santa Claus piñata dangling overhead. That's the classroom, folks, the only classroom for a one room schoolhouse covering six grades and around nine to eleven students, depending on the time of year.

The teacher was Mrs. Ireta Anderson, a young lady of twenty-three fresh from Sul Ross and recently thrown to the wolves; i.e. Yours Truly as well as my fellow miscreants. And yes, she always looked like a million bucks when she walked into that classroom and right through to the end of the day, no matter what fist fights, bloodletting, skullduggery or other assorted mayhem occurred in between. Some fifty years later, I am still in awe of her.

Flanking her is Hector Acosta and Willie Benavidez, two of my childhood friends and erstwhile fellow co-conspirators. Also identifiable is my younger brother Lyndon, seated behind Willie. Willie's little brother Tony is at the rear of the classroom near his sister Lupe, face partially blocked by one of those Christmas presents. Somewhere in all this is Virginia Benavidez, the eldest of the clan and often mother hen for us all. Virginia always had a special kind of heart.

416

I am seated behind Mrs. Anderson, mostly hidden from view and most likely up to no good. Some things never change. This was the first year of having a swamp cooler, you can see the opening on the back wall. Luxury, baby; pure luxury that sticks in your memory like a two part epoxy glue. I utilized the cooling breeze for assorted experiments and projects, not to be mentioned here specifically due to possible statutes of limitations.

That was a long time ago and Mrs. Anderson is now Mrs. Ireta Peek Ham. She is still as lovely and gracious as ever, and still possesses the same smile and great goodness shining from within. She, along with our prior teacher Mrs. Potter, made certain we received a proper education. No matter what difficulties they faced personally in accomplishing that onerous task.

When people ask where I went to school, they seem to have in mind some sort of high-priced private establishment with fine buildings, exquisitely manicured grounds and a staff representing some of the best universities extant. I don't know where they come up with such a thought, I suppose I should feel honored for them to think so.

But my mind turns to a one room ramshackle school house, sitting forlornly in the Chihuahuan Desert on the edges of a crumbling ghost town, surrounding by nothing but miles upon miles of lonesome in every direction.

Education should be a daily, lifelong process. I think I got a pretty good start.

418

"We're tenting tonight on the old campground,
Give us a song to cheer;
Our weary hearts, a song of home,
And friends we love so dear."
--Walter Kittredge

Even after four continents, thirty countries and having traveled most of these United States, the Big Bend is still my favorite place to be. And with that having been said, Fresno Canyon and its enveloping watershed remain as a depository for many of my favorite memories of this country.

Close to sixty years ago, my family had lease holdings up and down that canyon. The reason was two-fold: it was easier for us to access the bottoms and feeders from Lajitas than it was for the owners at the Sauceda, and the water available helped balance out the sorrier sections in our possession. Thus, I became intimately acquainted with locales such as the Smith, the Madrid, Buena Suerte and Fresno Farm, and most everything in between.

Ample amounts of good water can be found in the bed of Fresno Creek, as well as its tributaries running westerly up the escarpment. These are in nature often springs, while tinajas are scattered about the western reaches of the opposing *El Solitario*. This telling variance is due to the massive geological upheavals from a hundred million years ago. It is also why this land is referred to as a geologist's nightmare or paradise, depending on the individual's inclination.

But when you are ten going on eleven after a hard, blistering day of working cattle, you could care less about the scientific trivia. All that mattered was that water. That's me in the photograph, paddling along on part of a tree trunk from a downed cottonwood and having the time of my life. Swimming trunks were not required, you just stripped down to your jeans and bailed into

419

the waterhole. Sometimes you could get away with more (or more accurately less), but on this particular day womenfolk were present.

That moccasined right foot most likely belonged to my grandmother or my Tia Maggie, since this was taken with a Polaroid they both favored. The rope is a precautionary measure due to my occasional over exuberance when involved in such wet, wonderful pleasures. On the back of the photo is the handwriting of my mother, Rosa Lynn English. Mom was raised in Uvalde and brought her love for water to this seared land, so I guess I came by it honestly.

When I look at this photo and me at ten, I smile to myself down deep inside. It was a different time and a different place, as well as a different way of life and especially in raising kids. It was tough, it was isolated, it was primitive and in rare instances even a bit dangerous. Many modern parents and grandparents would probably faint dead away at the mere thought of their offspring being raised in such an environment.

For myself, I do not regret a single moment of the experience.

421

"One of the best things in the world to be is a boy; it requires no experience, but needs some practice to be a good one."
--Charles Dudley Warner

This was taken by my mom, Rosa Lynn English, as we were getting ready to work cattle along Terlingua Creek. From left to right is my youngest brother, Barry, myself, my dad E.B. 'Ben' English III, and my brother Lyndon. It was summertime and I can tell we were working the creek bottoms as Dad, Lyndon and I have our leggings on. Barry is only about five, so he is mostly here to learn.

Barry is riding a little-bitty black Shetland pony with a matching little-bitty black heart. That horse managed to throw Barry numerous times, bite most everyone and everything on the place and kick some of my mother's teeth loose. Dad figured he must have been some sort of carnival pony, as he always wanted to travel in circles to the left.

That was especially so when he was excited about something, like half-wild, crazy eyed cattle bigger than he was. This Lilliputian fiend on four hooves was given to Barry by 'Tio' Tull Newton, the youngest brother of a bunch of outlaws known as the Newton Gang. That Shetland could have been one of them reincarnated.

I am riding my Appaloosa we called Pepe, after a character played by Mexican comedian and actor Mario Moreno, better known as Cantinflas. Both Lyndon and I broke our own horses, given to us by our grandfather E. B. 'Ben' English Jr. Pepe was smart, surefooted and could run like the wind, proving that in wagers against full-sized horses and riders.

But Pepe had a flaw, too; he loved to run but reining him in could be a different story. You can tell we are making progress; he's wearing a bridle now rather than a hackamore. Still, once he got the bit in his teeth, he would often go wide open until he got tired of doing so. Even dad couldn't haul him in until we rigged up a jawbreaker.

Dad is riding his favorite mount *Pedernal*, Mexican colloquial for the flint point blaze on his forehead. Pedernal was a fine-looking animal; a well set-up sorrel with blonde tail and mane. He had plenty of speed, bottom and cow smarts but shared the same sort of black heart as Barry's Shetland.

That horse didn't like kids, women, spurs, or much of anything else, and would lay his ears back and bare his teeth at the drop of a hat. He was a hand full, no doubt about it.

Lyndon is riding his horse Sparky. That pig-eyed grulla matched the name, too, because there was always something happening with him. When Lyndon climbed into the saddle to start the day, the rodeo was on. That pony would hump up and squeal long and loud, pitching and bucking every step of the way until he got his kinks worked out.

Sparky had another bad habit, too, and must have been a fish in a prior life. When you came to a large-sized water hole you'd better bail off quick. Sparky was bound to take a roll in it, saddle and all.

Looking at this photo, I think of a story my Dad shared with me many years later. He said that one day, perhaps even this one, we were pushing some cattle to the rock pens at our headquarters. Nicknamed 'Fulcher cows,' these bovines were one of the few that not only survived but thrived in the lower Big Bend. That meant they were about half crazy, too, and gathering them was always an adventure.

Dad recalled that at one point he reined in to see me go flying by on Pepe like a Phantom jet on afterburner, doing my best Yosemite Sam of "Whoa, Camel, Whoa" as I blew past.

Meanwhile Lyndon was watering Sparky in Terlingua Creek. That grulla promptly jerked his head down before Lyndon could set himself, sending my brother over and into the waterhole head first. Lyndon hit the wet stuff moving, knowing that Sparky's next move was to take that roll of his.

All the while Barry was doing his level best riding drag on that black Shetland, circling around and around up the width of the creek.

Dad reminisced that all he could do was break out another Marlboro and take a long, soothing drawl as he eyeballed nothing but rough country, cows that looked like rejects from an Ace Reid cartoon, and his young drovers in different stages of distress.

He pulled the cigarette out of his mouth, shook his head and muttered, "Yep, you got yourself one helluva a cow outfit here."

423

"Oh, the old swimmin' hole!
When I last saw the place,
The scenes were all changed,
like the change on my face."
--James Whitcomb Riley

It was just an old cottonwood sitting in Terlingua Creek, deformed by the flashfloods which partially uprooted it and gave the tree a pronounced tilt downstream.

As with so many other gives and takes in this world, those same intermittent forces also sustained it through dry spells and drought; when lesser things of nature shriveled and died due to shallower roots. No one really knew how long it had been there, it seemed as old and gnarled as the landscape to which it was born.

But there was one thing we did know about that spot, its placement made for a pretty decent wading hole when the creek came down just right. I say that as it depended on which channel the rushing waters decided to use when the far too seldom big rains came. A hit-or-miss proposition, but usually reliable enough come a hot day and a bit of free time.

Each year we hosted a trail riding group from the Permian Basin area, a time that all our family looked forward to. There was good food, good conversation and the chance to share the rare sights found so readily in this area. Part of that excitement was also because several of those riders had young families, which made for new partners-in-crime beyond the list of usual suspects.

After an afternoon's ride, I sometimes took my visiting peers for a little cooling fun under that cottonwood tree. They held me in some awe as I not only already knew how to drive, but my dad trusted me enough to take our GMC four-wheel drive without supervision. He was a strict disciplinarian, though he tended to reward well when an exemplary job was done. If memory serves me correctly, this was one of those times. I could barely see over the dashboard.

We had only been at the water hole for about a half hour when dark, ominous clouds settled beyond Hen Egg Mountain. Rain of any sort is always welcome in this country, especially when there appears to be copious amounts of it. But that appreciation is a double-edged sword, as it instills a healthy respect for fast moving water when in the belly of a potential monster like Terlingua Creek.

Sizing up the situation, I began picking up my gear to head back to ranch headquarters. My companions asked what was going on and I pointed to the rapidly developing downpours. The time for us to leave was now, as a flash flood was likely already headed our direction.

Now these boys were not only 'flat landers' but a majority of them were town kids, who had no idea of the treachery this country was capable of. Not only that, but a few of them were older than me. Not understanding and perhaps looking to get in a 'dig' against the freedom I was afforded, they began ridiculing my caution as boys of bravado often do.

I retorted by telling them they could walk back because I was taking the GMC with me. Furthermore, I informed them to climb into that cottonwood when the waters came, as in my estimation they surely would. There were some other words and insults exchanged. Like I said we were all red-blooded sons of Texas and full of ourselves, as well as other things.

I drove back to headquarters and continued on with my afternoon. Dad was busy with the wants and needs of the trail riders, and it took a while to dawn on him that I had returned alone.

Finally, he got a break and asked "Son, where are those boys you were with?"

"Still at the cottonwood," was my answer.

Dad had been watching the clouds too, and upon hearing my response things went into overdrive. He let loose with a string of colorful expletives best not repeated and ran for the GMC, yelling at me to come on. Dad's cussing was nothing new, but to see him running anyplace was a revelation so I hit a high lope myself.

Down South County Road we went, dirt and rocks flying as we careened our way along, that odd-fire V6 screaming for mercy. We came to a shuddering, skidding halt on finding our way blocked by brown, frothy water. Both of us bailed out and moved to where we could better see the cottonwood, Dad fearing the worst and me fearing what Dad's reaction could mean to my continued good health.

426

Together we let out a sigh of relief, though for slightly different reasons. Those boys looked like a bunch of hoot owls nesting in the lower branches of that old cottonwood; nothing but big, wide eyes as the surging water rushed on below them.

I turned to my father and attempted to vindicate myself, saying; "Dad, I told 'em to climb that cottonwood when the creek came down."

He looked at me for a long moment with the intent of killing something, or more likely somebody, but it passed and he just shook his head. We waited for the creek to reach a fordable level and eased out to the weathered old tree to collect our low-hanging human fruit. Then back to headquarters we went, laughing now for the experience.

All except Dad, who had started to gray a bit.

"And I died in my boots like a pioneer,
With the whole wide sky above me."
--Stephen Vincent Benét

This crumbling heap of adobe, tin and rotting lumber, along with the decaying concrete slab that once supported it, is all that is left of what was once Study Butte Trading Post.

These general stores, or 'trading posts' as they were referred to, dotted the lower Big Bend area from Candelaria all the way down to Boquillas. By and large they were a phenomenon on our side of the river, but the Mexican population just beyond that thin ribbon of muddy water made as much use of them as anyone else. In fact, looking back I would have to say even more so.

You see, most of these establishments were true trading posts. Money for most anyone in this country during that time could be hard to come by, so many obtained what they needed through bartering. Thus these stores were often a combination of grocery, hardware, clothing and gun shop; as well as a pelts purchaser, candelilla buyer and social meeting place for people of the area. It was a time-honored tradition mostly gone by the 1980s.

The store here catered to the mining community of Study Butte while it was operational, and then to the locals until most of them went the way of the mines. This one was of particular merit to me, as my great-great Aunt Mag Smith ran it for a short while before passing on. And yes, this was the same Maggie Smith of local lore involving the Hot Springs back in the 1940s and 1950s, as well as many other places in the Big Bend.

The story of Aunt Mag was not only her own, but also of a time and way of life that has been dead and gone for nearly a half century now. One could say that when she was buried a part of Texas history, as well as northern Mexico's, was laid to rest alongside her. Within ten more years, the Big Bend would change dramatically from what she ever knew or experienced.

It was her time and her place in this world, and it will not come again.

429

> *"When the One Great Scorer,*
> *Comes to write against your name---*
> *He marks---not that you won or lost---*
> *But how you played the game."*
> *--Grantland Rice*

You are standing in a saddle on top of Wild Horse Mountain, looking west towards the Leon, the Sawmill and then the Black Mesa area in the far distance.

On the horizon is the southern part of *El Solitario*. A heavy layer of clouds have settled here, and long peals of thunder that sound like God's own artillery echoes about while a soft drizzle begins to fall. It is mid-September in the lower Big Bend and the rains have come again.

Many folks wouldn't give this shot a second thought, way too much variance in ambient light for my little Kodak digital to handle. Too much light and dark, they'd say, and they'd be right.

But this photograph is quite poignant for me personally and for several reasons. Everything was so verdant and green in this country, and that blessed moisture signified a lost hope for me. For if it had rained like this when I was a kid, we wouldn't have been forced to pull up stakes and move on.

The area encapsulated in the frame covers a lot of the land we once owned, which makes this circumstance a double irony. Some of it was highway frontage property, which at that time was more of a pain than anything else. We had to work doubly hard in maintaining the dilapidated fence lines.

Looking down there and at all those roofs made me think of my grandfather. My mind went back to the summer of 1970 and we had gone flat busted broke.

My mother had an idea and it was a sound one financially. She wanted to subdivide that highway frontage and sell it in lots much like Terlingua Ranch had done. Grandfather was dead set against the idea, commenting he couldn't do that to this country, it just wouldn't be right.

431

Mom persisted by pointing out "If you don't do it Ben, someone else will."

His reply was short and final, and left no doubt as to where he stood.

"Well, probably so. But it won't be me."

Now I'm not saying who was right or wrong, or bemoaning progress, or taking away from the fact that others found their own happiness in that land. After all, you could make the argument that one does not really own any land ever, it'll still be there a long time after you're gone.

Just like my grandfather.

And in some ways, the land actually possesses you and all that you are, just like my grandfather.

But I will tell you this: They don't make those kind of men anymore, those who can truthfully say that money isn't everything. Then prove out their words in that sort of way.

Carl C. Williams, former sheriff of Brewster County, was good friends with my grandfather. We were talking about him not too long ago and the old sheriff reflected and then said:

"Your grandfather was one to ride the river with."

I reckon that sums up everything else that needs saying.

433

"For man, as for flower and beast and bird, the supreme triumph is to be the most vividly, most perfectly, alive."
--D. H. Lawrence

This was taken about twelve years ago inside the Basin, along the inner loop trail after coming down from the Pinnacles. That's my younger son, Ethan L'Amour English, gazing north to the back side of Pulliam Bluff. It was summertime and we had some weather rolling in, so he was keeping watch with a practiced eye.

Ethan was only a teenager then, but you can tell by his gear and stance that even at a young age he 'tweren't no pilgrim.' Though I could never give my sons the kind of freedom I had while growing up, they were still crawling around in these mountains and surrounding deserts not long after being able to walk.

It made them lean and tough and strong. It also filled their hearts with an abiding awe for what God saw fit to create, and to give these spectacular gifts the care and respect they deserve. In its own way, the Big Bend made my sons into the men they are now as much as anything else.

Ethan L'Amour went on to be an Eagle Scout, a cross country and track powerhouse, valedictorian of his high school class, and like his older brother Benjamin Levi, a graduate of the Naval Academy at Annapolis. While there he competed in the Junior Olympics, placing well for the Navy pistol team.

He is now a lieutenant and skipper of a Mark Six patrol boat, stationed in the Persian Gulf. People ask me if I tend to worry about my sons much. Honestly, I don't, because I know what they are made of.

I write this not so much as a proud father but to give encouragement and support for today's young parents, struggling to make their child into a decent human being in an increasingly indecent world.

Don't give up, stay true to the course. For in the end your actions and good faith will become the brightest star in the heavens that your children will have to guide by.

This country will help you accomplish that goal, and in all the right ways.

"The love of Jesus does not separate us from the common necessities and infirmities of human life. Men of God are still men.
--Charles Spurgeon

My youngest brother Barry never had any children of his own, but that does not mean he didn't have real influence on many a young person who came his way. In this photograph are five of them, all nephews in his mostly all-nephew family.

Pictured from left to right are Ethan L'Amour English, Lieutenant, United States Navy, Foy Boyd, Logan English, Master Sergeant, United States Air Force, Layne English, United States Air Force veteran, and Benjamin Levi English, Captain, United States Marine Corps.

Each of these young men spent a goodly amount of time with their Uncle Barry while they were growing up, learning the way of ranch life in Texas that extends back in our family for some seven generations or so. In turn, Barry left his mark on each one in their minds, in their hearts and in their spirits.

Note that I said 'men,' not boys or guys or fellas. He helped see to that, too. In fact, he demanded it. They grew into tough, resourceful, caring, Christian individuals, and gentlemen to boot. Any one of them will do for any hard task when called upon, and have proven this repeatedly time and again.

Tuesday a week ago, Barry passed unexpectedly from this life at a far too early age. These young men came in from near and far, and from halfway around the world, to pay their final respects.

I don't think any man could ever have better living eulogies.

We'll miss you, Barry. More than you will ever know.

Vaya con Dios, 'Mano.

Ride 'em pretty.

438

> *"While we are on earth, we are subject to a threefold 'darkness;' the darkness of error, the darkness of sorrow, and the darkness of death."*
>
> **--George Horne**

In a lifetime of fond memories involving the lower Big Bend, for me the fondest of all would be north of Lajitas. Made up of the southern reaches of *El Solitario*, the neighboring Fresno Canyon, and the old military road that skirts Lajitas Mesa, these are the memories of my childhood.

Amid those boundaries lies Contrabando Canyon, shown in the photograph above. This was taken not too long ago, a bit upstream from the McGuirk ruins. From here it is not too far to where my Tia Maggie once resided, as well as in other locales in this immediate area.

Years later she would move away for good but her heart stayed loyal to this land. Like so many others no matter where one roams, the Big Bend is always home.

That does not mean life here was easy. Tia Maggie lived with no telephone and no electricity, and usually cooked on a wood stove. Washing clothes consisted of carrying them up into a nearby cleft, using a rub board and water from a secluded tinaja.

Her husband was often gone, which made my grandparents in Lajitas the nearest help available. As far as I know she never asked for any. She could ride, shoot and make do better than most men, much like my grandmother and my great-great Aunt Mag, whom Tia was named for.

In doing so she learned the sheltered secrets of this country as few others. Decades later, now half blind and of failing health, she could still describe events and locations in minute detail. God gave her a mind that came with an inner map and magnetic compass.

Tia Maggie was one of my most enthusiastic supporters ever, no matter what I might be involved in. She was always so grateful for our 'little walks,' as she put them, which I would post on social media. Many of you have followed some of the bantering between us on Facebook, some even commented and joined in.

She enjoyed that immensely.

A year or so ago on a bitterly cold February night, Tia's home caught on fire. Though her husband was barely able to escape with his own life from another part of the house, she was trapped inside. Ultimately her daughter and son-in-law forced their way in to get to her, but it was too late.

Tia Maggie did not survive.

The house itself was a total loss. Obliterated in that fire were irreplaceable family heirlooms, such as the pocket watch taken from one of General Orazco's tenientes following a gun battle in 1915. There were thousands upon thousands of photographs of the Big Bend dating back to a hundred years before, and the personal mementoes of four generations of my ancestors.

All gone, all turned to ashes.

Yet for me, my greatest personal loss is of my Tia and her memories. Everything else was just things.

Soon I will return to this area again, the land she loved most of all and could now only experience through my writing and photography. When I go I will be joined by her daughters, guiding them to a suitable spot to honor her oft-repeated request of having her cremated remains scattered north of Lajitas.

And for me, to add one very sad memory to so many fond ones.

"I hope that when you're my age you'll be able to say, as I have been able to say: We lived in freedom, we lived lives that were a statement, not an apology."
--Ronald Reagan

This is a story about a pistol. It is also a bit of the life story of the special kind of man who carried it, and of an era that has long since passed.

These stories, as well as so many others concerning the lower Big Bend, mean a great deal to me. A reader recently commented on that thought, thanking me for making the effort to tell them. He mentioned that as long as I tell these stories, the people involved and the times they lived in will never really die.

For my own very personal reasons, I hope that never holds so true as in the story I tell now.

First, the pistol. It is a Colt Commercial Government 1911 Pre-70 in .45 ACP, a fairly unusual variation in bright nickel finish. Fresh from the factory in late 1965, it came into my grandfather's possession on Christmas Day of that year.

The Colt was a special gift from two men, young men at that time who were federal narcotics agents. Both thought a great deal of my grandfather, which is evident in the presentation of such an expensive pistol. In that they took it one step further, the gun was fitted with a pair of Guadalajara silver grips and engraved 'Ben English 12-25-65 Ray & Cliff.'

That would be Ray Atkinson and Cliff Wilson. Cliff passed away some years back, but Ray is still alive and kicking after a very full and eventful life. We stay in contact and he sometimes regales me with stories of my grandfather, for which I am grateful. He knew him intimately on a man to man basis, while I did so only barely.

442

I never once heard my grandfather tell a single story of bravado on himself, he didn't have to. Others did it for him. These stories still survive in the memories of the men who knew him best, such as those related by Carl C. Williams in his book *More Than A Badge*.

Each of these individuals is a man's man in their own right, and each has said my grandfather was truly someone to admire as well as respect. The honored adage of being known by the company you keep never seemed more appropriate than when I hear them speak of him. He may have died a poor man, but he was as rich as anyone I ever knew when it came to friends that mattered.

For the remainder of his days this pistol was his prized possession.

Some years following his passing, I was home on leave visiting my grandmother. She excused herself for a moment and stepped out of the room. When she came back, she was carrying a large manila folder.

"Your Papa wanted you to have this, when the time was right."

I opened the folder and there was the nickeled 1911, placed in the holster he had made for it. Wrapped separately in soft tissue was his tie tack of tiny crossed Colt single actions, the one he wore during his two terms as sheriff of Zavala County.

More time passed. After becoming a certified armorer for the Texas Department of Public Safety, I carefully refitted the pistol to better suit occasional carry work. Better sights, a custom guide rod and an extended safety were added. This photograph was taken after the modifications were completed.

Exactly fifty years and a few months following the Colt being gifted to him, I stepped up to the firing line for my Special Ranger certification with his pistol in my hand. When the qualification was finished, the X-ring for the target was in tatters. 1911s have always fit me well, going back to my time in the Marine Corps. His fits me best of all.

One day my older son will inherit this pistol. He is the fifth Ben; the first born of the first born right down the line. In the meantime, I will continue to carry this Colt for certain events and occasions.

In our present age some might say the Colt is too heavy, too rare and too old, and that its time has finally passed. But I still do so, because it is my closest link to the man I respected most of all. I know this pistol can be counted upon, and that it will always shoot straight and true.

After all, it is my grandfather's gun.

> *"Well, I know some day,*
> *farther down the road,*
> *I'll come to the edge of the Great Unknown;*
> *There'll stand a black horse, riderless,*
> *And I wonder if I'm ready for this"* ...
> *--Chris LeDoux, 'The Ride'*

Since learning of my brother Barry's passing, folks have contacted me wanting to know more about him.

Barry was born in Alpine in 1963, likely about a century too late. An eighth generation Texan, he got his first taste of the cowboy life alongside our dad and granddad in the lower parts of the Big Bend.

That's he and I on those two mounts, Barry was barely five sitting atop a blazed-faced bay we called 'Grandpa.' But even at five, he could knock out my dad's tracks all day long up and down Terlingua Creek, into The Cottonwood and along the eastern reaches of *El Solitario*; hanging on like a blue tick to a hound dog.

You see, he always wanted to be a cowboy.

In later years people would marvel at how good a cowboy he really was, as well as a stockman. Not me. If you can keep from breaking your fool neck chasing after some half-wild, crazy eyed cow across half the lower Big Bend, you can cowboy most anyplace.

Now I haven't been on the back of a horse in decades, choosing instead to go straight into the Marines from high school and then a career as a peace officer.

Brother Lyndon went the cowboy way for a while and became known as a fair hand at breaking horses. Ultimately, he went the same way as I, a Texas peace officer and a darn good one at that. But though he still does general work on a ranch, his cowboying days are over.

But with Barry, it was a way of life and he never gave much thought to wanting to be anything else.

He knew who he was, what he was and what he stood for. He did what he thought was right, was strong for his Lord, and never took in a breath that wasn't free.

I'd call that bountiful blessings and a life well lived.

Some weeks later on a Sunday morning, I was sitting at the table with a cup of coffee listening to Red Stegall's *Cowboy Corner*. The sun was rising over Hancock Hill and peeking through the pines, the warmth signaling yet another spring coming on.

It was then it finally hit me: Barry was gone.

And with him a way of life that is going much the same direction. Sometimes it's hard to remember what this country used to be, even a few short years ago. It's never going back to what it was. When these big ranches in West Texas get busted up, they stay that way.

One thing's for certain, I'm sure glad Barry wanted to be a cowboy. Not only for him but for that way of life, for each was directly linked to the other in mindset, philosophy and ethics.

You know, my family and kin came to Texas during Spanish rule and helped get that way of life started. They were the ones who pushed those longhorns up the Chisholm, the Shawnee, the Western and the Goodnight-Loving.

They braved searing heat, bitter cold, flooded rivers and forty miles of hard, tough going with not a drop of water along the way, time and again.

They were the ones that books were written about, ballads were sung and legends grown upon.

They were the true believers, just like Barry and I find it fitting that he was around for the final act.

And when his time came, he mounted that riderless black, tipped his hat, and rode away into that Great Unknown.

A cowboy.

EPILOGUE

For those who have lived in and truly understand the soul of this singular land, the heart of the lower Big Bend is in the desert itself. To keep the heart beating, you need arteries to carry the essential nutrients.

In this case the major artery is the Rio Grande; fed in turn by three minor ones known as the Tornillo, the Fresno and the Terlingua. Mankind has clung close to these givers of life throughout his existence here, as evidenced by the numerous ruins from all eras found along them.

In the endless number of days I knew as a boy, I wandered along and through these arteries of necessity. Each to me were special in their own manner; I drank from their pools and streams, lazed in the shade of their trees and rock walls, camped along their banks and hunted the muley deer for physical sustenance.

But there was also the receiving of the most important sustenance of all, that for the mind and spirit.

Man has come and man has gone in his mortal haste and confusion since time immemorial, but those precious arteries of the desert carry on through all.

And now in seeing the September song of my own life just ahead, I long to be with them more and more.

And when I die my ashes will join them, for they are where I belong.

Thank you to all who have read this book and allowed me to tell of a Big Bend that existed 'once upon a time.'

And in some ways continues to do so.

May God bless you and yours,

Ben H. English
Alpine, Texas

ABOUT THE AUTHOR

Ben H. English is an eighth-generation Texan who was raised in the Big Bend Country of the Lone Star State. He attended schools in Presidio, Marfa and later, a one room school house in Terlingua. During this time his family had several ranching and business interests in the area, including the historic Lajitas Trading Post which was run by his grandparents.

Mr. English served seven years in the US Marine Corps and upon returning to civilian life, graduated college with honors. He joined the Texas Highway Patrol in 1986, where he served until his retirement in late 2008. He spent the following two years working part time as a Criminal Justice teacher at Ozona High School.

Mr. English has spent much of his life prowling about in the lower Big Bend. His first book, Yonderings, detailed just some of those journeys and was published by Texas Christian University Press.

Presently, Mr. English and his wife live in Alpine, Texas so they can be closer to the land they both love so much. To this day, he likes nothing better than grabbing a pack and some canteens, and heading off in a direction he has never been before.

THANK YOU FOR READING!

If you enjoyed this book, we would appreciate your customer review on your book seller's website or on Goodreads.

Also, we would like for you to know that you can find more great books like this one at www.CreativeTexts.com

Printed in the USA
CPSIA information can be obtained
at www.ICGtesting.com
LVHW022102081123
763417LV00005B/164